THE REIGN OF EDWARD VIII

A quarter of a century has passed since that dramatic explosion in English history occasioned by the King's decision to abandon his throne and his people in favour of a Mrs. Simpson, and the dust has now begun to settle on the memories of those extraordinary scenes — the quiet little divorce arranged somewhere in the Eastern Counties; the ant-like activities of American journalists; the comings and goings between No. 10 Downing Street and Fort Belvedere in Windsor Park; and the final speech of renunciation.

Now Robert Sencourt, a noted historian, has blown away the dust from those events and reveals them clearly once more in the searching light of his own personal acquaintanceship with most of the people intimately involved in the affair and of the revelation of many hitherto undisclosed facts. The result is a completely fresh and intensely interesting picture of one of the most astonishing periods in our history.

THE REIGN OF EDWARD VIII

ROBERT SENCOURT

With 32 pages of half-tone illustrations

ANTHONY GIBBS & PHILLIPS
LONDON

First published in Great Britain by
Anthony Gibbs & Phillips, Ltd.,
14 Kensington Court, London, W.8

MCMLXII

Reprinted March 1962

This essay in history is written in fealty to the Crown and inscribed to the memory of one who must live in history as one of its most devoted and most distinguished servants.

THE LATE LORD HARDINGE OF PENSHURST

"It is an abomination to the King to do evil; for the throne is established by righteousness."

The Hebrew Book of Proverbs

Printed in Great Britain by
Cox and Wyman Ltd.,
London, Reading, and Fakenham.

Appreciations

MANY people are now tending to forget what the Duke of Windsor did and tending to remember that they are rather sorry for him . . . Such will be inclined to say, "Good Gracious, why can't they leave the man alone?" . . . Your answer to this, which should be discreetly but quite plainly made, would be that you only wish to make sure that for history the simple judgment of right and wrong should not be obscured; and secondly, that the Duke of Windsor's book had done grave injustice to Baldwin and others, whose actions you desired, very properly, to vindicate. You have drawn together very well the various affairs of the reign.

EDWARD, EARL OF HALIFAX

That has been the great drama of our time, and I found your narrative absorbing. It fills a gap in history, setting forth the facts impartially, yet not without sympathy for the personages involved. Behind it is the weight of the high authorities, from whom you have gathered your information and to whom you have submitted your pages. As to your style, you know how often it has delighted me.

Signed: G. P. GOOCH, C.H., F.B.A.,
Trinity College, Cambridge

Preface

I HAVE felt that a biographer should live as much as he can in the heart and mind of his subject. History, however, whatever Carlyle said, is other than biography: mind has to be balanced against mind in the assessment of a situation and the object is much less psychology than the narrative of events. Here my object has been to make that as unbiased and objective as I could. Both the Duke and the Duchess of Windsor have presented their own points of view very skilfully in their two fascinating narratives: but autobiography can never be the complete material of history. No book has yet tried to take into account the pressure of public opinion on the reign of Edward VIII; yet it had an overwhelming weight on the Government.

However, I have not been content to take the books of either the Duke or the Duchess of Windsor as the final word on their side. I have sought the opinions of their friends and supporters and among those owe a great deal to Lord Brownlow who has kindly placed at my disposal his invaluable critique on *The Heart Has Its Reasons* and a later letter sent to the *Sunday Telegraph* and to others who being members of the Court should not have their names mentioned. All these have given me much authoritative information in favour of His Royal Highness and corrected false impressions from other sources. My hope is that no ungenerous word about him appear in this book, as it was that of the late Lord Halifax who saw more of the Duke in the Washington Embassy than as a Minister central in affairs in the reign itself. He read through my manuscript a month or two before his death and wrote finally the comments placed at the disposal of my readers. It was Lord Attlee himself who personally insisted to me that he had gone to Baldwin before any influence was brought to bear on him from the side of the Prime Minister. Sir Winston Churchill's assertion that the Government brought to bear on the Opposition an unfair influence has no foundation.

Although I never knew Baldwin himself I have seen much and learnt much from his son, the present Earl, as well as from his two secretaries Lord Crathorne and Sir Horace Wilson, G.C.B., G.C.M.G. Sir Rupert Howarth, K.C.M.G., K.C.V.O., has supplied me with valuable information about the function of the Privy Council in relation to a Royal Marriage. His friend Sir

Thomas Barnes, G.C.B., gave me the date of the "appearance" of Sir Francis Stevenson in the Simpsons' divorce proceedings. To the Lord Chancellor with Mr. Dermot Morrah I owe an elucidation of the position of the reigning sovereign to the Royal Marriage Act of 1772 and to Mr. Daniel F. Burlingham, J.P., the exact facts as to how the clocks at Sandringham were altered immediately after the death of King George V. To Captain Cecil Howe, C.B.E., R.N., the precise details of the departure of the former King after his Abdication. Mr. Arthur Mann has placed at my disposal the historic article which broke the silence of the press.

I have talked to Lord Simon and to Lord Somervell, the two high legal authorities in the Government. I was also introduced to Ernest Simpson by his sister Mrs. Kerr-Smiley who gave me the most valuable information as did also the Rev. Lambert Foxell who had been the counsellor and friend of Mr. Simpson from the time when in the First War Mr. Simpson held a commission in the Coldstreams of which Mr. Foxell was then chaplain. Thus the fact that Simpson in the whole course of his life always refused to discuss this affair did not prevent me from hearing of his view of the situation in which he was placed. In fact I have even seen a letter from the now Duchess of Windsor paying a tribute to Ernest Simpson in the period before she had ceased to be his legal wife.

Among the privileges that the preparation of this book brought me I value nothing more than the courtesy and hospitality of the late Lord Hardinge of Penshurst and Lady Hardinge. The further I went in my study the more I appreciated his judgment and discretion and the more valuable I found his elucidations, not least those published in *The Times* which he had been obliged to make when his work had been misrepresented. Their awareness of the part of the Court in our recent history struck me as unique and I am deeply grateful for their concern that my narrative should be just and accurate. My narrative will show what I owe to what Lady Hardinge has herself published and to her long knowledge of the Court.

It was they who, having each read through my pages, urged that I should talk to Lord Monckton and he indeed received me courteously three times. My chief object was that he should have every opportunity to correct what I had written about himself: but his only concern, with which I have done everything possible to comply, was that nothing should appear which should displease the Duke of Windsor, though he agreed that Baldwin had been on excellent terms with himself. Like a high-court official he has not seen my present narrative and is therefore in no way responsible for it. Another who supplied me with information for this subject, as he did for a biographical sketch of the late Lord Willingdon, was Sir Eric Miéville, who was Private Secretary to His Royal Highness the Duke of York.

Die Geschichteschreibung ist eine Gewissensache. Writing history, Ranke once wrote, is an affair of conscience. When one writes of recent or contemporary history one will have a number of authoritative printed pages on which to draw, including those of Hansard. One should have access to the persons who can speak with authority; but above all, in the course of years, impressions which come now from one quarter, now from another, join with personal observation and judgment to complete the work of which Newman called the illative sense, meaning a method of arriving at the truth through instinct playing upon impressions reaching us from many quarters. I do not mean that I wish myself to pass judgment on passing events. Almost all the judgments cited here are those of others, and especially Members of Parliament. But a narrative, especially when it relates to foreign policy, does reflect a gradual accumulation of experience. That experience however was moulded especially by two authorities who were very close friends of mine, the Duke of Alba and Sir Victor Wellesley. One element of my narrative is personal knowledge of the great majority of the people it mentions.

The background of this book is the hospitality I have in the course of years had the honour of receiving from members of the Court and the Royal Family themselves. I ought to make humble acknowledgment to their Majesties, Queen Mary, Queen Elizabeth the Queen Mother, of whom I saw much when the guest of her parents at Glamis Castle, Queen Victoria Eugenia, and to the Duke of Connaught, and Lord and Lady Edward Gleichen. Apart from the Royal Family I ought to mention the late Lord and Lady Wigram, and my generous host Mr. George Drummond who so often entertained the Prince at Pitsford Hall.

Both Lord Somervell and Mr. Hector Bolitho read through earlier drafts of these pages, and gave valuable help as did also Mr. H. D. Ziman, the Hon. Michael Berry, Mr. Dermot Morrah and Mr. Donald Adamson. I also owe a great deal to the archives of *The Times* and the courtesy of Mr. John Maywood who was already on the staff of that great paper when in 1912 I first met the then Prince of Wales at Magdalen.

There was much in 1936 to recall what Lord Acton had written in the reign of Queen Victoria: "The inflexible integrity of the moral code is to me the secret of the authority, the dignity and the nobility of history."

Authority, dignity, and nobility are proper not only to history but to the Court of St. James, and Her Majesty's Government, who well know what is essential to the prestige of the Crown.

I have sought to suppress what conflicts with it. Much therefore that I know is not set down here: suppression, nevertheless, should never go so far as to mislead the public who, if they cannot at a particular juncture know all the truth, have a right not to be hoodwinked by what purports to be a history. This point was pressed on me several years ago by another valued friend, the late Algernon Cecil. Nephew, while still at Eton and Oxford, of a Prime Minister, he received much authoritative yet confidential information he could not print. But he said that discretion should never induce one to write in a tone that seemed to deny what one knew to be true. We discussed the case of Wordsworth's liaison at Tours with Annette Vallon. The poet's brother, Christopher, then Dean of Lincoln, when writing a biography of Wordsworth would have embarrassed many, including himself, if he had disclosed the existence of Caroline, the illegitimate daughter. All he wrote of Wordsworth at Tours was: "He was subject to many temptations." That was not enough, said Algernon Cecil, he should have added after temptation the words "which he did not always resist".

PART ONE

The Royal Heritage

CHAPTER 1

ALTHOUGH the reign of King Edward VIII was within the span of a year, it was by no means the least significant in his country's history. On the contrary, it was pregnant with great issues for monarchy, morality and foreign affairs; and it came in a crucial period when the throne was involved with destiny in a campaign amid the hills and lowlands of the border between tradition and revolution.

In the complex character of this prince these opposing principles played their tournament, and he was called to the throne in a year when the strife which was to ruin Europe was already in sight.

But not only was Europe to be debilitated, and dethroned from its long hegemony. Great Britain was to fall from her sovereign rank, and to forfeit to social revolution the prestige of her ruling class: her Empire was to lose much of its coherence. But even in doing so, it was to enhance the role and prestige of the Crown, and make more demands than ever from the character and devotion of those it invested with the title, and attributes, of majesty.

It would be a mistake to peep at the reign of King Edward VIII as through a microscope fixed on the details of a personal melodrama. We miss its significance till we relate it to the idea of monarchy throughout his life, and also to the political situation which was the concern of his father.

The reign is also of interest to the United States, first because the person who had most to do with the King was an American, and secondly because in the supreme issues he preferred American standards to those of the Church and the tradition of his Court. His reign became in the end a duel between the spirit of Britain and the trend of America. It meant a crisis in the soul of Canada.

He first captivated the world by his spontaneous boyishness. With a look of unsophisticated innocence he combined a power to captivate and delight. He was unconventional and from the beginning he hated ceremony, and loved an escapade. He was shy but his shyness almost added to his delightfulness. He subjugated the world as the embodiment of simplicity; and from the moment he came to know America he found that it suited him right down to the ground. In his instinctive reaction to the demands of royal state he persuaded democracy that here was a Prince after its own heart.

Not less than formality he hated files; nor did he ever care to study either books or state papers for the truth of the stories they divulge. His art was to learn through people and what they were doing in practical life. He had an instinctive flair for business and was at one with people in their ways of earning their living. His approaches were direct, easy and informal. But while this gave him a swift popularity among the masses, it meant a break with the atmosphere into which he was born.

The Prince was so well aware of the tide—and of the need—of change that he anticipated a reign in which his instinct and convictions would deal boldly with affairs. But though he was quick to observe he was little given to deep thinking, and in his psychology there were certain conflicts: the conflict of temperament which in its craving for freedom pushed convention to one side. Liking easy relations, he combined the enormous privileges and distinctions of royalty with a certain immaturity—a temperament furthermore in which naïveté, or at least a good intention, was at war with discretion, and at the same time modernness with respectability.

He sometimes chose his friends from unexpected quarters: he was from childhood strained and nettled by both the example of stern duty and its precept which came to him from the warmhearted common sense of his father and the imposing queenliness of his mother. As he grew to manhood he was rushed from engagement to engagement and never left silent and alone to gain what a normal youth gains from his freedom; and since society made voracious demands of him it would have been surprising if he did not form instinctive defences. But as soon as he grew up to see what was required of him he displayed a rare gift of arousing the enthusiasm all were longing to feel for him: and wherever he went people, as they feasted their eyes on him, admired and loved him.

And yet, because in the end he proved to have in his expansive nature instincts more American than British, he finally imperilled his tenure of the Crown.

But even if the story is centred on the nine pregnant months of his reign we will understand neither him nor it unless we realize the Court of his parents.

THE earliest years of the boy Prince were passed in the shadow of a great-grandmother who towered eminent over her family, as over all her people, with a gleaming massiveness like that of a lofty mountain over plain and ranges. Queen Victoria inspired reverence and awe. If as they took their walks in the grounds of Osborne, any of her children, though well on in years, saw her in the offing, they dashed behind bushes to avoid meeting her: all who visited her remained standing in her presence. After dinner she took her stand on a carpet trod by no other feet than hers. But it would be a mistake to think that the Queen was always dour or a terror to children. Far from it. For the last years of her life the grandchildren who lived with her always came in for her to kiss them good night, and sometimes with the Mallet boys, the sons of her wittiest maid-of-honour who had been Marie Adeane. She loved them all to have a good time: for them brought "Buffalo Bill" to Windsor. At Balmoral she would have the carpet rolled up for her to dance with her grandsons.

If, hearing a risqué story she did say once: "We are not amused." This must not be taken as typical: for the most part she was amused almost too easily. Once at dinner she asked an admiral about his sister, Miss Seymour. His answer: "She is doing pretty well, Ma'am; she is lying on her side on the beach and tomorrow we hope to scrape her bottom" brought tears of laughter to her eyes. (The admiral who had not quite caught the name thought she was referring to a vessel under his care, *The Sea-Mew*.) And her laugh was always a joy to hear—her smile too was of the sweetest and her voice had a silvery ring quite delightful. She was indeed a dear old lady, pouring out beneficence on her beloved people and saying from her heart: "May God bless them."

But as we each have two grandmothers, so we have four great-grandmothers—what did this mean for the new Prince of Wales?

If one was Queen Victoria, another was Queen Louise of Denmark, daughter of the Landgrave of Hesse-Cassel: but on his mother's side came two more—a German Duchess of Cambridge, and then, quite different from the small German Royalties . . . a Hungarian Countess who had captivated Prince Alexander of Wurtemburg into making a morganatic marriage. Edward VII was a King who had harked back to a grandfather who had long lived with the Canadian Baroness whom he called Madame St. Laurent before, by his marriage with a Coburg, he begat a daughter to inherit the throne of England. "It is only my life", Queen Victoria used to say, "which separates my son from his wicked uncles"—that is why she felt she had to be so watchful over his bringing up.

As for her son Edward VII he did not inspire a similar awe— or love—but he and his winsome Queen were immensely popular. Feeling he would like to be a son of Napoleon III he enjoyed Paris, his society, his state, his food (the cold chicken at midnight, the ham and eggs for tea) but he was prompt and able in the dispatch of business and had an instinct for foreign affairs. His favourite in late years was Mrs. George Keppel, but she was never allowed to embarrass Queen Alexandra or imperil the decorum of a Court in which no one whose name was smirched by scandal was ever allowed to appear.

King George V came to present, in a more modern form, an ideal imbibed through thirty-six years of veneration of the widowed Victoria. She had even chosen for him—and with masterly perspicacity—a wife marked as much by her figure and deportment as by her virtues and strength of character to grow into a Queen impeccable and beloved.

Nevertheless, if one of Queen Mary's grandfathers was a royal Duke of Cambridge, the other was this romantic and handsome Prince who had put love before the claims of royalty and had produced a son to whom was given the name first of Prince—then Duke—of Teck. Queen Mary, who was a high-spirited girl, passionately interested in her family history as well as in the prestige of the Crown, never ceased to feel interest in her Hungarian grandmother, Claudine Rhedey, whose name she bore; for this reason, doubtless she better understood when it became apparent that there was something neither conventional nor Teutonic in the temperament of her eldest son, as indeed there had been an element distinctly tempestuous in her youngest brother. Knowing her heredity, she was aware that she could transmit a strain of something which through her sense of royal dignity few could discern in herself, or in her other children.

But when in 1910 the new reign of George V began, it was seen at once that the King and Queen would keep intact as they approached the age of fifty the regular tenor of their lives, lives circumspect, British and dutiful. King Edward had loved to dazzle the *nouveau riche* with a welcome into his splendour. King George took more notice of the busy men who had not made money. The glint of cosmopolitanism faded from the household and presence of a pair who spent little time abroad. Both King Edward and Queen Alexandra had spoken English with marked foreign accents; Queen Victoria had felt herself as much at home in German as in English. But King George V and Queen Mary cared no more for foreigners than for life on the Continent. Though their court had nothing of the stillness of Victoria's widowhood it became at once more staid and circumspect. The King's ways and tastes were those of a naval officer who had joined the *Britannia* on the River Dart in Devon in 1876. Queen Mary who had romped about as a healthy girl was not without a taste for the Continent. For early in the eighties her parents had found it advisable, on account of their bills, to leave Britain for Tuscany.

But by 1911 Queen Mary felt herself fully adequate to the position of supreme woman of the world. She too was "Erect and Obvious, the Queen of England".

She never discussed politics with men of affairs: she never made a speech. It was not for her to work on state papers. But the King consulted her on every point, and it was she who by virtue of her personality and her bearing upheld the dignity of the husband to whom she invariably appeared to defer. She never clashed with any person in any position. If she had trouble with any of her children, or even with so close an attendant as one of those personal maids who in the Court were known as 'dressers' she left it to the King to administer the rebuke; and all knew he would not mince matters.

Although she came forward as an authority on nurseries and on needlework, on maternity homes, on families as on furniture, she nurtured a secret instinct for the conduct of affairs with the royal prerogatives secured at the centre of them. Ever conscious of the throne and its prestige she was not one with whom even children could relax; nor did she ever really understand them or mother them. Her fine figure and her bearing were so majestic that her presence dominated any scene with the sense of obligation, of rightness and of reverence at the same time, as she showed herself to be very good and yet more kind.

So Buckingham Palace and Windsor changed once more: if neither sumptuousness nor gaiety was obvious, everything was of the best; the Americans and the Jews faded from the Court: it seemed less concerned with money and amusement, more with worth. Duty was its note; it became fully aware of the sufferings of the poor: it won a new esteem from its closeness to the people.

But it would be really absurd to think that either King George or Queen Mary were either unceremonious or partial to austerity. Their princely homes were all the reverse of Spartan—the cuisine was excellent, the sauces delicious, the comfort complete; and the Queen never came down to dinner but wearing a tiara and superb jewellery, while at dinner all men at the Court wore the Windsor uniform: an evening dress with scarlet collar and cuffs over knee-breeches.

The King looked back to the days of Victoria and was no

lover of novelty. When he saw a change he would say: "We never did that in the olden days." He no more liked women to smoke or paint their fingernails than he liked cocktails or jazz or Bolshevism. Nevertheless he so far accommodated himself to a changing world that when a Labour Government came in, he was so considerate and kindly with its members that the head of it, Ramsay MacDonald, said that, having come to the Palace to complete an anachronistic formality, he soon realized, as he confessed to M. André Maurois, that he was in the presence of a man who was immensely his superior.

CHAPTER III

PRINCE EDWARD had suited himself to the part of a Naval cadet, and the authorities had sent in a very favourable report. He expected to continue in the Navy. So he was surprised, and in fact annoyed, when as he turned seventeen he was told he was to give up his ship, travel to the Continent, and go on to Oxford. Most young men in the Navy have been delighted to live for a while as undergraduates. This one had an instinct that he would not be quite at ease with the demands it would make on him.

He came to Oxford not only younger but smaller than almost any other undergraduate, and added to this he was both shy, and averse from books. He was soon aware that his personality was hardly equal to his unparalleled prestige. Who could fail to observe the future King? Yet the youth they saw looked a babe. His features were as small as his stature, and unformed. He moved among the maturing *élite* of England as a child strayed from the nursery, a fledgeling fallen from the nest. It would have been a strain for any boy: how much more for one who was heir to the Imperial Crown!

It had been planned that he should have suitable companions and chief among them was Lord Stanley, heir to a princely position in Lancashire and to the massive Lord Derby. Stanley therefore was given rooms on the same staircase as the Prince, rooms looking on one side to a still cloister and the college Hall and the tower of Magdalen, on the other over green sward to the Colonnade and groups of seventeenth-century buildings still called 'new'. But the Prince at this time saw very little of Edward Stanley. Rank made little or no difference to his choice of intimates—the friend he preferred was a musical undergraduate, Eric Cipriani Dunstan, apart from whom he was seldom seen in the street. In a short time he was noticed wearing a fur collar driving a large open Daimler—that was what marked him among undergraduates who knew him as the Pragger

Wagger. To guide his work he had the most distinguished scholars, foremost among them, the President of Magdalen. Their report was kindly and favourable. "What a true sense of duty he has," wrote the Grand Duchess of Mecklenburg-Strelitz after he had stayed with her. "What a warm heart for what is right." But neither from Oxford scholars nor from his tutor Hansell, who now came back to keep an eye on him, did he amass the normal amount of book-learning. With the informal friendship he had found at Oxford, the Prince was happy to put in a second year. Then came the war.

As that long costly campaign wore on, it exhausted the country's financial reserves and bled the finest youth of England in the tragic attrition of trench warfare which Sir Winston Churchill and Lord Montgomery have justly denounced for its unavailing toll of promising life in an almost complete lack of strategic objective. The Prince in the uniform of a Grenadier moved through those scenes of blood and mud, courageous and unassuming, lithe in his body, not without cynicism in his mind. As the wastage wore on, it occurred to certain wise men that a move should be made to end it. Lord Lansdowne who had been both Foreign Secretary and Viceroy of India wrote in this sense a letter which *The Times* refused. It was then published in the *Daily Telegraph*, because in the very highest quarters pressure was put upon Lord Burnham, the proprietor of that paper. It would never have done to suggest that the King was not giving full support to his country's war: but a prudent man can sometimes sense a disaster to which party leaders are blind. The King who much preferred his generals could no longer give full confidence to Ministers who refused any helping action when his friend, ally and cousin was shot down with all his family in a dreadful cellar at Ekaterinburg. On the subject of war, the Prince, like his father, was under few illusions. He had, however, learnt the knack of getting in touch with common men because he shared in the hardships and dangers into which war forced them. He lived at close quarters with endurance, cynicism, mud, licence and death. And he gave the sympathy of his heart to those who in doing so suffered in years to come.

Sir Ronald Storrs says of a visit he made to the Nile that he entered at once into the spirit of Egyptian Cairo and all fell under "the fascination of that quiet human directness acclaimed later by the Empire and the World".*

When the war had ended, the Prince no longer showed the signs of physical immaturity which had so often embarrassed him at Oxford. In a phrase too often quoted and only partly correct, he avowed that he had found his manhood. In fact by the time of the armistice in 1918 he was already twenty-four.

* Storrs: *Orientations*, p. 193.

In general he had shown few signs of deep attraction to the opposite sex. But it was widely believed that he was in love with Lady Rosemary Leveson-Gower, a daughter of the Duke of Sutherland. In 1919 she married Lord Ednam who in time became Lord Dudley. The general belief in the Court was that if this romance had been duly encouraged, it would have saved the anxieties which the King and Queen, and not they alone, felt about the question of the Prince's marriage in later years. But did she return his interest? One can hardly think that Venus played her steady radiance on his youth. The very fact that wherever he turned he charmed and that the girls around him could hardly look at him without falling in love with him was only one of the things that made it so hard for him to choose one in particular who had the gifts and inclinations which would not only suit forever his special temperament but fulfil what it required for Princess of Wales, for Queen of England. It never occurred to Lady Elizabeth Bowes-Lyon as she grew up at her father's castle of Glamis in Forfarshire that it was she who was reserved for this role. In fact she was told not to think of anything like it. Her father, who had seen a good deal of King Edward VII had thought him too stout, believed that the simple ideals of a Scottish patrician were finer than those of the Court. "No," he used to say, "if there is one thing I have determined for my children, it is that they shall never have any sort of post about the Court."* But a few years later Prince Albert, the Duke of York, was resolutely in love with her and while she still hesitated as to whether her father's inclination was not right, the Prince of Wales said to her: "You had better take him, and go in the end to Buck House." Although both the Prince and the lady he finally married insist that he intended to take and keep the crown, those who could see into the deeper currents of his consciousness were constantly aware that something in his mentality gave him a secret warning of another fate.

As for the Prince of twenty-four who returned from the grim attrition of the trenches, his tastes were simple; he began to dance; he preferred films to the theatre and never read. What he learnt he learnt from talk. The best of companions when hilarity was loud around him, and the drink flowed, he was lifeless at ceremonies and nervous, with his fingers always at his collar and an itch for a cigarette. He was far from enjoying the brilliant functions of society. But when he spoke, he pleased, not because of wit but because he said the things that others say and ordinary people felt that he was one of them.

His hatred of dressing up and ceremonial, his thirst for ease, intimacy and cheeriness made him at home among people who, knowing little of rank and of what servants at that time added to

* It was said by Lord Strathmore to the author.

European life, gave his personality a power to evoke a boundless enthusiasm for what he personified—the glory of the crown—to which he added the glamour of freshness and youth, and a very easy way of giving a thrill to all sorts of girls who, turning up from nowhere, followed him—intimate and entranced. After a tour of Canada, he made a visit to Washington where Sir Edward Grey was Ambassador and combined a radiant charm with a dignity that suited his hosts.

Nevertheless, he was at times worn out. Then he turned to something to buoy him up while he coped with the scrutiny which could too easily denounce him as thoughtless, ungracious or unpunctual. Arriving now and again at some big house where social prestige gave an entry to the British Court, he could not always flatter his hostess. At some functions boredom blocked his memory; he had only to smile, but few can always smile. Close observers "never noted in him any study, any retirement, any sequestration from open haunts and popularity". But unless princes can escape from their Falstaffs to sages and some solitude, how can their characters solidify or their minds ripen?

There was already in the Prince of Wales a conflict between enthusiasm and whimsicality, between heart and inertia. He had few reserves of stamina and none of dignity. And already came a foretaste of the familiarity with which American newspapers were to headline their interest: among these were:

OH WHO'LL ASK THE PRINCE OF WALES WHAT HE WEARS ASLEEP?
HERE HE IS, GIRLS, THE MOST ELIGIBLE BACHELOR YET UNCAUGHT

Called Prince, he was a slave; by the time he left Australia—so he himself tells us—half killed by kindness, he was physically and mentally worn out. The weariness of it all! The foundation stones to lay, the trees to plant, the deputations to meet, the hospital wards to visit where men maimed by the war waited for the word of royal sympathy, the thousands, thousands of hands that pressed his own to ache and cramp. That was what it meant to be Prince of Wales in the Dominions.

The strain upon him was unfair, and unnerving. He could not stay to know anything; caught, he says, like a man in a revolving door, he was pushed on from behind. No matter how he would have liked to stay, no matter how tired he was, his tyrant programme lashed him ruthlessly on. He could not help reacting. That is why at times he felt the need of whisky, or of rest. Twenty years before, his dutiful father, in a like access of disgust, had burst out as he drove through the streets of Ottawa: "I've had enough of this—I'm not going on with it." His faithful spouse nudged him sharply and said: "Don't be a fool, George! You've *got* to go on with it." But who was there to nudge this Prince of Wales?

By 29th April, 1922, King George V had become aware of difficulties. He saw in the Duke of York, who had now succeeded in pressing his suit on Lady Elizabeth Bowes-Lyon, a prince not only sensible and easy but one who agreed with his own opinion about people and things. "We have always got on well together. Very different to dear David."*

To tell the truth the way the Prince of Wales had won the favour of youth and of the masses was rather by appeal to sentiment than industry on which judgment could base the approval which is won by careful work. In 1926, a veteran journalist, A. G. Gardiner, had interrupted the chorus of adulation with a warning which echoed the opinions of many who had to curb their instinctive respect with what comes from observation.

In 'Certain People of Importance' Gardiner wrote that the test of a governing machine is whether it functions widely and efficiently. He noted the acclaim which met the Prince on his various tours, and the amusement aroused by his horsemanship, and his rollicking diversions. Then—asking "what next?"—he went on that it would be idle to pretend that there was not an increasing note of anxiety in the question. The Prince, Gardiner said, has now passed through that phase in which it was sufficient to regard him as the Prince Charming of romance, a sort of visitor out of a fairy tale whose engaging ways so won all hearts and from whom nothing was asked but that he should appear ... "his spirits are high, his smile instant and responsive, his manner, boyish and impulsive, is certainly free from any of the calculated restraints. He can deliver a speech as gallantly as he can ride a horse." Though Gardiner refrained from mentioning the role of Prince Charming, he could not but observe the lack of seriousness. "What is excusable and of course natural in a youth," he wrote, "can be disquieting in a man," and it seemed that even at the age of thirty-two the Prince had not really attained the manhood he thought he had found in the trenches. On the *Renown* he had been photographed when acting in amateur theatricals. Of course these photographs should never have been published, and it worried Gardiner to see the papers splashed with pictures of the heir to the throne in undignified poses. He asked—even then in 1926—whether the general and admirable friendliness of the Prince could not be combined with a little more discrimination in the matter of his particular friendships. "The nation", he said, "would be gratified and relieved to find the heir to the throne settled in life."

Yes, that was the increasing preoccupation of those who knew most about what the Court required from the Prince, as his heart seemed to hover in butterfly flights from one woman to another: and so in fact he continued to do for the next five years.

* Sir John Wheeler-Bennett, *King George VI.*

And many a mother still had ambitions. "I am not a snob," said a certain Duchess when she saw him dancing at her country house, "but I confess I would like to see my daughter the Queen of England."

CHAPTER IV

A FAMILY, linked like the Royal House by blood relationship to the courts of Europe, had inevitably an interest in Foreign Affairs, and with that interest an instinctive sense of any revolution that could threaten a throne.

Among the things which King George noted were the large amount of unemployment and the growing dissatisfaction of the working classes. As far back as 1921 Lord Stamfordham had written to the Prime Minister (then Lloyd George) about the King's concern over such things. "The people are discontented and agitators seize their opportunities, marches are organized, the police interfere; resistance ensues; troops are called out and riot begets riot and possibly revolution." The King was deeply troubled about it. It was not enough to give little doles of fifteen shillings a week for men and twelve shillings a week for women. They should have productive work provided. If the government could always find enormous credits to pay for the military victories which were now turning out to be vanity, why should it not find smaller sums in order that those who wanted work should have it? Was the work of the soldier, the sailor, the airman the only employment for which Conservatives were willing to pay—or the only heroism for kings to honour?

That concern and question remained with George V. On 21st June, 1925, he told his Private Secretary to write to the Prime Minister (now Baldwin) how disturbed he was that trade should be going badly and men be out of work. He met people of every class: he heard on all sides how grave things were. Whatever were the causes, whatever the remedies, let the government have a fitting policy to deal with the crisis.

The King was not wrong. The next year a coal strike began. This soon led to a general strike which was taken as a challenge from the Trades Unions to the Government. Could they coerce, or at least intimidate it, and if so were they to have access to funds either from Banks or from Russia?

Once again the King acted as mediator. He advised the Ministers not to do anything that looked like confiscation. If foreign governments sent in money to cause or to maintain the strike, one could complain; but it would never do to hold back money which saved miners' families from starvation.

In settling this affair, Baldwin acted with great ability. Brought up to deal with personal regard for three hundred workmen all of whom he knew personally and whose welfare he had constantly at heart, he had the art of adjusting the reasonable demands of his employees with the business enterprise which secures contracts and brings income. He proved able in ticklish negotiations, and to complete these he found he had a man of remarkable powers of conciliation in his chief industrial adviser, Sir Horace Wilson, whom the King also learnt to appreciate personally.

All these affairs were watched closely by the Prince of Wales. He lent his car and chauffeur to circulate *The British Gazette*, edited by the Chancellor of the Exchequer, Winston Churchill, who had stood by his side when in robes of satin and velvet he had carried his golden sceptre at his investiture as Prince of Wales at the Castle of Carnarvon.

In the following year, 1927, both the Prince and the Prime Minister were invited to Canada to celebrate Canada's sixtieth year as a Dominion with an independent government. Baldwin was himself just sixty years of age in that year. He took with him his wife and his younger son, Windham,* while the Prince had as companion his youngest brother, the Duke of Kent. Thus the Prince and the Baldwins were constantly travelling together, with excellent opportunities to get to know one another.

The Prince has since written that he was irritated by the Prime Minister's mannerisms; and, to tell the truth, Baldwin had several. Not only had he a curious trick of stretching out his arms and clicking his fingers. He would put his hands in his pockets and take one out to shake his forefinger to drive home the point he wanted to make. Sometimes he would open his mouth and move his tongue from side to side without speaking; he would twist his face awry by pulling up one corner of his mouth; his pipe was always in his hand and he would polish it on his nose. All these were odd tricks to find in a Conservative Prime Minister who had been educated at Harrow and Cambridge.

But the two Princes seemed at the time to be on excellent terms with the Baldwins. As for the Prime Minister he was enthusiastic about the Prince, feeling for him that particular affection which an older man can offer to young royalty. His son too was very fond of the Prince, both then and when he met him at house parties in succeeding years. As for Mrs. Baldwin she made the Prince a hero of romance. Did he, as his book would suggest, reciprocate nothing of this? At the time he was cordiality itself to his father's First Minister and seemed very much to appreciate the curious mixture which all found in Baldwin of sagacity, warm-heartedness, sincerity and nerves.

* The present Earl Baldwin of Bewdley. The Prime Minister saw very little of his elder son, Oliver, who indeed became a Socialist; he died in 1958.

Passing in England's general opinion as a bucolic John Bull who wanted to get back to his pigs, Baldwin was in reality a man taut and complex, with a chaos storming within. Fundamentally kindly, he by no means lacked the guile with which the politician calculates as he balances the issues out between what he thought right and what he thought the country would stand; and those who watched him from day to day in Parliament were very well aware of it. His eyes glinted indeed with a steady humour. Yet in spite of that, his face looked often tired, tired by the baffling questions which he asked of time and eternity as he looked into the depths of his being or of his country's life.

That face was not easy to read. It was that of a prosperous businessman in the country who was the father of six children and the head of a big manufacturing firm. Somehow he had found when he came to live in London that people trusted him. He plunged into politics, yet he knew their limits. Like Cavour, he knew that, if politicians were to do for themselves what they were doing for what they called their country, they would be denounced as rascals. And when asked by Curzon in 1922 what he thought of the government's programme, he said: "It looks to me like the prospectus of a fraudulent company-promoter."*

The Prince, too, had his doubts of the existing order of politics: behind his boyishness, he too was puzzled by the complexities of the world. He, too, suffered from a recurring conflict. His quick mind, his business flair, and his unrivalled gift of popular appeal were countered by a restless moodiness which rendered incalculable the impulses of his already headstrong will.

In 1928, the year after his return from Canada, the Prince embarked upon a tour of Africa. In the midst of it he was recalled because the King, his father, was dangerously ill with septicaemia. At Brindisi he found two letters from his brother, the Duke of York. In one of them he read: "There is a lovely story going round about from the East End that the reason of your rushing home is that in the event of anything happening to Papa I am going to bag the throne in your absence."† The Prince's return, as we shall see, was not without other strong ingredients of personal drama which were a prelude to that of his reign.

Though the old King slowly recovered, he was never so strong and energetic as he had been before. In the remaining years of his life his character seemed to soften and ripen; he rose to higher levels as a man. His old readiness to call those around him devils and every other name under the sun did not leave him. But until 1931 he had one companion, Sir Charles Cust, who had abused

* Hon. A. W. Baldwin. *My Father*, pp. 138–40.
† This story was told to the author at the time by Charles, Viscount Halifax.

him since the time they were midshipmen together and even now would answer the King's tirades with the comment "I never heard such nonsense in my life". After Cust died the only person left who could speak to him in the tone of equality was his sister Victoria. And he loved to tell the story of how when at half past nine in the morning—the hour when His Majesty regularly telephoned to her—she heard the bell ring and taking up the receiver said, "Hullo, you old fool", the operator, knowing that there was only one person to whom this greeting could be addressed, broke in, "Beg pardon, Your Royal Highness, His Majesty is not yet on the line."*

When she died on 3rd December, 1935, it was a fearful blow. "No one", he said, "had a sister like her." After that even his writing changed.

During the King's illness he got to know of the solicitude and regard of his countless subjects. It was with the gravest concern that they watched the progress of his malady and his slow recovery. This consciousness warmed his heart and deepened his strong sense of responsibility in fulfilling in his simple way the functions of the Crown, to which he and his Consort were in fact giving a new and immensely significant development.

One of his preoccupations was that he was the personal owner of huge properties—Britain's biggest landlord by far, and that ownership meant always responsibility: he was the head of a wide family connected with many thrones some of whom still survived: he was the head of society, not only in Great Britain but in the whole Empire which still included India, and its many potentates.

But beside all this he was the pivot and centre of Parliamentary government carried on in his own name. It was for him to execute every document to which the state seal is affixed. He must have instant knowledge of every event which touched Britain's relation to the powers. Without the signature which witnessed his approval none could hold high office in Army, Navy or Air Force, in Church or State. There was a moment when the Archbishop of Canterbury was inconvenienced because the King was not well enough to sign the document which enabled the Archbishop to draw his salary of fifteen thousand pounds a year. The King must know not only his Ambassadors but all those who were accredited to his court. He did not meet his Ministers in Council, but he must know forthwith the minutes of every meeting of the Cabinet. He was advised by Ministers how he was to act; but, on the other hand, he was bound to know of the matters which they laid before him. For the King's right to be informed means the duty of digesting the information so that he may exercise his right, which is no less than a duty, to advise

* John Gore: *King George V.*

24

and to warn. King George V saw them all: both Ministers and State Papers, as his grand-daughter, Queen Elizabeth, sees them still, dealing with both with faultless regularity and dispatch.

As Mr. Gore admirably said of the King: "He is the head of the State. Everything that is done in his name is his personal responsibility still . . ." and with George V conscience required that he should give formal approval to nothing which his judgment—strengthened as that was by unique experience—urged was unsound or unwise in the interest of the country as a whole until he had said all he could for a reconsideration. The King, "is above party and beyond controversy, and these conditions with his continuity of office assure him the opportunity to gain an experience greater and to exercise a judgment cooler than any of his Ministers. Within the compass of his abilities, a constitutional King would always influence his Ministers and the history of his country; and the more conscientious he is the more will he try to master the intricacies of the problems which face his governments and to decide for himself if the solutions which they propose are the best and wisest." The Sovereign reproduces in himself—or herself—the advisory function of the heads of the services whether civil or military. Now King George was extremely conscientious, some thought too much so. The Prince Consort's decision that Ministers should submit to the Sovereign all papers of importance had such weight with him that from the moment of his accession, with his Private Secretary beside him, he was busy with his boxes. "Rare indeed was the occasion", writes the Duke of Windsor, "that I went to his room without finding him poring over their contents." He used to say that his Private Secretary, Lord Stamfordham, taught him to be a King.

When he could, he spoke out with the wisdom of the man who values what he inherited: when he had to face an unwelcome change, he would say: "There's nothing I can do about it." On affairs he was voluble and his voice was loud. He might not have been a reader of history, he might not always have been fit for a spelling bee and to the end of his life he was floored by such words as mausoleum, business and academy. But gradually—always with precious help from the Queen—he had mastered the essentials of government, his native simplicity buttressing the intuition which is so often the possession of a man who has to do the work of an immense position. Thus he had with the years come to exercise the power of a mind of extreme uprightness and at the same time shrewd.

This had got through to the people: they had come to know the King as a man all their own, devoted to his duty and exercising in his bluff way the same sort of benevolent suzerainty which their grandparents had recognized and venerated in Queen Victoria. He liked his own choice: if things displeased

25

him he let people know it, and his talk, the sailor idiom of Victorian days, was flavoured with words which name perdition to express annoyance. When these were too loud on public occasions Queen Mary would say: "Not now George—wait till you get home." "Good God, how should I know?" he answered a visiting royalty who asked where one could find the Prince of Wales. He was through it all a very religious man who from his boyhood had read his daily chapter from the Bible, and he recommended others to do likewise. In times of stress he would cherish and quote an old naval saying: "Keep your hair on!"

PART TWO

The Preceding Complications:
Hitler, Geneva and Mrs. Simpson

CHAPTER V

By 1931, King George, at the age of sixty-six, and after reigning twenty-one years, was extremely well informed about the government of his Empire and the people who ran it. Two years before important things had happened. The Baldwin government had lost the election; and there had been a sudden collapse first on the Stock Exchange of New York, and then in the whole trading system of the world.

The year 1931 was also to prove of great moment in the story of the British Crown. Both Court and Government saw an immense increase in its prestige and function. In the preceding year there had been an Imperial Conference to discuss the relations of the Dominions to London. Now their aspirations were embodied in the Statute of Westminster.

This made the Dominions of Canada and New Zealand, the Australian Commonwealth, the Union of South Africa, and the Irish Free State into states absolutely independent of Great Britain. Their only link with the Mother Country was in their fealty to the Crown. The preamble to the Statute of Westminster expressly stated that "the Crown was the symbol of the Free Association of the members of the British Commonwealth of Nations and that they are united by their common allegiance to the Crown."

Henceforward, no law passed by the British Parliament would extend to a Dominion unless with the request and consent of that Dominion.

Henceforward, too, it would be in accord with the established constitutional position of all members of the Commonwealth that the Parliaments of each should ratify any change in the succession to the throne, or in the royal style and titles.

But the Statute embodied in law a principle which had been growing stronger all through the reign of George V. Though strengthened by tariffs, commerce, tradition, culture, and above all by language, *the cohesion of the British Commonwealth of Nations depended finally upon the Crown.* It was therefore of enormous importance that its occupant should be worthy of the regard with which his office was invested. The sovereign embodied more than ever both the legal and the human elements of the Imperial Unity.

Hardly had the Statute of Westminster been passed than the stress of a financial crisis which shook America, Britain and Europe became more acute. In August of that year the state of British finances was so critical that the King felt obliged to consult leaders of all parties, and at the suggestion of one of these he took the big step of inviting them to form a coalition.

By the beginning of 1931 it was plain that the crisis involved not only the banking but the government of Britain, the credit of which was now in danger, with her pound. All depended on loans from the United States. American bankers, who had worries enough of their own, were in no mood to advance money to finance what they considered Socialist extremes. It was a question of cutting allowances which had eased the lot of the poor—that on one side and on the other securing enough confidence from the masters of finance to enable Britain to obtain the goods without which her people could not live. It was because the King saw that danger for the people from the Socialists insisting on their theories that he felt that there must be a compromise between the parties. He decided that he must see the leaders of them all. Leaving the seclusion of Balmoral, he came to London to do so, and insisted that they should face reality.

No doubt it was the King's own thought that the Liberal, Sir Herbert Samuel, who was deputizing for Lloyd George, was voicing when he spoke for a coalition. Baldwin arrived later and agreed. Ramsay MacDonald, after a stormy meeting with his Labour Cabinet, decided to become the leader of a coalition government in which few of his former colleagues were prepared to take a place.

Together the new Government coped with first the slump and then with the political portents which resulted from it in 1932: the rise to power in Germany of Hitler, in America of Roosevelt. The régime of the rich had suddenly overreached itself. Here were the two men who, embodying the reaction, were in their time to lead the world to the triumph of Russia and of Revolution. Each of these men was out for a New Deal: each wanted to curb capitalism, each was influenced by Moscow. Hitler while denouncing it secretly offered it the flattery of imitation. Roosevelt on the other hand made his moves in the Socialist direction with due regard for the enterprising spirit of the United States. But he was the first American to recognize the Moscow government, saying that Russia and America must get together (before he had finished, indeed they did!) and he espoused Russian causes in China. Of all this England as yet recked little. The King, however, soon saw that there was danger brewing in Germany. At the same time he was anxious to explore the possibility of an agreement; for after all one basis of Hitler's thinking was admiration for Great Britain. The answer that the King got from his Permanent Under-Secretary for Foreign Affairs was not encouraging. There was also Italy. He knew from Sir Ronald Graham that Mussolini had also for twelve years made friendship with Britain a cornerstone of his policy, and that he had freed Italy from the menace of revolution. In any case if Germany was becoming warlike again, it would be better to have Italy on the right side.

In these broad views of Foreign Affairs, he and the Prince of Wales were inclined to agree.

Such was the state of British government under Ramsay MacDonald whom Winston Churchill designated at the time as the 'Boneless Wonder'.

Neither MacDonald nor Sir John Simon, his Foreign Secretary, took any decisive action on Foreign Affairs. They put their trust in the League of Nations which, though it might have set out to right the wrongs of the world, was sometimes used as a means of coercing the defeated into longer subservience. It never gave a constructive lead to solving Europe's major problems; worse almost than that, it had a sense of its own prestige which impelled nations towards war to defend that prestige when by their traditional diplomacy they would have worked for equitable adjustment. While flattering the idealists that it provided the stronghold of a just peace it placed at the disposal of intriguers a contrivance for hiding their designs under a cover of virtue.

With regard to these great issues which lead to wars, it was only the more dangerous because it could justly claim that it did useful work in dealing with certain special abuses. But the Prince of Wales, like many Conservatives of the time (not only in Britain), had no patience with it. It was exploited in fact as an insidious appendage to the Treaty of Versailles. And he saw through this exploitation.

Into his interest in foreign affairs came five far-reaching complications: his intense sympathy with the lot of the poor, and especially those who could find no work: his interest in trade and business, as distinct from the services, though of course he knew these too: his dislike of books and documents: his fancy for the latest style of diversions, not least in night clubs, tangos and jazz, especially those American favourites of the early twenties, the 'Charleston' and the 'Blackbottom' which had come from negroes in the Southern States, with accompanying cocktails. Then in the daylight a point-to-point and steeplechase—but far more serious than any of these the way his predilections turned from the society that pleased his parents, and his brothers of York and Gloucester to occupy himself and his heart with friends such as gay Gertie Lawrence and the lovely Mrs. Dudley Ward. Through and after the First World War, the world was already changing fast—though not yet at the giddying pace it changed through and after the Second World War. But in his family it was he alone who with 'a hydra-headed wilfulness' defied both his parents and their friends in his choice of intimates.

If any of his brothers had choices which their parents depre- cated, personal attraction gave way sooner or later to the counsels of their parents, and so as the years went on the example given by the spontaneous choice of the Duke of York was followed. The Princess Mary had been married to one who was then one of Britain's wealthiest noblemen who easily adapted himself to the role of son-in-law of the King. The Princes had married young ladies irreproachable in character as in lineage: daughters of an earl, of a duke, of a royalty of Greece. But the Prince of Wales, so quickly friendly with the girls who attached them- selves to him on his tours, had not, since that early case of Lady Ednam, evinced any real interest of the heart *except in women already married*. There was not only Mrs. Dudley Ward. Many thought he really preferred Americans—others noticed how he took to Argentines, and Thelma Lady Furness was so often at his house that she gradually and tactfully assumed the role of a sort of hostess there.

But now in this year of 1932 when Hitler and Roosevelt rose in their rival orbits of revolutionary leadership the Court and society of London realized that there too a fateful personality had appeared upon the scene. Fashion seized the fact that the Prince of Wales had a new and central interest in his friendship with an American friend of Lady Furness—this friend was the wife of a London magnate in Marine Insurance. The rapid growth of this interest titillated the taste for innuendo among those in the know: it soon caused anxious concern to the Court and the King.

Both the Prince and this lady have now given us their stories, stories in which there is no attempt to hide what caused the element of scandal which became more and more marked, as the two had more opportunities of meeting. Both imply that they very soon ignored any claims of loyalty. The truth is that he chose to depart in several important respects from the tradition of the Court. They are therefore at a loss to explain what really happened when the Prince ascended the throne. There were salient points where the Prince departed from that tradition of the Court which had come to play so great a part in the con- stitutional life of both Britain and the Commonwealth.

Since he felt himself thoroughly at home in the United States, he soon suited himself to the headlines which had disconcerted his father. His free ways, his lack of conventionality, the veil of

30

wildness he was apt to spread over his duties, his distaste for ceremony and state all helped to make him at one with Americans; and he thought it would be a good thing if he, and those like him, paid a visit every two or three years to this new, rich, powerful, innovating country.

Then, when it was discovered that he could do something for British prestige and British trade in the New World and especially to counteract the enterprise of Fascist Italy in South America, he had gone with the Duke of Kent to do a tour in the Argentine and Chile. He had learned Spanish for the occasion and he exerted himself to secure popularity for Britain and things British. He became known as Britain's best salesman. He was the Ambassador Prince who could exert the skill and represent the enterprise and claim of London better than any commercial counsellor in an embassy. He could in fact suit himself almost as well to an America which looked towards Mother Spain as to one which spoke—in its own way—the language of England. He was not always easy to manage; and from time to time there was a scene. Yet wherever he went he soon learnt, and always kept, the technique of putting himself in touch with people who in their struggle with material conditions had flung off the conventions and constraints of Europe. Brazilians were surprised to find that in a sports club at Rio de Janeiro, he insisted on changing in the general clubroom, and taking his shower with others. He saw with his own eyes that linked with the prosperity of the new world there was a life of hardship which put a discount on squeamishness and catered for comfort both with new inventions, open shirts, and living for fresh air and a sensible freedom. All that suited him finely, whether in South America, North America, or the British Empire.

From the freedom of the New World he came back to Old England to meet face to face the conditions of the masses of the people and the woes of the unemployed. These after the slump of 1932 mounted to the grim figure of *two millions*. Here were people wanting to work and kept idle, living on a pittance. A Prince who had his home in palaces and moving among homes where all was of the best in comfort and style, saw under grey skies, and in the hideous conditions of industrial poverty, with its desolate streets, its fetid mines, its noisy factories, the squalor of the masses of Great Britain. What a contrast between that, and the lives of those boys who went, say, to public schools —or to the very few whom he was in the habit of visiting who lived in the amplitude of great homes as the ruling, the privileged class of England! There was about one in every hundred who could have a comfortable and amusing time, with the sustenance and solace of class superiority. What was one to say of those odd fifty millions who made up the rest? The Prince had spoken in

31

strong terms of what he saw when he went among the very poor and saw their needs; he spoke of how little had been done for them in a country so obviously wealthy and with certain displays of riches irresponsible and blatant.

Moved as he was from place to place and scene to scene which made such demands upon his attention and his heart, he was, as we saw, often worn out. When he was so, he turned for repose, not to quiet but to distraction. His distractions were those of an age which lived in an uneasy pose between its dope and its stimulation, its cocktails, its cigarettes and its cinema. Had he been an intellectual, or a very strong character, he might have turned to purer founts of refreshment. But there was in him a temperamental, an instinctive reaction against the standards and habits of his parents.

For part of that his father was no doubt to blame. King George V with those virtues of simplicity, sincerity, heartiness, kindliness, strong sense and love of duty which the British loved because such things were in the compass of the average man—with all these never arrived at mastering the new parental art of putting himself in touch with his own children.

Sensitive in himself, the King did not get so far as to realize what would make his children uncomfortable. He was, says Sir Harold Nicolson, "frequently pragmatic and sometimes harsh".*

For the language of the King was, as could have been gathered already, anything but veiled or formal when he wanted to express disapproval. His voice was loud, his words were rough.

That this impaired the King's relations with his sons was only too well known in the circles of the Court; and at last Lord Derby, as an intimate friend of His Majesty, ventured to say that he found his sons' companionship one of his greatest pleasures: Why should the King also not be on good terms with *his* sons? There was a pause of some minutes before the King answered. Then he said: "My father was frightened of his mother, I was frightened of him, and I am damned well sure that they are going to be frightened of me."

Does that do? The comment given by a Prime Minister to the present writer was: "He didn't know how to bring up his sons." But his task was made more difficult by the passionate enthusiasm with which the Press chronicled every move of the Prince, who was given the idea that no matter what he did, it was right. This was in its way just as unfair to him as his father's bullying. Between them they made him a man to whom none cared to offer counsel. For the crises to come newspapers were piling up drama for their darling.

* H. Nicolson: *George V*, p. 365.

CHAPTER VI

WHO can wonder if the Prince of Wales who was greeted on one side with adulation and worship was abashed when he faced in his father so bluff and fierce a disciplinarian ? Recoil, not without a certain obstinacy, was only to be expected: and there was in the character of the Prince that other strain—that turned for distraction to violent exercise, to daredevil riding, to dancing in the new restless negroid style which swept the English-speaking world and which sought in cigarette and cocktail relief from the strain of living. Just when the Prince needed steadying and tranquillizing habits he met the swift but unsettling changes of his set. Even before 1930 he had lost that freshness which once added so much to the charm of his naïveté: he looked strained and was at times moody. His character had been subjected to a tension too unique, too subtle, too varied and continuous for it to ripen and strengthen from those first immaturities which had made him both difficult to manage and odd in the choice of companions. In his nature there was something which cried for relaxation—but also an impulse which lured him to risks and inclined him to take them.

He was, if not at war, at issue not only with his parents but with his whole position as Prince of Wales. On the one side, it was of course infinitely flattering; but, taken as a whole, he was seeming to lose patience with it. The result was on one side an inclination to escape from it into distracting noise, or to give it an unprecedented flavour which might appeal to the masses in a modernized and in fact disintegrated world. Nor was this restlessness astonishing. If memories can haunt with horror, so anticipations can be ghoulish too. Danger was in the wind, Europe had found no solutions to the issues which in 1914 had led to war. On the contrary, it saw in every direction millions of men on the edge of starvation. It complained now of overproduction, now of under-consumption. Half of it wanted to sell what the other half did not want to buy: and the result was that not only in Britain, but yet more in Germany capable men starved when they wanted to work: youth went too often from disgruntlement to despair.

In 1931, the year of the Statute of Westminster, the Prince made another tour of Africa. Returning in the autumn, he established himself in a new home which from henceforth became the centre of his relaxation and the background of the personal drama which at the same time began to dominate his life. Here George IV had lodged one of his favourites. But no one

33

of note had lived in it till the Prince made it his own, now in 1931. It was ideally situated—six miles from Windsor, twenty-five from London, placed among woods to the south of Virginia Water.

The Prince tells us that he delighted in its seclusion, and expended on it the art of the creator. It had been surrounded by funereal yews: he cut them down and changed laurel to rhodo-dendrons with vivid flowers. He made an overgrown pond into a swimming bath; he worked his gardeners hard and in their absence at weekends he threw his own energy into clearing away the undergrowth, replanting shrubs, peopling the herbaceous borders with the bloom of flowers and cutting winding paths through groves of pine or birch.

He had not been there a year before he began inviting that new friend who for the years succeeding has been the over-mastering influence on his life. We shall learn how he met her. She was the second wife of a London business man, Ernest Simpson.

In the Prince the passion of gardening thus replaced that for riding riskily and hard: as in earlier years squash had given way to golf, now golf found its gracious rival in this garden. He even forced his guests to pour their energy into this new venture; while he made the house itself comfortable and modern with hot water and central heating, to which he added showers and a steambath. Here in England was a house with those physical *agréments* which defy the English climate and emulate America.

The old Greek adage tells us that 'character is fate'. Here the Prince's character found a frame in which hardening in its strength it gloried. Here he prepared month by month for the fateful years of his reign. For here his new friendship with Mrs. Simpson transformed into standing enmity with his father, a secret but obstinate warfare.

Yes, Mr. Bolitho gives us the key to the situation when he tells us that "frequent chastening made the Prince of Wales secretive, stubborn and more self-willed than ever". He came to look upon his father, the Archbishop of Canterbury, and some of the older Ministers as critics and unsympathetic company designated to frustrate his natural eagerness, and his apparent success with the newspapers. He therefore made his own life as he wished in "a circle of friends of which his father did not approve".*

And now—out of this set which they could not like came the woman who in her story, her definiteness and her personality was the epitome of a smartness which regarded nothing as superior to itself, and had engaged against the standards and rules of the past.

In herself Mrs. Simpson was anything but noisy: she was

* H. Bolitho: *Edward VIII*, p. 150.

34

quiet, sensible, slim, shrewd.* Though described by an admirer as gay, she could interest and please good and cultured men. But she was very much the American out for adventure, the American who had long ceased to be accepted by her family's set in Baltimore. Her polish was of steel, well rubbed by knife powder. She had cut sharply into the fruit-cake of life. She appealed to the Prince, as she maddened his servants, by the ways of the little woman who busies herself with the small things on which a house's efficiency depends; she also kept in her own way abreast of affairs in those critical years of history. In the closing years of the reign of King George V, the Prince's attentions to this lady were so marked that they occasioned wide comment in the world of fashion as well as in American newspapers. It was but too clear that he had placed at her disposal the heart which some had believed attached to Lady Furness, and this in spite of the fact that she was living with her English husband after divorcing for desertion another husband yet alive.

The King had long been concerned about his son and his circle; but even he was ill prepared for *this*. He was shocked, affronted, alarmed. He turned to the Duke of Connaught who combined a genial command with the courtliest manner to say a word so bland that even the Prince would listen. He sought counsel in his bluff direct way of his Prime Minister. He poured out his heart again and again to his Primate. He spoke out freely to Sir Horace Wilson and Mr. Walter Monckton. But who was to counsel discretion, who to moderate or guide the passion of a headstrong Prince, a passion like a charger let loose on the highway and the open field with the bit between his teeth, and hurling forward in the saddle a figure clinging, frail, unnerved and fitful in his charm?

By 1934 it was now six years since Ernest Simpson had awoken in the lady's heart what she called deep feelings of love. She avows that now those deep feelings came once more into her life. What is certain is that she soon saw she had the Prince of Wales as a new admirer.

During that summer new feelings came into the heart of the Duke of Kent. He succeeded in fixing his affections on a beautiful Princess whose grandfather had been King in Greece and whose sister was married to that elegant cosmopolitan, Prince Paul of Yugoslavia. The Duke accordingly was married to Princess Marina on 29th November, 1934. The Prince of Wales arranged that the Simpsons should be invited to the state reception at Buckingham Palace before the wedding. He not only presented her to Prince Paul, but took her up to speak with the King and Queen themselves. She tells us that she was impressed by their gift of putting people at their ease. Of *their*

* Elsa Maxwell, quoted by W. B. Wells, *Why Edward Went*, p. 31.

impression there is no record—but they did not receive her again. She was wearing a striking dress—so striking that Prince Paul made it the occasion of a compliment. But was he really so favourably impressed ? Few were, and he was a man of exquisite taste. It was not until afterwards that Mrs. Simpson learnt the lesson that the height of success in garb is less to be striking than correct—that in fact the only way the trained eye is won is by the elegance of plainness. She was present in Westminster Abbey for the Duke's wedding. Her story from now on was that of *Wallis in Wonderland.*

This wedding cut the Prince of Wales from the closest friend in his family, so Mrs. Simpson tells us. Others, and the Duke of Kent among them, said it was not his marriage but the Prince's occupation with Mrs. Simpson which cut him from every member of the family circle. Certainly the Duke of Kent was the one brother, eight years younger than himself, with whom he was on terms of comradeship with the flattering addition of finding the young man if anything gayer and more of a jazzboy than himself. "Handsome and gallant", Sir Winston Churchill was to call him at his death. None ever accused him of being too serious. He was gallant whichever way one pronounced the word. He was, says Mrs. Simpson, "tempestuous", adding that "in the years before I knew him he had sowed his share of wild oats; but the Prince of Wales had taken him in hand." If this is intended to imply that either the Prince or Mrs. Simpson were responsible for the change that settled him as a happy husband with Princess Marina it would give not quite the exact idea of what happened. What did happen is that as the Prince became more and more preoccupied with Mrs. Simpson, his brother, though once saved from great dangers by his eldest brother's intervention, turned back from an errant love to the traditions of the Court.

The devoted brothers separated—and the Prince felt himself further and further away from every member of his family. At times he felt it and yearned for the good simple soundness of a tradition he had flung over; at times he remembered a religious phase when he had actually sought a spiritual counsellor to whom for a time he made confessions, seeking absolution from the life he led. And sometimes, on Sunday afternoons, he would go over for evensong to St. George's Chapel, listen to its excellent choir and fine acoustics, and sitting in his stall as Knight of the Garter, would find "an inner comfort of the Spirit" he had seldom known elsewhere, and certainly seldom sought. His was a simple mind but a complex nature. How could he be without nobler cares ? For he believed that he could give monarchy a new scope and power in connection with this changing world to which he suited himself; he had evanescent ideals, with hankerings after higher things he sensed yet could never quite make his own.

36

While he thus looked before and after with a craving for what was not within his grasp, he turned more and more to that something, partly wonder and enchantment, partly elfish and princely impulse, and all subtilized by the alternations of satisfied and unsatisfied longing—that something which he found, and exchanged, in the scintillating companionship of this frank, informed, open, direct, understanding, piquant American woman who had gained social experience as she flashed from friend to friend, becoming more and more skilled in the art of making swift approaches to men, and giving each what he found amusing; who was gay as a lark and who was now married—in the Register Office—to a British subject, the able, well bred, highly honourable and cultured master of marine insurance, Ernest Simpson who had once been in the Coldstream Guards.

She knew the better how to talk to this Prince in that she had peered into the forces and ideas working in his world, now in Bolshevism, now in Fascism, now in changing China: she was informed, adroit, witty and discriminating: and, since never without a dash of daring, she was spirited and surprising in the vigour of her views and in the deftness with which she voiced them. She mixed her cocktails well. She knew just how to make a party a success and give her guests the food they would enjoy. She was always the little woman who could see to all the little things. Each of her menus was a masterpiece. She knew when to put in the squeeze of lemon. She would put her finger under the mantelpiece to see if it had been properly dusted. She was keen as a knife, and sharp as a needle. And she helped the Prince tremendously because when he stated a view she could correct for him in argument without ever trying his brain with things that would be out of his depth. He was fascinated by the lissom leanness of her short figure, by the brown waves of her hair, by the blue gleam of her intelligent eyes, by the wit that darted, like deer from bracken, out of her demure naïveté. Her talk was as pointed as her dress was neat. Her highest praise was to add to blame the confiding wink which belied it.

His feelings about her were summed up in the simple phrase he got more and more to repeat: "Wallis is a wonderful woman." And he repeated this phrase like a sort of incantation as the devotees of Coué used at that time to say "In every way on every day, I become more gay and more gay and more gay".

Those who criticized his friendship never spoke: the newspapers' talk was in reality destroying his judgment: he grew unable to distinguish between the wounds of the friend and the flatterer's kisses which in the last resort would prove fatal.

CHAPTER VII

BOTH the Prince and his favourite have, as we saw, told their story, and hers was written with what Lord Brownlow calls "an almost blinding veracity", with candour and constant wit, often at her own expense. So we know much, though perhaps not all, of the past of the lady whom London then addressed as Mrs. Simpson. Born in 1896 on the borders of Pennsylvania, she was the daughter of Teacle Wallis Warfield (who was the son of a merchant interested in Republican politics) and of his wife Alice Montague. There are plenty of these families left today in and around Baltimore; and the details of her bringing up are not hard to canvas.*

But she has told us sufficient herself. She was given at her christening the names of Bessie and Wallis. When she was three her father died; and her mother, after preparing dinners for paying guests, secured means enough to send her daughter to Arundel School where the smarter girls of Baltimore went. In 1908 when little Bessie was twelve, her mother was married again, being given away by her sister, the Bessie after whom the daughter was named, the lady known in Baltimore as Mrs. Buchanan Merryman, married to a man in comfortable circumstances. From then on money was not lacking in the girl's education. She went to a finishing school. She learnt to ride, to play golf and tennis, and then on leaving school came out in Baltimore in 1914 under the wing of an uncle who had made money, Solomon Davis Warfield.

The Warfields and the Montagues were both very good families with inherited properties, backgrounds, and a love of horses; but the position of Mrs. Teacle Warfield at that moment was not such as to make the social standing of the young Bessie secure in her own city.

In 1916 down in Florida she met a man whom she called the world's most fascinating aviator, Earl Winfield Spencer. They fell in love and were married before long at Christ Church in Baltimore. Her complaint, however, is that his taste for drink offset his charms. They quarrelled, but when he was stationed in China she agreed to follow him. But there, she says, his drinking bouts again disturbed her—though they did not disturb his career as an airman: in any case, she separated from him. Although she does not say so, she must have known what it is to be uncertain of one's income, and men were sorry for her. Her

* What follows in the next pages is based solely on the autobiography of the Duchess of Windsor.

38

husband, she says, gave her two hundred and twenty-five dollars a month out of his naval pay and she asked for further help from her uncle Solomon. She does not speak at this turn of seeking regular employment.

But she went over to America and Europe, and returned to the China Coast, settling for a time in Hong Kong. Then she remembered that she had the address of an Englishman in Shanghai. They met in a bar; they spent the evening together, and at the end of it she had established a friendship which opened to her the doors of many interesting houses in Shanghai. It will be enough—she tells us—if we know of this kind young Englishman as Robbie.

After she had tasted in his company the hospitality of Shanghai, she went on to Pekin. There she met a woman she had known before, now married to Herman L. Rogers. In Pekin the foreign men outnumbered the women by ten to one. In such circumstances, a smart young American woman separated from her husband can have a very gay time, and gay it was for Mrs. Spencer. As she herself puts it, "The incidence of honourable men with dishonourable intentions was undoubtedly higher than a Sunday School teacher might knowingly have tolerated for long . . . every woman could be Cinderella and midnight never struck. . . ."* In fact she tells us that it was her conscience which compelled her to seek a change, and that when she returned to the purlieus of Baltimore she had become in her uncle's eye the black sheep of the family. When he died he left his money not to her but to found a home where women could retire when they had no visible means of support. In this book to quote Lord Brownlow again, "there is no attempt to gloss over mistakes or to file down the rough edges of fact". What is the object of writing such a frank and flavoured narrative ? Surely to show that in the most perilous risks, this lady was always mistress of her poise. Hers was no frail vessel to capsize in a sudden squall: this elegant craft could look on arctic tempests and be never shaken; or if sailing to seas where tropic sunset

> Streams o'er a rich ambrosial ocean-isle
> And overhead the stately palm-trees
> Whisper in odorous heights of even

she would be far too skilfully steered for a coral reef to scrape her keel.

She was still waiting to put her divorce case through, when, on a visit to New York, she met with an old friend, Mary Raffray, now married to a French officer. With Jacques and Mary Raffray was an Englishman, Ernest Simpson, who had

* Duchess of Windsor: *The Heart Has Its Reasons*, p. 131.

been in love with her. But instead he had married the divorced wife of another man, and this already led him to tragedy.

Mr. and Mrs. Ernest Simpson were, in fact, finding marriage a strain and considering how they could dissolve it.

Sad evidence had convinced Simpson that he could not live happily with her. Much distressed at the plight in which he found her in Paris, he went back to seek counsel from Madame Raffray who could only advise divorce. So it was that each on the point of obtaining a divorce, Mr Ernest Simpson and Mrs. Wallis Spencer met in the house of Madame Raffray who appreciated to the full the gifts and personality of the old friend to whom she had been bridesmaid in 1916. She asked Ernest Simpson if he did not find this his solution: here was a woman who should give him consolation, companionship and love.

This is the true story of how the two Simpsons found their way to the Register Office: and later it became of the greatest moment to each of them. The time was to come when just as Mary Raffray had counselled Ernest Simpson to marry Mrs. Spencer, so this Mrs. Spencer, as Mrs. Simpson, was to counsel Ernest Simpson to marry Mary Raffray.

About the time that Mrs. Spencer met Mr. Simpson, she consulted a clairvoyant, who filled her mind with wild surmise. But she was now the legal, secure and happy wife of Ernest Simpson.

All that she tells us of her early life is essential to the story of the reign of King Edward VIII. "Her youth and earlier years in the States and the Far East," says Lord Brownlow, "might at first appear irrelevant—but they are not—since to my mind they provide the whole answer to a question of vital importance. How did she allow herself to become the flash-point of a great crisis?"

The new Mrs. Ernest Simpson was now thirty-two. She had the reassuring conviction that she was establishing herself in a solid position—the more to be appreciated after her preceding trials. Her restlessness left her. Her husband was comfortably off: he was quiet, cultured, well-read, kindly, pleasant. He had had a commission in the Coldstream Guards. He knew what was what and he cared for her. His sister had a high social position in London with a great house in Belgrave Square where she often entertained the Prince of Wales. But she did not invite her new sister-in-law at the same time: she did not think it would fit in.

Nevertheless a few months after Wallis Spencer married Ernest Simpson in 1928, she caught her first glimpse of the Prince. Slim and youthful, though not without a look of strain after his rushed anxious journey from Africa where, as often before, his interest had been attracted by a lady from whom he had been suddenly parted, he was being driven through London to the sickbed where his father lay between life and death.

The Prime Minister, Mr. Baldwin, had that same day met him at Dover to welcome him home. As they rode together in the train the Prime Minister, who was not without information about the Prince's tour, had an intuition that the day would come when he would have to remonstrate with the Prince, and that the subject of his objection would be a woman.* The Prime Minister, of course, had never breathed a word about the nature of the Prince's response to the damsels whom he had seen a year before chasing him from town to town in Canada. He was anything but a Puritan. In fact one of his principal troubles had been that at Harrow after he had gone up in the school he was found reading a dubious book. What more natural? Few are the boys who have never done so. But a Puritanical Headmaster had ordered him to the Fourth Form Room, that place of condign punishment at Harrow where upon bared flesh is inflicted the laceration of the birch. A proud, virtuous, sensitive boy did not easily forget it, and when he found the same Headmaster was Master of his college at Cambridge, he was disheartened from the search for academic honour. When, however, in 1908 he entered Parliament, he was very happily married and indeed the father of six children.

After Mrs. Simpson—as she now was—settled in London she found in the American Embassy men she had known in Pekin. Among them was a Thaw whose wife's sister had married a big shipowner, Lord Furness. This was the Thelma Furness who was so often hostess at Fort Belvedere. Lady Furness, finding Mrs. Simpson amusing, arranged that she should be asked in the winter of 1930 to a party at Melton Mowbray to meet the Prince of Wales and the Duke of Kent. The Prince particularly liked animated strong-minded women whose attractiveness was other than that of clinging femininity: he liked such women above all if they belonged to the United States.

Then at a party given by Lord and Lady Furness Mrs. Simpson met him again and he gave her a lift home.

In January, 1932, the next year, he invited the Simpsons to a weekend at Fort Belvedere. Lady Furness who continued to be often his hostess there and judged well the type of American woman who amused him, had arranged this visit. It appeared to succeed: several times in the course of that year the Simpsons were invited back to Fort Belvedere. They saw how the Prince liked to live, and how he took his guests out with him to slash undergrowth before, as evening drew on, he came in to take his steam bath in the basement where he invited them to join him.

He felt that in his new friend at last he had found the sort of understanding woman he needed: and from that time on he was always arranging to meet the Simpsons. Later, her husband

* A. W. Baldwin: *My Father*, p. 299.

41

being engaged elsewhere, Lord Moyne took them both on a cruise in his yacht the *Rosaura* which sailed from Biarritz down the coast of Portugal into the Mediterranean. And on that cruise, it appears, the Rubicon was crossed. It was the summer of 1934, and the Prince coming to forty years of age.

He was beginning to be more in love than he had ever been with Mrs. Dudley Ward. Mrs. Simpson succeeded in giving him the impression that she was the woman who understood him as no other had done in the whole course of his life. There she was, one who could talk to him freely with point, with gaiety, and with spirit, on every subject that mattered to him. When Lady Furness was about to leave for America, her friend Mrs. Simpson said suddenly, "Oh Thelma, the little man is going to be so lonely." "Well, dear," was the answer, "you look after him for me while I'm away. See that he does not get into mischief."

When Lady Furness returned from America (receiving attention from Aly Khan as she came) the Prince wanted at once to see her. He had sent her in telegrams while she was away what she calls: "All the little sentimental things so dear to the heart of a woman." And now she was back he hurried to dine with her, but he seemed distrait. It was not until 2nd April 1934, that she was able to go out and stay at Fort Belvedere, and then she noticed that when the Prince took some salad in his fingers, "Wallis playfully slapped his hand." Lady Furness caught her eye. One cold defiant glance in return told her what she calls "the whole story."

Lady Furness went to bed without saying good night. "So much," she writes, "had suddenly cascaded on my head." A little later, the Prince himself was in her bedroom. "Darling," she asked him: "Is it Wallis?" His features froze—he walked out of the room.

Lady Furness left the Fort the following morning. She did not return. When she wrote her story she puts a query about what Mrs. Simpson meant by keeping a man out of mischief.

CHAPTER VIII

THE next year, 1935, proved to be a year of crisis in more ways than one. During that year the Prince's relationship with Mrs. Simpson became so obviously his chief preoccupation that it caused grave concern to the whole Court. In international relations the year also brought up affairs of the highest moment. Some in fact have called it the turning point of that pregnant decade. In it the leading issues of the reign of Edward VIII loomed up already vast and palpable.

The years of Hitler's power had seen a roaring revival of German industry: what filled the factories with workers and noise was the building up of weapons of war, and foremost among these a huge air-force which by the summer of 1935 claimed to be as large as that of England and was increasing at a much higher rate. Few could ignore the threat implied by Hitler's rearmament—it was the subject of instant concern to the British Government which felt bound to increase its own resources. In this campaign, one Minister spoke out after another, the strongest speeches coming from Neville Chamberlain.

In the latter part of the year, the people were still more strongly excited about the moves of another dictator: Mussolini was pressing his case against Abyssinia which he had urged to come into the League of Nations; and the Negus was resisting him. This affair was already brewing when the British Empire prepared a magnificent celebration of the jubilee of King George's accession twenty-five years before.

The jubilee was the grand event of a shining month of May in London. It was an occasion of impressive celebrations in every corner of the Empire: it even turned the borders of the Nile into fairyland: it transformed London and flooded her nights with coloured fire.

Now—when King George was seventy—his far-flung peoples had come to realize how much it meant to them when they turned towards him their respectful affection. That warm dutiful heart, that honest common sense at the centre of things was what they wanted. "There are times when the finest intelligence in the world is less serviceable than the broad common sense of a *grand seigneur*."[*] Cleverness so often gets a nation nowhere; goodness is what counts. "The power of the Throne", wrote John Buchan, "lies in what it is: but the authority of the King lies both in what he is and in what he has done. With the Queen and his family to aid him, he has made Britain not only a nation but a household."[†]

So much of personal tribute was indeed general, in the acclaim and functions which marked the jubilee. But these were also an instinctive response to what they looked to see the crown to give them—a share in glory and greatness. It is not enough for human hearts to live a routine, even a prosperous routine, from day to day. A nation can demand sacrifices as it does in war. But alas! the sacrifices of war fail too often to lead to the betterment of peoples in the solidity of peace. That had been proved too true when, after 1918, Europe and the British Empire faced the danger, the injustice, the malaise of a vindictive peace conference; blind to economic realities, that conference had

---

[*] F. S. Oliver: *The Endless Adventure*, III, p. 109.
[†] Buchan: *The King's Grace* (1936), pp. 319–20.

expressed a stubborn hatred contrary to the true advantage of every nation engaged, and oblivious to that justice on which alone can be laid the foundations of peace and that commerce which means the increase of riches in the exchange of them.

But while nationalism, when it asks for sacrifices, may be employing it for the most dubious of purposes, it may also offer a people splendour and success through the spectacle of what they can bring forward to honour a King. So the British Empire did in 1935 for the Royal Jubilee.

And although the King was not a man who cared for fashion any more than he was a scholar or a genius, although his way of speaking was the sailor's and his bearded face had nothing in it of handsomeness, nor his figure of princely proportions, yet he proved to be both what the people understood and what they wanted: to represent an aspiration within their reach, at the same time as his reign—in spite of its dangerous stresses—had led them further into shared well-being.

For all these reasons they gave themselves to celebrating the jubilee till the King's heart was moved to its depths. He thanked them in those simple words and touching phrases which, joined to his strong vibrant voice, always made a speech of his a masterpiece of simple power: "I can only say to you, my very very dear People, that the Queen and I thank you from the depths of our hearts for all the loyalty and may I say—the love— with which this day and always you have surrounded us. I dedicate myself anew to your service for all the years that may yet be given me." The voice was not a melodious voice. But the British peoples, as they listened to it (and they came to love doing so) felt themselves in close touch with one who, doing his duty in a way they understood, really and deeply cared for them; here was a man who had indeed surrendered his heart and body to their service; and to the service of God.

And by his side although she never spoke was the great lady who, as she moved among them in her royal grace, was this exemplary woman who at every turn spoke and moved, shrewd, kind, wise, interesting herself everywhere as guest, or hostess, as collector, as friend and making all—unless perhaps her own children—feel that at the height of the Court was the heart of the mother. But while the Sovereigns, and their Empire, shared glory in this royal festival, the effort demanded of His Majesty took toll of his reserves of strength. As, at the end of them, he looked back into his daily round of duties, he was very tired.

CHAPTER IX

Two heavy anxieties now bore upon the declining strength of King George from separate quarters. The first was that, as he felt his strength to fail, he could not rely upon, or approve, the conduct of the Heir Apparent; the second was that the League of Nations to which the voters of Britain had pinned their faith was proving itself inadequate to deal with the problems of the two dynamic powers in Central Europe: Italy with a vast increase of population had the doors of emigration now closed to her; Germany under the tyranny, only too widely welcomed, of a headstrong and dangerously abnormal leader who saw in the revived energies of his cohorts a chance to surge forward, in the militance of state socialism, on a career of national ambition which would give them the hegemony of Europe.

The British and French, secure in the control of 20,000,000 square miles of territory looked to Geneva to guarantee their privileges against the resurgent Italy and Germany, leaving these in a living space of hardly more than half a million square miles between them.

Fundamental problems of this kind were never dealt with—they were hardly mentioned—at Geneva. Geneva spoke on the other hand of Collective Security, as though all nations were ready to rush to arms to restrain an aggressor, when as a matter of fact no nation would ever think of going to war unless in defence of an immediate danger to itself. Nor was it ever considered that even in a case of aggression there might also be an element of provocation.

Is it wrong that people are loath to fight? With regard to both Germany and Italy there were profound difficulties, demanding real thought and resolute far-reaching decision. Then it was remembered that in former years Italy had been allowed a zone of influence in the virgin and enormous tracts of Abyssinia. It was to these that Mussolini now turned his glowering eye. If Italians were now to develop Abyssinia, as a hundred years before Britons had developed huge virgin tracts in other parts of Africa—not to mention Australia, Canada, New Zealand; and Americans had swept across their continent—not always disdaining the use of the word Empire as they did so—might not this prove a solution as much to the advantage of the Abyssinians as of the Italians? That was the Italian contention; both in Downing Street and at the Quai d'Orsay many considered it a feasible solution.

Plain warnings came to Buckingham Palace of what Hitler

might have in view. The King had taken cognizance of them. The corollary was plain: if Germany was growing dangerous, the Abyssinian question must be handled in a way not to endanger Anglo-Italian friendship. So the Foreign Secretary wrote to the King on 21st February, 1935. The King agreed. "We mustn't let old Musso down", was the way he put it. He knew very well from his former Ambassador, Sir Ronald Graham, that Mussolini had for twelve solid years acted in every particular as the loyal ally of Great Britain: this was not the time to change him from a friend into an enemy.

With this trend of thought the Prince of Wales strongly agreed. He had no patience with the idea that young men should lose their zeal for military service. The Court could hardly feel enthusiastic to hear that the Union Society of Oxford of which the Prince himself had been a member passed a resolution that they were unprepared to fight for King and Country. But, at the same time, he was aware that there were real needs and hard pressures in both Italy and Germany, and though he was well aware of the needs of housing in Britain, his desire to improve the lot of the masses in his own country did not mean that he restricted his interest in the well-being of men and women simply to the slums of Great Britain.

The argument of the Labour Party was that support for the League of Nations would save the need for expensive armaments, and the money thus saved could be used for improving the lot of the poor. If all nations could come together and agree to maintain the settlement of Versailles, and the enormous preponderance in the world of Great Britain, France, and the United States, how excellent it would be! Alas! the trouble was that Europe as a whole was suffering from an economic anaemia which meant for millions weakness through idleness and hunger. For these the League did nothing. What was the result? In Portugal, in Turkey, in Rumania, in Greece, in Bulgaria, in Poland, in Hungary, in Austria—as in Germany and Italy—democracy had been superseded by dictatorship in order to deal masterfully with the crucial questions of work and distribution. Until peoples were nationally organized, their breakdowns were complete.

This tendency was viewed with misgiving by the peoples of the British and French Empires and of those United States which, though they hardly recognized it, were an Empire under another form. Secure in those reserves—those gigantic reserves which were won for them in the nineteenth century—they were still sufficiently pleased with the then state of affairs to talk always of democracy and collective security.

Knowing that this was the mood of these peoples, the British Government, now under the astute, but wearying leadership of

Baldwin, put this issue before the electorate in the autumn of 1935 when the jubilee had left them well content. The Government indeed spoke of the need to rearm; but it spoke with more insistence and zeal of the League of Nations—and for that the electors voted. On 14th November the results were announced. Although the Opposition had gained sixty-nine seats, the Baldwin Government still had the enormous majority of 431 against 184 in a total of 615, in other words a margin of 247.

Now the problem arose of what they were to do with it. The essence of the situation was that, while Baldwin had the subtlest knowledge of the mood and mentality of the British public, he disliked the intricate negotiation of Foreign Affairs.

But even while the election was being fought, the League of Nations for which the electors felt so warmly, had been subjected to the severest strain. Italy had marched into Abyssinia. Fully alive to the increasing German danger, the Foreign Office, largely under the direction of the Permanent Under-Secretary, Sir Robert Vansittart, had been busy with the Quai d'Orsay in working out a compromise to deal with the result. Two able diplomats, Maurice Petersen and the Comte de St. Quentin, had been at work for weeks in the work of adjusting the varying interests of the nations involved and the claims of principle. Such work of adjusting different needs and urges is the traditional business of diplomacy. They found what they believed to be the right technical solution: it was to hand over to Italy a large tract on those borders of Abyssinia where the authority of the Negus had never been an administrative reality.

Anthony Eden signed this draft, as League of Nations Minister; and the final agreement was ratified in Paris on 10th December, 1935, between Laval and the Foreign Secretary. It was an effective example of technical professional compromise, according to established tradition. Both the King and the Prince of Wales were in agreement with it. The King was strongly against any attack on Italy. "I have been through one war," he said, "I cannot have another. If you are to keep me in it, there must be no war."*

The trouble was that the country had not been given the slightest inkling of the diplomacy required. Looking for peaceful solutions in their traditional way, the diplomats, as we have seen, had arrived at an adjustment which they deemed the most equitable at their disposal, and the most prudent. If it gave Italy some tracts of Abyssinia which the Negus did not in fact control, it offered Abyssinia an outlet to the sea: it would keep the Negus on his throne while it offered progress and order to immense stretches where his authority was not recognized. It gave the Italians an outlet for energy and population and kept on their

* Lord Templewood: *Nine Troubled Years*, p. 159.

47

side France and England in the approaching tussle with Germany.

But in all this there was a fatal flaw: *the Foreign Secretary, who also was tired, had entirely omitted to instruct or prepare public opinion.* He had not even made the issues sufficiently clear to his own colleagues. Mussolini had critics enough in England, men who from the first had been disgusted by his violence, by his contempt for Parliament, by his outrageous treatment of opposing leaders. Had he not encouraged bandits to maraud the property of Count Sforza, and thugs to murder Matteotti? Laval, too, was deeply distrusted. The British on the whole were enthusiastic for the League and sympathetic with the Negus.

When therefore they found that the Negus was to cede territory without the League being consulted, and that this was done under the name of a French politician friendly to Mussolini —and very likely in his pay—there was an outcry. Then it was found that as the French owned the railway which connected Addis Ababa with the sea, there was to be no railway in the track to the sea which the Negus was to have. As Geoffrey Dawson summed it up in *The Times*, it was to be a corridor for camels.

CHAPTER X

BALDWIN came into the House of Commons and made the unwise statement that his lips were sealed, but that, if all knew what he knew, there was not a Member who would not vote for the proposals. He said afterwards that the meaning of this phrase (which was used very effectively against him) was that he knew that Laval had been bought by Mussolini! He must also have known what again he could not say, that if this proposal were rejected, the Italians would race on to a victory which no nation showed the slightest readiness to prevent—that, in other words, 'collective security' had proved a farce. But, whatever he meant, he certainly did not intend to resign when his party had a majority of 247. And each Minister is technically responsible for the policy of his department. In his resignation speech to the House of Commons, however, Hoare refused to pretend that he had not given support to the policy of what has since been known as the Hoare-Laval agreement—refused also to pretend that he saw the slightest hope of any other policy availing for the defence of Abyssinia.

The Prince of Wales, who tells us that he knew what had been happening behind the scenes and that he had no love for the League of Nations, slipped into the Peers' Gallery to hear his father's old friend make his speech. This is what he heard:

That Italy was already at war with Abyssinia and that France

48

was determined not to fight Italy; that the war must not be made into a European conflagration; England taking up arms against Italy with France on Italy's side. In other words if war was to be waged with Italy it would be waged by Britain alone, and, since no other nation would support her, such a war would smash the League of Nations.

Nothing could be more unfair to the Negus than to buoy him up with talk of support from a League which in the event had shown that it would not raise a finger to give him practical help. A war had begun. Once any war has begun there are only two ways to end it. The one is negotiation; the other is surrender, which means collapse.

Not a ship, not a machine, not a man had been moved in support of the Geneva stand by any country except Great Britain. How could one member save the League, how secure peace if no other would support its contentions? All that in effect Great Britain could do for Abyssinia was to bring forward a basis for negotiations. Sir Samuel Hoare saw no other way of giving practical support to Abyssinia than the one to which he and Laval had put their signatures. He resigned because public opinion would not endorse it.

The Prince listened and agreed: in fact none could dispute the resigning Minister's contentions. But the Government decided to allow ill-formed opinion to overrule skilled diplomacy. In other words it sacrificed Abyssinia and the balance of power in Europe to the appearance of fulfilling its election pledges. What, then, was the result? Sanctions were applied to Italy: their only effect was not to restrain but to exasperate and alienate her. The Italian people who up to that time were rightly sceptical of Mussolini's venture now rallied to him as to a victim of intrigue. He pushed on with the war and won it.

But in doing so he changed his country from a friend into an enemy of Britain and ranged her on the Hitler side. The whole affair gave the world the impression that Great Britain was powerless as an enemy, and quite untrustworthy as a friend. Her prestige was fearfully weakened, that of Germany strengthened, and all this at a time of crisis in the situation of Europe.

The King, however, had been anxious for the prestige of his Government: the Prince, after hearing Sir Samuel Hoare, felt cynical about its methods. "I was all for Mr. Winston Churchill in his campaign to rearm Britain although I was against anything that might tend to throw the Italy of Mussolini into the arms of Hitler."* So wrote the Prince. He felt himself a realist who saw that while the League of Nations stood for an ideal, it lacked compulsive force: it was "a will o' the wisp in pursuit of which

* *A King's Story*, p. 299.

my country might foolishly neglect what had been its sure recourse in the past against aggression."*

This view was strongly to affect his attitude when in the next year he became King. Without explaining his view we could not understand the foreign affairs of his reign.

CHAPTER XI

IT was already the Christmas week of 1935, the last Christmas that King George V was to see, the last time he was to speak to his people from Sandringham. The family gathered once more, the nation listened and the Prince, desirous to save his father at such a time from any further strain, said nothing on what he could not but know remained one of his father's heaviest anxieties.

In the preceding February he had invited the two Simpsons to join him at Kitzbühel for winter sport. The wife tells us that when she mooted this to her husband, he answered that he did not care to ski and had at that time urgent business in New York.

"Have you definitely made up your mind to go?" he asked.†
"Of course," she answered. "Why not? I wouldn't dream of missing it." Rising from his chair he answered: "I rather thought we might have gone to New York together. I see now that I was wrong."

He was indeed.

So, just as Mrs. Simpson had in the preceding summer gone without her husband on that yachting expedition where—it is she, herself, who tells us—she had crossed the frontier into something more than friendship with the Prince, so now, without her husband—and indeed definitely against his wish—she had become the Prince's guest in a Tyrolean hotel. They stayed there a fortnight, and then he announced that he would take her on to Vienna that she might enjoy a waltz to the music of Strauss. From Vienna, in turn, he announced that he was going on again to Budapest to exchange the swaying music of Vienna's dance for the fiery surge and passion of gipsy music as it vibrated from the strings of Hungarian violins. On the waves of this music, first sentimental and seductive in the mood of Austria, then riotous in that of the Hungary of his great-grandmother, Claudine Rhedey, the lady, so she tells us, was carried away into realms which she calls those of dream, of illusion.

A situation had now arisen which indeed asked the question: 'Where did she belong?' Yes, where? That is the question many

* *A King's Story*, p. 299.   † Duchess of Windsor.

people had begun to ask; and none can be surprised at what she tells us that when she returned to the roof of her husband, a barrier had risen between them. It is not easy for a woman to live with a man who is forced to recognize that she had shown marked preference for the company of another, while she is still eating his bread.

At the same time she found herself taken up by certain ambitious hostesses, especially Lady Colefax and Lady Cunard. To these was now added Lady Oxford. This meant that Mrs. Simpson's close relation with the Prince was now recognized in London society, and that it became the subject of general gossip of which little failed to reach the ears of the King and Queen, the more as it was now becoming the subject of comment in American newspapers.

Not only did the Prince continually invite the two Simpsons to stay with him at Fort Belvedere. Mrs. Simpson always spoke of her loyalty to the cause and interest of her husband. He seemed on good enough terms with her and he could enjoy the company of his old friend Madame Jacques Raffray, who had been as we saw the bridesmaid of Bessie Warfield when she married her first husband, and in whose house Mrs. Spencer had met Mr. Simpson.

At the end of that jubilee summer the Prince went to pay a long visit to Lady Cholmondeley, Sir Philip Sassoon's sister, at Cannes, where she had a luxurious villa and was entertaining Mrs. Simpson. She and the Prince not only stayed at the villa but they went on expeditions in a private yacht over the sparkling Mediterranean to the lonely shores of mountainous Corsica, and to the sparsely peopled Iles d'Hyères which offered specially lonely beaches.

And then suddenly, the Prince decided to take her once more to Vienna, and on to Budapest where his ancestry beckoned.

So in 1935, as they both tell in their books, they were together for two whole months on the Continent, from 3rd August to 4th October. Even after her return she was frequently invited to stay at Fort Belvedere, and still her husband was invited with her. Nevertheless it must not be thought that Ernest Simpson was merely a complacent husband. Flattered by the Prince's invitations he still maintained his standards of honour: yet he could hardly feel lonely in the company of Mary Raffray whom he had loved earlier and was to marry later. If to outward appearance the relations of wife and husband were surprisingly little strained, it began to be taken everywhere for granted that though she lived under her husband's roof her greater interest was in the Prince of Wales who found in her so wonderful a woman.

CHAPTER XII

DAY after day, the King received details of the progress of the affair, the widening noise of its scandal.

By Christmas it was already seen that his health was breaking up. He knew what he had represented as an example and pivot to his people: he knew how much they approved of his honour, his virtue, his fidelity. What would be the result if he were suddenly to die and his place be taken by a Prince whose constant association with another man's wife—after each of these had already been divorced from other partners—was not to be kept secret but the subject of incessant comment in London, as well as of notices in French and American newspapers?

The King knew how difficult it was to deal with the problem. He was apt to break out to those he knew best with the words: "There's nothing I can do with the fellow." Neither he nor the Queen were on such terms with the Prince of Wales that they could so much as mention this personal complication which weighed so heavily on the mind of George V in those last weeks of his life.

For Christmas day, the Royal Family gathered once more at Sandringham to celebrate the festival with the worried and wearied King. Through frosty air they went as usual to Church, and came back to eat their Christmas dinner together. Then, at three in the afternoon the King went to his room to speak to his people with the wonted urgency of his regard for them, and the air vibrated for the fifth and last time with that deep clear moving voice: "We wish you all, my dear friends, a happy Christmas. I have been deeply touched by the greetings which in the last few minutes have reached me from all parts of the Empire. Let me in response send to you each a greeting from myself. My words will be very simple but spoken from the heart on this family festival of Christmas.

"The year that is passing, the twenty-fifth since my accession, has been most memorable. It called forth a spontaneous offering of loyalty—and may I say love?—which the Queen and I can never forget. How could I fail to notice", he said, "in all the rejoicing, not merely respect for the throne but a warm and generous remembrance of the man himself who—may God help him—has been placed upon it.

"It is this personal link between me and my people which I value more than I can say. It binds us together in all our joys and sorrows as when this year was showed your happiness in the marriage of my son and your sympathy in the death of my beloved sister. I feel this link now as I speak to you. . . .

"In Europe and many parts of the world anxieties beset us. It is good to think that our family of peoples is at peace in itself and united in one desire to be at peace with other nations, —the friend of all, the enemy of none. May this spirit of goodwill and mutual helpfulness grow and spread. Then it will buy not only the blessings of peace but a solution of the economic troubles that still beset us ... I add a heartfelt prayer that wherever you are God may bless and keep you always ..."

He was already ill: his strength ebbed fast in icy winter. Three weeks later he was dying. A council took over his powers; the family gathered once more. The end had come. After breathing a last word to his Private Secretary, Lord Wigram, of his regard for the Empire, the King died at five minutes to twelve on the night of 20th January, 1936.

His death faced his eldest son with the fact that there was none left to maintain a decision about his marriage. He would have to decide himself on the choices before him. In the sense of shock he found the strain too great: even before King George had died his successor had given an order to King's Lynn that the man in charge of Sandringham clocks should put them back to normal time.*

This in itself, done by his order and so quickly, shocked faithful old servants. Not to leave an hour before he showed this recoil from his father's amiable idiosyncrasies! They shook their heads and wondered what was coming. They shook their heads still more when from the coffin of King George, part of the crown was dislodged and fell to the ground. The orb on it was actually picked up by a Guardsman who put it in his pocket.

Early the next day, the new King announced he must leave Sandringham to confer with the Prime Minister. The time he gave to Mr. Baldwin, however, was short in comparison with that he gave to Mrs. Simpson. But the words of his Minister were warm and evoked a touching response. Both Baldwins, in spite of some inevitable misgivings, were full of affectionate hope that at this turn of history they had been given the man who would give what the time required for a new interpretation of the role of Sovereign. "We have faith in you," Mrs. Baldwin said. The King held her hand in his, and pressed it for a noticeable moment.

"I had rather hoped," said Baldwin to his friend, Tom Jones, "to escape the responsibility of having to take charge of the Prince as King. But perhaps Providence has kept me there for that purpose. I am less confident about him than Lucy." (Lucy was Mrs. Baldwin.) Baldwin went on to say to Tom Jones that the subject of Mrs. Simpson had never been mentioned between

* The clocks at Sandringham had been put forward by Edward VII as Prince of Wales to get his guests up in good time for shooting. Neither Queen Alexandra nor George V had wanted to change what the old King had fixed.

them; nor could anyone handle him—as those closest to him knew best.

Baldwin confided to his secretary, Tom Jones, that when he was a little boy in Worcestershire and read history, he never thought that he would have to interfere between a king and his closest friend in circumstances so invidious as these.*

He was indeed a master of taste in effective and, when the occasion required, noble phrase. But it was the Socialist leader who in the funeral orations in the House of Commons pointed out with most precision what King George V had done already to suit the monarchy to a swiftly changing world. His reign, said Mr. Attlee, as he then was, had seen years of sweeping change. Even without a world war, they must have been years of stress, through an advance of science, the spread of education, the progress in the ideas of self-government at home and overseas, the pressure of economic forces. The war was a forcing house of change.

In such an epoch, said Mr. Attlee, two things "were required of the Sovereign of a great state. The first was sympathy with new ideas and readiness to accept change, and to adapt himself to altered conditions. The second was to give society, bewildered by the rapid progress of events, a rallying point of stability. These things were found in King George in full measure. They are not common . . . He knew and understood the people and the age in which he lived and progressed with them . . . He allowed his nominal sovereignty to be diminished apparently, but by so doing he established his real sovereignty in the hearts of his peoples of the Empire.

"Equally important," went on the Leader of the Opposition, "has been the power of the King to offer a point of stability in a distracted world. The movements of mass hysteria which have been noticed elsewhere have passed this country by. One reason has been the presence of the King who commanded the respect and affection of his people and who was beyond the spirit of faction. There was no need to elevate some individual party leader into a national hero . . .

"He sought, as soon as the war ended to do his utmost to heal its wounds and to re-create good relations between nations. No less in the difficult post-war years he shared in the work of reconstruction. He was a real social reformer and took the keenest interest in the problems of the day . . .

"The duties of kingship have to be reinterpreted in the modern world with the passing years. King George showed an incomparable understanding of what is required of a King in the modern world."

If such words could be used by Labour's leader of the man

* Thomas Jones, C.H.: *A Diary with Letters*, p. 164, where a stronger term is used.

54

who had just ceased to reign, it was obvious that his successor did not need to make violent changes either in adapting the monarchy to a world already trembling on the brink of more violent upheaval, that the opportunities of personal intervention must not be seized with a hasty hand. This in other words was no time for personal. impatient or arbitrary action. Many therefore wondered: some remembered a prophecy printed years before by "Cheiro", the astrologer and palmist, that an over-whelming passion for a woman would drive the King from the throne. And a clairvoyant, we remember, had told Mrs. Simpson she was, after divorce, to play her part in history.

PART THREE

The Reign: First Months

CHAPTER XIII

TWO days after the father's death, his eldest son, with ancient ceremony conducted by uniformed officials of the College of Heralds, was proclaimed his successor as Edward VIII. Trumpeters rang their thrilling notes over the Friary Court of St. James's Palace, where Mrs. Simpson, by special invitation, was watching the ceremony in a private room in which the King —to the surprise of all—rapidly joined her. An enterprising photographer snapped them as they looked together from the window. Such was his first appearance after his proclamation in those sweeping and sonorous words which told both how old in history was his heritage, how wide the dominions which looked to him as Sovereign Lord. But as far as word and proclamation caught his attention they were submerged in his fealty to his married friend. He accompanied her as she descended. And it is from him as witness that we hear of the avowal he made her: "Wallis, nothing can ever change my feelings towards you."

"Nothing can ever change my feelings towards you." Then the doubt whether the gossips were right when they said he was in love with her should be dissolved into certainties. But what was now to happen? She was living still with Simpson in a flat at Bryanston Court. Her admirer at the head of the pageantries of a King's funeral and a King's accession was caught up in the prestige and prerogatives of the head of the British Empire.

His short, tense, startling reign had now begun. The red boxes, that he should duly read from them, came to him: he should have been the pivot and finger of government. He could see everything he chose to see of state secrets. He received the Ministers, and at once he must move, central and chief, in the funeral ceremonies which, in their impressiveness, told him once more what rank he had inherited and what an additional weight of glory had been placed upon his head in the heritage of personal sympathy and regard which his father's faithfulness had won.

All were prepared to see him accept it and enjoy it while giving a modernized world his experience of not merely those who inherited rank or who attained eminence, political or official, but of the masses of the people in their need and in their work. Ministers, and great newspapers which spoke with a voice hardly less authoritative, greeted him with tributes of enthusiastic deference. All realized how special had been his opportunities of estimating both the productivity of his dominions and the miseries of its unfortunates. They saw in him a man of forty-one in whom experience and enterprise either joined or contended in tournament. No word was breathed of misgiving, let alone of scandal. No suggestion was ever made, no hint given, that at various functions, the way he presided had been perfunctory: that he was often ill at ease in society: that his face had exchanged freshness for strain.

A new photograph by the leading firm of Vandyk in Bond Street, presented well-cut features, marked with endearing leanness; and he appeared still to wear the rosebud of youth.

Let us cite two impressive testimonies of his enormous reputation. The first is from Lord Simon: "When he first ascended the throne he was the most widely known and the most universally popular personality in the world. As Prince of Wales he had travelled through every part of his future dominions, and his qualities of easy affability and ready enthusiasm had endeared him to everybody. By general consent his charm was irresistible ... he had the happy knack, when inspecting factories, or housing estates, or depressed areas, of making manifest his interest in the lives and lots of ordinary people. In him the unemployed thought they had a friend; the followers of every kind of sport recognized in him the Prince of sportsmen. If his effort in the first few months of his reign to introduce more informality into occasions which were essentially formal was not everywhere approved, this was a reaction from the correct atmosphere of his parents' home."* So much from Lord Simon, the Home Secretary. Now let us add the appraisal of that distinguished journalist, Sir Philip Gibbs: "To young men of that age, whether in the services or in the factories, the King supplied the need for their hearts and souls to admire. They gave him not merely loyalty but hero-worship. They looked to him as their hero and their friend. He seemed the individuality and the spirit they most admired. They would follow him at his beck unto the world's end—they shared in his sport and in his state as though it were their own. They liked to think of him as doing the things they would like to do. 'He's one of us', they said. 'He understands us. He knows how to talk to us. He sympathizes with any of us down on our luck. He wants to make the politicians get a move on—he's on the side of the people. He hates humbug. He's the only man in England we can trust, and, by God, we trust him.' "†

Dismissing criticism, therefore, all who wrote or spoke of his

* Simon: *Retrospect.*
† Sir Philip Gibbs: *Ordeal in England,* pp. 99-100.

accession appeared to be waiting for him to accomplish something both royal and novel. If they had a cognizance of any past deficiency they cherished the expectation that he would say with Henry V

> the tide of blood in me
> Hath proudly flowed in vanity till now;
> Now doth it turn and ebb back to the sea
> Where it shall mingle with the state of floods
> And flow henceforth in formal majesty.

Respectful courtesy silenced criticism. Loyalty buttressed hope.

In the new King, nevertheless, there could not but be a conflict of motives: on the one side the endeavour or at least the dream and fancy to give a new significance to kingship not merely in meeting the masses and their needs but in asserting for himself the political prerogatives which constitutional government still reserved to the Sovereign. Such was one expression of King Edward's will. The other was to follow his inclinations in his choice both of methods and of friends.

These conflicts in his character were new factors in the drama of royal prerogatives in relation to mounting forces of national peril. On the one side the masses were not getting due advantage of the country's capacity for production; more urgent and immediate, however, was the question of an international policy for the welfare of Europe as a whole, so that in the heart of the Continent there should not be—as there had been, owing to hunger—the canker of grievance. The idealists were the victims of outmoded schemes: the two odd portentous masters of the crowds—one in Italy, one in Germany—who took to themselves the name of leaders had ambitions which were also out of date. For, though they were very different, and in fact the two had only just ceased to be in personal conflict, they had, in saving their peoples from chaos and misery, tied up party organization on socialist lines with national aggressiveness and indeed with actual brutality: their violence had not stopped short at murder. We saw how such lurches into crime could not but shock—and at times outrage—the free man's love of order and of law.

Here then were the problems which confronted the government, and therefore the King, of England in 1936. Like the preceding year, 1936 was to prove crucial in the development of European crisis. The drama of the new reign was not only that of a spate of gossip about a Prince personally admired. It was the complications which personal scandals added to the menace of upheaval in Europe. Neither the great war which began in 1939 nor the revolution which followed it can be fully understood till we relate both to the reign of King Edward VIII and the remarkable set of men with whom he worked.

CHAPTER XIV

WHO were the principal personages with whom he had to deal?

First there were those of the Court. At the head of this, there was his mother still living in Buckingham Palace among the treasures she had there arranged around her. On the verge of seventy, she was unwearied and undaunted; her eyes had still a diamond brilliance; and moving, as she had done for twenty-five years representing in gentle but unquestionable sovereignty, in quiet efficiency and shrewdness, as in inflexible uprightness, the majesty of the throne. There was her daughter whose shyness was so much more obvious, the Princess Royal, Countess of Harewood, appearing from time to time at her side, and now mother of two boys, and suiting herself to times when the great wealth her husband had inherited was dwindling. There were three brothers most successfully married, the two elder more serious and conventional, each showing their father's virtues in unobtrusive ways, and taking opportunities of social service. Each had his happy home, though as yet there were no children born to the Duke of Gloucester. Then debonair, but no longer what the French call 'volage', was the Duke of Kent whose eldest son had just been born.

Here then were five royal households, secure in an atmosphere of deference and prestige, with duties accordingly. Here were Princes and Princesses playing the part expected of them with quiet correctness at the head of society. Edward VIII was on good enough terms with each and all of them, though he had been much closer in sympathy with the Duke of Kent and his Duchess whose Parisian chic bore witness of her Continental connection: her links with Greece, with Belgrade, with Paris itself.

So much for the Royal Family. Then came the immediate staff: Lord Wigram as Private Secretary, with his tall figure and easy yet courtly manners and the elegance of a beautiful wife. Assisting Wigram was Major Alexander Hardinge, the son of a great diplomat who had been selected by Edward VII as Viceroy of India and who after giving up the Paris Embassy was still living at his attractive home at Penshurst. Major Hardinge was married to a stepdaughter of Lord Milner, who was also a niece of Lord Salisbury. Here in the Court already sixteen years was a friend of his own age and trained in the best traditions by the remarkable man, Lord Stamfordham, who had served for decades with Queen Victoria, and after her death had been with George V. His was a direct, uncompromising, conscientious efficiency in dealing methodically with an immense mass of detail, of which he said plainly what it required. This was the standard of Lord Stamfordham; and so thoroughly had he learnt it from Queen Victoria for whom in turn the Prince Consort had set the highest standard in dealing with State papers. Then as Lord Chamberlain responsible for the functions of the Court was Lord Cromer. These were the people immediately responsible for the administration of the Court. They were all men of character as fine in their efficiency, as they were easy and pleasant in their ways, for they all had perfect manners.

Sir Alan Lascelles represented the more formal tradition, Sir Godfrey Thomas who had been much with his new master, excelled in a tact so self-effacing as to seem almost shyness, but was perfect unselfishness.

So much for the Court. What of the Government? Here, too, were men not only secure in their immense majority in Parliament, but for the most part able and well tried.

At the head of them, in the enjoyment of such power as he chose to exert (for the most important of the Royal prerogatives had gradually fallen into the hands of the Prime Minister) was Stanley Baldwin who, the year before, had taken over from Ramsay MacDonald the leadership which had already been his from 1925 to 1929. Here was a man of high character, ample wealth, impressive speech and long experience. Ambition had played less part in his long career than kindly shrewdness which men of England knew and trusted. Though secure in his popularity with his party, he had come loyally at the King's request to serve under Ramsay MacDonald. We have seen through the affair of Abyssinia how slack was his grasp of Foreign Affairs. His mind worked busily in certain spheres; though his grasp of detail often flagged, this had led so far but to one great difficulty; for difficulties have often a way of solving themselves, and the men he had placed in the various ministries were competent enough.

He had, as we saw, got into immediate touch with the new King, who coming on to him from Mrs. Simpson on the morning after his father's death had been with him in Downing Street on the first Sunday of the reign.

A man of heart who had long been a little cynical, and eased his acumen with a sense of humour—such was Baldwin. He dealt with ticklish situations in the light of wise saws of his own invention, such as "He who sleepeth with a goat spends the rest of his life plucking out fleas,"* to which he added this: "Never stand between a dog and a lamp-post."† We can see how he came to be described by some who knew him well as "a dear sweet simple soul". Sweet simplicity could be but one attribute of a man who had been chosen to oust Lloyd George, who had made Winston Churchill his Chancellor of the Exchequer, and for five years blandly listened to this Churchill discoursing with his

* Sir A. Bryant: *Stanley Baldwin*, p. 158.   † ibid., p. 159.

fluent brilliance on departments outside his own; who had served for years as a Conservative under a Socialist and Pacifist Prime Minister and who had extricated himself from the consequences of not giving enough attention to the complex affair of Abyssinia.

His party remained very pleased with him because to many Englishmen he seemed so like themselves. They did not see beneath to the nervous strain of inner conflict. They liked to think of him as the amateur in politics. But he was really nothing of the sort; he was "the highly competent professional, a professional all the more effective for being disguised as an amateur".* In his sincerity and good will was hidden such a mastery that in the words of Tom Driberg, he "foxed so many of those who seemed on the surface far smarter than he". "I can understand them calling me a fool," he would say, adding with a smile: "But what I can't understand is why they want to work under such a fool and a slacker."

He was a man who liked to do good by stealth. Long years passed before it was known to be he who had destroyed a fifth of his fortune of a quarter of a million pounds in order to give an example to others to whom the war had brought wealth while it had weakened the financial strength of the country. It was he who when out once on a walk through the Cotswold Hills of Gloucestershire heard of a home for incurables which might have to close for lack of funds because the old ladies who had run it could no longer afford what it needed. Going to a bank in the neighbouring town of Stroud he cashed a cheque for five hundred pounds. Then he gave the notes to a messenger he deemed reliable to take to the old ladies with a message that the money came from an unknown person who thought he might one day need to shelter in their home.

Having lived from boyhood close beside the three hundred workmen of his family factory, he had been taught to have a personal care for each of them in weal and woe. That was the background of his understanding of England, and his personal concern for the plights of the poor.

He had appointed as Chancellor of the Exchequer not indeed again the brilliant Churchill but a man who could sum and weigh issues and speak on them with trenchant finality, a man of decisive energy in the conduct of both private and public business—Neville Chamberlain. His marked features, his beautiful handwriting, his impeccable dress joined with the traditions of his family and the distinguished reputation of his brother to give him a special prestige in the Cabinet. He was already regarded as the next Prime Minister whom the Sovereign would choose. His problem had been to reduce taxation at the same

* T. Driberg.

time as he obtained more money for defence. But though, in face of the German danger, he insisted on heavier armaments (and therefore was classed with Winston Churchill as a warmonger) he could boast that Britain was recovering from the slump to eighty per cent of her former prosperity. "And if you want one hundred per cent," he said, "then leave this government in a little longer." The secret of his efficiency was to call for full evidence from different points of view, to balance them to obtain a conclusion that would be generally acceptable and, having made it, to apply it with decision. Once his plan was made he was determined to go through with it. He used to say that if he had been Prime Minister, the imbroglio over Abyssinia could never have occurred. This was a well-founded claim. Before endorsing the agreements at which the diplomats were arriving in Paris, Chamberlain would have had his eye on them and co-ordinated a policy which would command agreement, within those limits of the possible which are the terms of reference in every problem of diplomacy and government.

Beside him was Ramsay MacDonald whom George V had helped and liked when he first became Prime Minister in 1923. The years had not altogether mellowed this handsome old Scotsman who in his rise from schoolmastering with a stigma on his birth had come to view himself as something like infallible on the vast range of issues which are within the personal power of a Prime Minister. In other words the schoolmaster temper had survived the years of politics. MacDonald had made his compromises when he found himself heading a team of whom most were Conservatives—but he could not forget that twenty years before he had been a Pacifist; he still had, with a hatred of war, a distrust of armaments.

Then of very different type from him was the tall figure of Lord Halifax, whose father had been a gentleman-in-waiting to the Prince who was to reign as Edward VII while he himself had been chosen by George V from the Tory Ministers of 1924 to be Viceroy of India, as Lord Hardinge in earlier days had been chosen by his father. He had come back to take an inevitable place in the government because with his background of family and wealth he combined the widest sympathies and a character so elevated and upright with a manner so simple and confiding that he was secure of general confidence. He was one in whom the Royal Family had long trusted as a personal friend of a rank as high as his integrity, the sort of man they liked and relied upon as they did upon Sir Samuel Hoare who was their neighbour at Sandringham and who, if not actually a peer like Lord Halifax, was a baronet married to a sister of another prominent, if questioned, Churchman, Lord Beauchamp. Then at the Home Office was the National Liberal,

Sir John Simon who, though he might have been a failure as Secretary of State for Foreign Affairs, was so judicious, so experienced, so authoritative that he could not but have an important place in any coalition Cabinet. With a Liberal background he had done much to destroy the strike of 1926. He was the embodiment of administrative and legal ability. All these men had been much in the eye of the late King and looked back to a Victorian past. These were all men of strong religious views. Sir John Simon, a son of the Manse, Chamberlain a Unitarian married to a devout Anglican, the others rooted and grounded in the ways of the Church of England.

Now came two younger men with an outlook freer and more modern. One of them, born four years before the new King, was Duff Cooper, now at the Admiralty. Himself a grandson of an Earl of Fife, he had married a lady who combined being the more beautiful daughter of a beautiful Duchess with features which enabled her to portray a saint on the stage. They came together in a realm where pictures and politics, idealism and success glittered in a galaxy. With this pair, to whom, after long waiting, an heir had just been born, the new King found a mentality with which his gaiety could compromise and who would not take too ill the association which was inevitably distasteful to men older and more staid. Here was a man of culture, a writer on Talleyrand, linked with great houses in England and Scotland and especially with those younger members of such families as had the most modern tastes in amusement.

At the Foreign Office was one of the few Ministers who was younger than the King, the Anthony Eden under whose aegis had been the League of Nations and who had now replaced Sir Samuel Hoare as Foreign Secretary. As a speaker he was uninspiring; for it was beyond him to pass the conventional phrase. "Anthony," so Sir Winston Churchill is reported to have once said, "you have given us another of your fine speeches: you have brought in all the clichés except 'Please adjust your dress before leaving', and 'God is love'." But he did say "Mutual co-operation between the peoples is the only sure way to peace." The new King had seen him often enough, called him and his wife by their Christian names, and found them in social circles where the doors were flung open wide for Mrs. Simpson. But, all the same, the resignation of Hoare had, as we have seen, caused misgiving in the Royal Family, and the new King looked with displeasure on the role which the new Foreign Secretary was playing. Eden's first speech in his new position—a speech on his belief in the Collective system, which was dear to English hearts but which in point of fact was not working—had been made in the House of Commons only two days before the old King died, and was already far too ill to know anything about it.

On the side of Labour was a personality as shrewd and able as Baldwin himself and like him a man who combined with quiet ways mastery of the technique of manoeuvre. This was the Clement Attlee who had succeeded Ramsay MacDonald as Leader of the Opposition. A man whose small stature was not compensated by anything remarkable in features, Mr. Attlee had the power which is the heritage of a fundamentally honest man. He had begun as a Conservative, but experience of the lot of the poor in London had convinced him that what was needed by a Christian worker was Socialism. Though he had once raised the clenched fist to give the salute with Reds in Madrid, goodness and sympathy shone from the soft brightness of his eyes. He had already proved, and was long to prove, that he had ability to contrive and manage, with a skill in dealing with the House of Commons that made him a better leader of his party than the representatives of the working class such as the mighty Ernest Bevin, the great international negotiator of the Trades Unions, or Herbert Morrison, whose square form had long been a power on the London County Council.

Like Stanley Baldwin, and even more, Clement Attlee was the most regular of churchgoers. A brother had been in charge of a great London parish, a sister was a missionary.

The Liberal leader was the hatchet-faced, half-American, half-Scottish baronet who had a fiery belief in the traditional ideals of his sadly diminished party; among these ideals was certainly the League of Nations. The other figure in the Liberal Party, though he had long ceased to represent more than himself, was Lloyd George. Secure in the possession of the Party Funds, and with a brain of inexhaustible resource, he was now at the age of seventy-three to show that he could weigh in on subjects of the day. He had been hailed in former years as the master spirit in politics with a power of brain which Winston Churchill had said he would never aspire to rival.

But as an independent journalist of personal acumen, gleaming eloquence and enterprising vigour, intermingled at times with fairy-tale heroics, Churchill, if not more widely trusted than Lloyd George, could diffuse winged words with more success—as in fact he did week by week in the *Daily Telegraph* —still to denounce—as he had steadily denounced for sixteen years—the nefarious works of Russian Bolshevists. At the same time he was fully awake to the danger of Hitlerized Germany, and to the pace at which it was rearming. His argument was that the British must steadily support the League of Nations, yet not trust too blindly to it for their defence. He knew that collective security was more a chimera than a practical reality. If nations wanted to be sure of effective action, that must depend on the efforts of each. If we follow Hansard for those years, we find that on each point Churchill stated with great ability the two sides of every case, afterwards to recall which had proved the more prophetic. The Conservative governments were thinking on the same lines as himself, though practical considerations prevented them from doing things with a rush.

Such were the most prominent members of the Parliament and the government with whom the new King found himself surrounded. With those of the Government he had to work from day to day in that crucial time, when unemployment, though reduced from 2,000,000, was still at the fearful number of 1,600,000, which was 12·6 per cent of those insured (it had been 26 per cent in 1932). Miners and many others were living in conditions of such discomfort that they would have to travel miles in wet and filth when they had finished a day of arduous and dangerous work. As far as Foreign Affairs were concerned the chief event was the rapidity with which Badoglio's Italian army was invading and conquering Abyssinia, and Hitler taking advantage of the rift with Britain to win Italy to his side.

CHAPTER XV

THE new sovereign has set it down that it had never occurred to him to abrogate the succession. He denies flatly the rumour that he never meant to resign.

In a character so complex as his, there were springs of action of which he was perhaps only very partially conscious. His deliberate conscious intention was one thing, the trend of character which in the event decides action in a crisis is another. Those who worked most closely with Edward VIII observed much that suggested his responsibilities sat lightly on him, and that he was hardly ready for the element of drudgery in those duties of the monarchy which his father had so effectually adapted to the needs and mood of the age.

The odd thing was that King George V combined these idiosyncrasies of taste with a complete elasticity in meeting the revolutionary trend of affairs in such a way that a labour leader could cite him a model King for a Socialist scheme. The old man could do this because of his success in convincing the people as a whole that he understood and loved them. But the new King had often changed the circle of his confidants, friends and servants. And by this time the court was well enough aware that the one person who swayed his first choice of friends was Mrs. Simpson.

He says not only that he intended to reign but that he had in mind no far-reaching reforms. The rules of the Court were there for him to accept—where tradition was firm it was not for him to dispute it. It was an authority over the sovereign, as public opinion was the mistress of ministers. Nevertheless he intended to make the Court easier and broader: he wanted to live a simpler and more unconventional life. All expected in fact that he would do a useful work in adapting the monarchy to himself as the first King who had moved amongst and understood ordinary business men. If his staff were astounded by his ignorance of history—and he knew, if possible, still less of the arts and literature—bankers were impressed by his grasp of the essentials of finance; and his ability in uniting with the impact of big interests. He had been both able and conscientious in regard to improving the town properties of the Duchy of Cornwall. He was more at home in the new world than the old. This meant that he not only now adored Mrs. Simpson but that he had a general penchant for Americans—and also for Argentines.

In him the Empire could expect and could welcome a man much less conventional than his father. But among the circles closest to him were those who suspected that his unconventionality carried with it a disregard for rules of life the Court had cherished.

What he himself writes is "I was what I was: a man with a profound faith in God and an ingrained sense of duty." Yes, but at what point did inclination dispute the sense of duty? Did faith in God go so far as accepting the rules that the Church to which he belonged shared with Christian tradition? In what sense could he be termed 'Defender of the Faith'? These are the questions which underlie the unfolding outward events of that year of history.

But meanwhile it was a rule that for the six months of official mourning after the King's death all the Court officials should remain in office. So there they were, as before. Lord Wigram as Private Secretary, with Major Alec Hardinge as second in command; Lord Cromer as Lord Chamberlain, Lord Shaftesbury as Lord Steward, the Bishop of Oxford (a man who had passed years of his life as a don at Christ Church in Oxford) as Clerk of the Closet, while Queen Mary remained in Buckingham Palace. Outwardly in those months little in the conduct of affairs seemed to alter their course.

At the first possible moment he drastically reduced, not only the staff, but the pay of servants in every one of his establishments. The defence is that he was nervous about his budget; but the staff naturally resented it, the more so as there were other things that gave an impression of extravagance.

But meanwhile both passing and pregnant events continued on their course—what were they?

In Britain little of moment occurred. On 29th January, a Naval Conference was accepted to discuss British suggestions for reducing the size of warships, but on 13th February Italy announced that she was not ready to sign any such treaty. On 2nd March, the British Government, now secure in its majority and forced to face the result of no longer being on friendly terms with Italy, started on its great new defence programme. For the first time Britain began to be organized for war production as Germany had been in the preceding two years. At Geneva, almost immediately after the succession, Anthony Eden had vindicated the authority of the League in Danzig.

Meanwhile to avoid decision on the Oil Embargo, which Italy had said she would regard as an act of war, Italy and Abyssinia were urged to open negotiations for peace within the framework of the League.

But meanwhile Laval had resigned in France. Sarraut formed a new government with the polished and portly Flandin as his Foreign Minister: this government appeared secure, for on 31st January it obtained a vote of confidence of 361 as against 164.

Public opinion in Great Britain was not excited by these events as it had been in preceding months over the whole question of Abyssinia. But in fact the repercussions were much more ominous.

Almost immediately the French Government opened negotiations with Moscow with which, taking up the heritage of Laval, it made a pact which on 27th February the Chamber approved by a vote of 353 to 164. Taken together these two moves were to lead gradually to more and more immense disaster; and one needs to be related to the other, as both to the League of Nations.

We have seen how the League, from which the United States remained steadily aloof, was a body of interests dominated by certain powers and parties to the exclusion of others. Though it was the focus of nobly intentioned idealism, it never dealt with fundamental questions of justice for Italy and Japan in which the rise of population meant a hurrying drive towards need and hunger.

It was also unduly affected by the *Petite Entente* which, always insecure and soon divided within itself, represented a body of opinion mostly Slav which was hostile to tradition in general, and to German tradition in particular. Having done nothing for Italian claims from the beginning, and still less for Austrian or German ones, the League had been involved in 1935 in the question of coercing Italy in regard to Abyssinia. It paid no attention to previous agreements, going as far back as 1894, and strengthened in 1896, and then renewed in 1919—that there in the neighbourhood of Eritrea was the appointed field for Italy's economic expansion.

A time had come when Mussolini made a final and characteristic push to exploit its weaknesses. As the Negus disputed his demands and the League supported the Negus, he determined with temperamental audacity to show that he could flout the two of them, and to do so by a display of merciless force. The reign of Edward VIII had hardly begun when he put in charge of the Abyssinian campaign Italy's ablest commander, Badoglio.

The effect was startling: while bitter complaints were made of Italians bombing the Red Cross, their troops and aeroplanes moved forward at a rate which amazed neutral experts. It had been expected that the embargoes already put on Italy would join with ineffective war in country barren, tropical, primitive, and mountainous to debilitate and exhaust her troops.

Neither proved true. The masses in Italy suffered hunger and hardship for which alas! they thought Britain mostly to blame. But their troops were conveyed on wheels over rough mountain roads while their mustard gas annihilated opposition. They pressed onward in the wake of their aeroplanes which were soon bombing Dessie, the Abyssinian headquarters. At the same time the resentment of the Italian people and of their leader made them easy prey to the crafty and cajoling Hitler. It was already evident by the middle of February that France had no more support from Italy than she—any more than Abyssinia—could find effective support in the League of Nations.

In these circumstances, the Radical-Socialists of France bethought themselves of the foreign policy of France forty years before. As they had then turned to the old corrupt Czarist régime for an ally, so now they turned to its Bolshevist successor, certainly not less sinister. The Czar had been honest and amiable: who could say that of Stalin? Laval a year before had prepared the Franco-Soviet pact. But it was now found that whereas with the Czarist Russia there had been a common frontier with Germany, now there was no such thing; Russia, therefore, could no longer impinge direct on Germany.

Between these two nations stood other states: not merely a Poland even more hostile to Moscow than it had been to St. Petersburg, but between the Soviet Union and Czecho-Slovakia which was friendly, stood not only part of Poland but an extremely suspicious Rumania.

In the balance of power this made a crucial change. A pact with the Russia of 1914 and before had offered immediate succour against Germany: now, because of the buffer states between, a pact with the Soviet Union did not. It had a much greater disadvantage. As Hitler was always preaching the danger of the Soviet menace, it gave him the excuse of saying that he must take measures against it on his western frontier, where, by the Pact of Locarno, the Germans were bound not to march their troops across the Rhine.

Thus Edward VIII had hardly been six weeks on the throne when his Government faced a huge strategic issue. He found Hitler defying the arrangements into which the German Government had in 1925 freely entered. He did march his troops over the Rhine. His object was to prepare himself so that he would be free to attack in any quarter, and if turning eastward would be safe from any reprisal on the West. Germany had already denounced one clause of the Locarno agreements when in March, 1935 she introduced conscription, raising her army from 100,000 to 550,000 and embarking immediately afterwards on a programme of gigantic rearmament. That first threatening breach of agreement had been too easily condoned. How firm were the nations to be now?

Two big questions were involved. There was, first, the principle of keeping treaties, the more urgent because the treaties were meant to keep a balance of power, with armaments reduced. The second was strategic. If Hitler's troops were in the Rhineland, they could not only mass against the frontiers of the West, but they could also prevent the Western Powers from making good any claim to assist an ally on the Eastern side of Germany. And France had three allies there: Poland which was separate and whose hold on the Danzig corridor was bitterly resented in Germany, as the King of Sweden had warned the Prince of Wales some years before. Secondly, Czecho-Slovakia, which as a friend of Russia had a special energy in the *Petite Entente*; and now, thirdly, Russia itself. But the question of Czecho-Slovakia rivalled Poland in danger because there were within its frontiers some 4,500,000 who had good reasons for resenting Czech domination. Among these were 3,000,000 known as Sudeten Germans, living close to the frontiers of the Reich. Such a group like those specifically German territories near Danzig were extremely dangerous elements in a situation where 6,000,000 Germans were now being harnessed to arms with that efficiency with which Prussia for two hundred years had prepared for war and had waged it.

The opinion of the strategists was clear: when Hitler's troops marched over the Rhine this was the crucial moment—and so, arguing on technical grounds, the German General Staff had discountenanced this move: for it seemed to them that the professional experts of the West must at once demand resistance. It was believed—and it is still believed—that so strong was this conviction among the German generals that they were prepared to act against Hitler the minute that the Western Powers took arms to defend the Rhineland area. They had discountenanced the move and he had overruled them. If such were their reasonings and their resentment, then indeed the Western Powers threw idly away the supreme occasion to rid themselves of the demonic force which three years later was to embark on courses which ruined both Germany and themselves.

Such was the contention of Mr. Leo Kennedy, then Correspondent of *The Times* in Berlin. Such an idea was behind the strong adjurations of Mr. Winston Churchill in the *Daily Telegraph*. Hitler, he said, had set in motion a train of events which offered mankind their choice between blessing or curse. "Never till now were great communities offered such ample means of measuring their approaching agony. Never have they seemed less capable of taking effective measures to prevent it. Chattering, busy, toiling, sporting, amused from day to day by headlines, and from night to night by cinemas, they can yet feel themselves slipping, sinking, rolling backward to the age when earth was void and darkness moved on the face of the waters. Surely it is worth a supreme effort, the laying aside of every impediment, the clear-eyed facing of fundamental facts, the noble acceptance of risks inseparable from heroic endeavours to control the hideous drift of events and stop calamity upon the threshold. Stop it! Stop it! Stop it now!!! Now is the appointed time."*

But the whole current of opinion in the West was against a violent move. This was true of both Holland and Belgium, the small powers most easily overrun by German aggression. It might have been thought that Belgium at least would call upon her powerful neighbours at once to hurl back the approaching troops. But no! no party in Belgium wanted that,† and when later their Prime Minister, Mynher van Zeeland, spoke, it was in guarded terms which, though they sounded strong, called for diplomatic solidarity, not for definite action.

Such, too, was the weight of opinion in Great Britain. There very few had as yet envisaged the danger from Hitler's Germany; the immense majority felt that in the past decade or so the Germans had been roughly treated, and that it was natural enough if, after eighteen years of peace, paying reparations all the time, they now aspired to be masters in their own house. And so, though Mr. Kennedy might feel disturbed in Berlin, the tone of *The Times* was that this was no moment for concern. On the whole, the English papers agreed, though the *Manchester Guardian* advised them to be wary of a man who spoke of peace while he made ready for battle.

But the way the thing was worked was so subtle as to dope diplomacy.

---

* Churchill. *Step by Step*, p. 19.
† Of this King Leopold himself assured the author.

Hitler introduced the coup with speeches of extremest cunning: he said that the Franco-Soviet pact was a departure from the spirit of Locarno. Locarno had already given international guarantees to France. The new power linked her with a power which had aggressive designs on Europe, and was hostile to its system. Besides that, the Franco-Soviet pact left the *Soviet* with the decision when France was to act, and so could invite her at its own perverse will to join her in aggression.

In such tones Hitler spoke of the provocation he had received. But he was equally astute in explaining the moderation of his aims; he pretended he was not sending across the Rhine any force with power to strike. He was merely assembling in that area—with its population (as we have seen) of 14,500,000, a little army of 35,000, including police. Although in fact it came with tanks and nine brigades of artillery, with anti-aircraft guns and ear-afflicting roar, it was proclaimed to the world to be merely a token force. In addition to that Hitler joined his move with further and stronger avowals of peaceful intentions and especially of his own pledges to the League of Nations. Even to the trained diplomats, and especially those who set store by Geneva, these proposals seemed impressive and alluring—how much more so to people who, having expended their reserves of venom on Italy, were now glowing with good will towards Germany!

That is not all. When it is argued, as it often has been, that the Western Powers should have acted at once, then men forget a capital point which Mr. Churchill's adjuration absolutely ignored. But we must recall it now: *The Locarno Pact argued that against an act of aggression the League must first be invoked.* Now in the first place Hitler's offence was not technically an act of *aggression*. Like his rearmament in the preceding year, it was the breach of a treaty. But to deal with the breach of a treaty, which was not an attack, it was first necessary to invoke the League and seek a means of adjustment. And that, of course, is exactly what Hitler himself proposed. Why? Because if France and England were to rush to war without support from the rest of the League, that would have been itself a breach of the Locarno Pact. This was a point to which all supporters of the League were simply *compelled* to defer.

Even had the opinion of Britain been as strategic in its instincts as Mr. Churchill, the Government was bound to do what the Foreign Secretary, Mr. Eden, did: resort first to diplomacy. So negotiations began; as to that, there was really no choice; and once begun they dragged on from week to week, and men very soon forgot Churchill's stentorian call that now was the time to strike. On 26th March he and Sir Austen Chamberlain renewed their warnings, but in a guarded tone;

for they could not but be aware of the diplomatic complications.

There can be no doubt that the Government was alive to the crisis involved, and felt great concern. The King actually reports that while some counselled conciliation, others came to him with words of war. War, he actually says, seemed very close. According to the report of Fritz Hesse, a German journalist of high repute, Herr Leo von Hoesch, the German Ambassador, regarded the situation as so critical that he decided to go to the King and ask him to intervene. He went by night and secretly, and persuaded the King to send for Baldwin. Before long the German Ambassador had his reply, and Hesse claims that he was with the Ambassador when this reply came—by telephone,* and that he was given one receiver so as to listen. This is what he claims to have heard:

"Hullo, is that Leo? David speaking. Do you know who is speaking?"

"Of course I do."

"I sent for the Prime Minister and gave him a piece of my mind. I told the old so-and-so that I would abdicate if he made war. There was a frightful scene. But you needn't worry. There won't be a war."

If this story is true, if there had never been any attempt to deny it, it accords with what Hoare reports of the attitude of King George towards the idea of war with Italy. The moment when bellicose pressure was strongest was when M. Flandin was asked in Paris on 10th March if he would go to the length of military sanctions. After a whole minute of tense waiting the French Minister hissed out the word "Oui."†

He afterwards came over to London and talked to Ralph Wigram of the Foreign Office who himself agreed with Mr. Churchill and Mr. Leo Kennedy against the counsel of *The Times*. M. Flandin had many energetic talks in various quarters; for he, too, had an instinct that now if ever was the time to strike: now was the moment to show Hitler that wanton contempt for treaties was intolerable.

But opinion even in France did not support him. There, too, it was against a war which still had the appearance of being avoidable. It believed that the opportunities Hitler offered were promising.

As for the King, whatever the truth of the German journalist's report (and it is very circumstantial) he certainly was wary of war: he "saw but too clearly that it could only bring needless human suffering and a resurgent Bolshevism pouring into the vacuum of a ravaged and exhausted continent."‡ Distrust of

* Hesse: *Hitler and the English*, translation of *Der Kampf um Deutschland*.
† *Contemporary Review*, 9th May, 1936, p. 616
‡ Duchess of Windsor, op. cit., p. 309.

72

war, as harbinger of revolution, was in his bones. When at last on 3rd September, 1939 he heard that Britain had actually engaged with Germany, his comment was, "I am afraid that in the end this may open the way for world Communism."* He and Sir Winston Churchill, as the latter freely admitted, had not always seen eye to eye on Foreign Policy.

In March, 1936, this view coincided with a feeling almost universal among the peoples of Europe. The West, trusting in the League of Nations, had neglected to arm, and was everywhere unready to strike. Only in the minds of a few experts was it clear that the leverage on Eastern Europe was an empty Rhineland. There seemed no other reason why Hitler should not station there a modicum of troops—and these, so he promised, without the accoutrements of mechanized attack.

Such was the engagement (false as it of course turned out) that Hitler made. And with it he gave fresh guarantees, and made fresh professions of his love of peace. Did he himself not know the evils of war? Had he not proposed general disarmament before he also made concrete proposals to stop all use of poison gas, all bombing aeroplanes? Yes, so much was undeniable. Hitler had made all these proposals before he set out upon his armament scheme. It was Britain who had refused to give up bombing aeroplanes, and it was an actual fact that Hitler had not begun his portentous rearmament till the other proposals had been turned down.

So all this *sounded* plausible enough. One would have needed an uncanny insight to know just how far those strong and eloquent words were just deliberate deceit, hiding an aggressiveness even more sinister. There had been warnings of course—warnings clearest in the wholesale murders—by his connivance, if not his ordering—of *his own adherents*; a warning yet more arresting and grim in the fact that from his very embassy in Vienna had gone the assassins in 1934 to murder the Chancellor of Austria; warning still stronger in his murderous onslaughts on the Jews.

So, on the one side you could get words of protest and denunciation from one newspaper after another, or even from Flandin and Sarraut themselves. But it is a weakness of the French to take strong words, and well-contrived plans for accomplished deeds of arms. On this occasion much was said by the French Government, nothing whatsoever was done. The attitude of the French was that they had their Maginot line of impregnable defence along the French frontier, and that was enough. They were oblivious of the fact that even this line did not extend to the whole of their own frontier, and there was none on the Belgian frontier.

* Duchess of Windsor, op. cit., p. 309.

And there was yet another question in their minds: how far could they rely on help from Britain? Had the British mobilized to send troops to the Rhineland? No attempt whatever had been made in that direction. Also, the French were conscious of another thing that caused profound misgiving. It was that the British had forgotten those designs of a united front against Germany which they had put through at Stresa. In order to press sanctions and reject the Hoare-Laval agreement they had alienated—had indeed flung on to the other side—the powerful makeweight of Italy, whose position in the Mediterranean was of the highest moment in the strategy of Europe. With the islands of Sicily, and of Pantellaria (soon to be armed) between Sicily and North Africa, she could bar naval movements in and through the Mediterranean almost as effectively as though the Suez Canal itself were cut.

If Germany were really growing dangerous, asked the French, why make so rash a move as that?

The British answer—that it was because of Abyssinia and because of the League of Nations—ran counter to the trend of public opinion in France. Was Flandin expecting a decision by arms when he pressed Britain for military action in the Rhineland? Not really. To tell the truth, public opinion in France on that question tended to reflect that of Great Britain. "Rightly or wrongly," wrote an experienced British authority, "the French people left to themselves do not attach great importance to the effort to keep Germany under unilateral disabilities. They cannot understand why Germany should not be as free to do what it pleases in its own territory . . . as the French on their territory."*

Three years before, when Hitler came into power, they had discussed whether it was advisable to have a preventive war; but their instinct had been against it; they did not want then to pick a fresh quarrel with Germany. They had realized by now that they could not continue to override the Germans as beaten enemies. Then what were they to do? The only thing was to come to terms with them. Their feeling was not that they should hang on to enactments of the past, enactments which each abrogated at the moment convenient. It was to make a fresh start.

The sudden rearmament in March, 1935, had called up the spectre of invasion; the answer, however, had been the Stresa pact between Great Britain, France and Italy. And when the powers met at Stresa, they had winked at Italy's African designs. "What did you say about Abyssinia?" This was a question

* Sisley Huddleston in *Contemporary Review*, May, 1936, p. 524. Huddleston was then Correspondent for the *Manchester Guardian* and the *Christian Science Monitor*. In later years he sided with the Vichy Government against the Resistance, but in 1936 his reputation was high everywhere.

which a naïve young Scotsman asked Ramsay MacDonald on his return. The question was answered with an angry glance and the words, "Young man, your question is irrelevant".

So Mussolini had had good reasons for thinking that none in Europe would disturb him as in the summer of that same 1935 he had prepared, before in 1936 he actually launched the Abyssinian campaign. His armies were so strong that nothing could save the Negus but that negotiated peace which the professional diplomats and public opinion in Great Britain had scorned. The French, having seen that pretty clearly all along, were now feeling cynical. While Sir Samuel Hoare had been resigning, and Anthony Eden taking over from him to further what the British public in their well-meaning ignorance had been demanding, the French were aware that the Italian troops were pressing on. So had it been all through February.

The French absolutely insisted that there should be no oil sanctions. When, however, Mr. Eden reached Geneva on 2nd March, the first thing he did was to propose them on Italy! M. Flandin was both astounded and indignant. The space for negotiations on this subject was extended to seven days—from 4th March to 11th March.

It was exactly in the middle of that week, on 7th March, that Hitler made his specious peace proposals and, with these words of conciliation on his lips, sent his troops into the unpromised land on the borders of the Rhine.

Why had France gone as far as she had done in walking with Britain in the matter of Abyssinia? Not because they liked doing so. That we have seen clearly enough. Nevertheless they had imposed certain sanctions because they believed that by doing so they would engage Britain to give them similar support against Germany. Since 7th October, 1935, when Mussolini first attacked Abyssinia London had been exerting a constant pressure on Paris, and there was a constant issue between the two as a result. London had always been trying to drag Paris with her.

Now on 7th March it was Paris which tried to drag London to do against its former enemy, Germany, what London had been doing against its former ally, Italy. Hitler had changed the situation. On 9th March in the House of Commons Mr. Eden spoke to propose a doctrine of appeasement, a doctrine which the Prime Minister proclaimed. He said he desired to bring France and Germany together in friendship with ourselves.

In a most important debate in the House of Commons on 26th March, Mr. Eden made another and longer speech. This was hailed on every side of the House as one of the most successful he ever made. Negotiations were to go on: there were to be no new commitments. Britain was not to be drawn into a quarrel not her own by the Franco-Soviet Pact.

None spoke of any immediate threat of war. Mr. Churchill, in characteristically effective words, spoke of the change of atmosphere since Hitler came to power. Five years ago all had felt safe: all were looking forward to peace: five years before to talk of war would have been not only a folly but a sign of lunacy. But now, how different! The need to arm had become imperative. He then spoke of the strategic dangers which this move had added to those of Germany's resurgent ferocity. He went so far as to say that the new thrust forward offered at once a menace to Holland, Belgium and France. Much more. "It will be a barrier across Germany's front door which leaves her free to sally out eastward and southward by other doors."

After this Neville Chamberlain spoke. His call was clear and practical, naming the nations gathered in the League. Nine or ten maimed people he said might gather together round a roaring lion, but that would not help them against it if they had nothing in their hands. He insisted that the only way for the nations around Germany to be safe from the tooth and claw of the wild beast was also to be armed.

The next day, 28th March, at the Quai d'Orsay, M. Flandin and M. Litvinoff signed the Franco-Soviet pact! A day later still and Flandin hurled at Vézelay an answer to all that Hitler had been saying about the eternal rights of the German people being superior to the rights and regulations in ephemeral peace treaties. Flandin put the question:

What value will any treaty have in the future, if Germany reserves the claim to repudiate it in the name of the German people's rights?

And then he asked about Hitler's further designs—Danzig, Memel, colonies. There was Nazi propaganda in Austria, Schleswig, Sudetenland, those parts of Upper Silesia now belonging to Poland, and even in German Switzerland.

George Glasgow, considering all this, asked in the *Contemporary Review* where the next move was to come: there was a Henlein party in the German-speaking part of Western Bohemia. Might not that soon provide Hitler with a temptation? And what about the oilfields of Rumania? These at that time looked to be the danger spots.

In Paris it seemed Flandin would like Britain to join in some support of their joint policy in Eastern Europe. But at that time no British government would survive which pledged itself by making guarantees in Eastern Europe. Nevertheless, Englishmen, like Frenchmen, now saw clearly that the victory of 1918 did not mean any solution of the German problem in 1936. That was more acute than ever.

When George Glasgow wrote of what was happening in March he felt it not inapposite to recall that his words would appear in a review coming out on 1st April, All Fools' Day.* He was right. On that day the papers were discussing Hitler once more. He had come out on 29th March with yet another pronouncement, making detailed peace proposals, enunciated at great length. He spoke of a preliminary period to calm the atmosphere, a second period for definite negotiations, a third for the elaboration of more far-reaching plans. In the meanwhile he argued that aerial warfare should not be waged against non-combatants: that gas with poisonous and incendiary bombs, along with heavy tanks and long-range guns should be abandoned by the general staffs of every nation.

What did all this mean? Opinion wavered between suspicion, credulity and relief. To some it seemed the answer to the deep longing of peoples. It seemed to others to surpass all one could have imagined of impertinence and hypocrisy.

On 3rd April, Mr. Eden made yet another pronouncement, repeating his guarantee to both France and Belgium; but Lord Zetland, speaking the same day in Manchester, spoke sharply of the danger always more urgent: the huge armament in Germany: the German propaganda in England that France by her Soviet pact had been to blame; that Germany had asserted herself not by negotiation but by force, and that the mass of the German people are very different in psychology to the average German individual. Besides all this, Goebbels was himself boasting that Hitler controlled the army, the Nazi organization, the police, the writers and the press!

CHAPTER XVI

It is a feature of English life that in the newspapers one urge in affairs thrusts out another. Hitler's march into the Rhineland occupied the attention of the capitals of Europe for just on a month, and then the subject fell into the background while all eyes turned towards the rapid advance of the Italians in Abyssinia.

In the first three months of the year, they under Badoglio had consolidated their position. On 25th March they began a great offensive in the Ogaden region of Abyssinia. A few days later their aeroplanes had bombed the provincial capital of Harrar, and practically destroyed it. The Negus based all his hopes on a pitched battle at Dessie where his military

* Contemporary Review, April 1936, p. 624.

headquarters were placed, but in this battle his forces were routed, and the Italians entered Dessie on 15th April.

Meanwhile another Italian column operating along the Sudan frontier had reached the Lake Tana from which issued the waters of the Blue Nile. The British Government could not be blind to what this meant. It was the one point at which their strategic interests were directly involved. So Baldwin prepared to adjust public opinion accordingly.

For already on 20th April he had said in the Worcester Guildhall that sanctions are slow in action and lose their efficacy unless they are to be supported by blockade and force. Collective security was yet far away, because to make it effective *all* nations must be ready to fight an aggressor. Then he went on to mention Germany. Hitler, he said, had at that moment more than any other the power to lift from Europe the black shadow of war. He had the power—had he the will?

In any work of peace the peoples of Europe would co-operate: to that work the Government, the House of Commons, the country would—how eagerly—devote themselves. He did not want to work against Italy: all that he wanted was to support the Government of the League.

So much from Baldwin who manifestly spoke for the Government as a whole.

Yet the very next day, 20th April, Eden at Geneva said it was Britain's manifest duty to maintain those economic and financial sanctions which had been put in force. On the very day after that, Marshal Badoglio, having established his headquarters in Dessie, prepared to advance with a mechanized column on Addis Ababa. On the 22nd their general advance was checked by fierce battles; but once again the Abyssinian forces were unequal to the modern equipment at the disposal of Badoglio. The engineering genius of the invaders made itself felt at every turn. Never before had an Italian army shown such efficiency in a campaign. Their commissariat, their water supplies, their transport and their hospitals, their wireless and their postal arrangements were thoroughly organized, and functioned without a hitch.

The experts of other nations had considered the obstacles in front of the Italians insuperable: Badoglio, in some ten weeks, had surmounted them all. He also found the discipline of his army excellent: the men showed not only ardour but enthusiasm and endurance, while the officers led them forward with skill and courage. "With such troops", wrote the hard-headed Badoglio to Mussolini, "we shall go to the top of the world."*

A track now led onward direct to the capital. In this Italians worked with furious energy, in sun and rain, by day and by night, and a string of vehicles proceeded over the improvised road; on

* Martelli: *Italy Against the World*, p. 231.

the 24th, the 25th and the 26th April Badoglio's columns moved forward under the Marshal's personal supervision. As the armies drew near the capital, Haile Selassie returned to it—but he was both exhausted and devoid of resources. The country was in disorder, and many tribes likely to rise against him. He decided to take the train for Djibuti. As soon as he departed Addis Ababa was given up to riot and loot.

As soon as this was reported to Europe, Paris wired to Rome that Badoglio should arrive in the capital as soon as possible: on 5th May he drove into the city in a Ford limousine, less as a conqueror than as a saviour.

Such was the end of the Abyssinian campaign. Mussolini hailed it as a triumph. He had waged war for seven months and could announce at the end of them that from 1st January to 31st May he had not lost more than 1,273 white troops killed with 31 missing. The death of labourers totalled 453, and of native troops, 1,593. For this price in blood a territory as extensive as France and Italy together was annexed to Italy, her King proclaimed its Emperor, while Mussolini said that he would bring civilization to redeem the miserable from the slavery of a thousand years. He could say more—that his victory had been achieved without disturbing the peace of Europe: for to "disturb the peace of Europe means to bring about the collapse of Europe".*

What was the effect on international politics and on the Britain of King Edward VIII ? To Europe it showed that the King had been right in declaring the League of Nations utterly ineffective. To Britain it brought embittered division. For while the Government of Baldwin was relieved that by having to accept a *fait accompli*, it could renew normal relations with Italy, all those who had espoused the cause of the Negus and of the League of Nations against Mussolini's obstinate determination first to attack, then to conquer were outraged by the sense that wrong had been victorious over right. Meetings were held to argue that sanctions against Italy should still continue; and when after a visit to Jerusalem the fallen Negus arrived in London, he was welcomed with warmest sympathy by those whose hearts were with him as both the darling of the League and the victim of Mussolini.

In due time his dignified and appealing figure was even seen in the Palace of Nations at Geneva; in eloquent words he spoke there of the great principles which had been at stake: collective security, the validity of treaties, the right of small states to maintain their integrity. "In a word," he said, "it is international morality which is at stake."†

Mr. Eden suggested that he should be received at Buckingham

* Martelli: p. 299.   † Martelli: p. 284.

79

Palace by the King. Edward VIII distinctly preferred not. He did not want to identify himself with the hero—and the victim—of the Geneva nations. He made a tactful compromise, suggesting that the Duke of Gloucester who had gone as Royal Envoy to the coronation at Addis Ababa should call on his dethroned Majesty to offer courteous words of personal sympathy.

Baldwin had now, if he could, to adjust himself and his people to some sort of reconciliation with Italy. He must try and join with France to win her back to their side in the tussle with Hitler. That was the steady plan of Vansittart and of professional diplomats.

They knew that Mussolini was not really hostile to Britain as a whole. He had been friends with influential Englishmen for too long. On 27th May, therefore, he interviewed the Foreign Editor of the *Daily Telegraph* to make many soothing and re-assuring statements: he was to make no big black army, he aimed at a liberal solution for foreign trade, harmonizing the interests of France and Britain with those of Italy. "Not only is Anglo-Italian rapprochement desirable," he said, "but it is necessary, and for my part, I will do everything in my power to bring it about." He did not intend to destroy the League of Nations: all that he required was to abandon sanctions.

Now although the League idealists insisted on retaining these they were already against the policy of the Government. This was soon made clear by Neville Chamberlain. He spoke on 10th June to an influential Conservative Club which contained many members of both Houses of Parliament. This was the '1900 Club'. He analysed the situation with characteristic clearness. For definiteness of thought and decision was the secret of the administrative success on which depended his succession to the Premiership.

The aggression, he said, had been patent and flagrant, and it had been thought that there was hardly any country on which a policy of sanctions could be exercised with a greater chance of success than Italy. That policy therefore had been tried out, but it had failed. It failed to prevent war: it failed to stop war: it failed to save the victim of aggression.

There is no reason, he went on, "why because the policy of collective security in the circumstances in which it was applied had failed, that we should therefore abandon the idea of the League or give up the ideals for which the League stands. We must admit, however, that we have tried to impose upon the League a task which was beyond its powers."

So the time had come, he argued, to decide what the League could do, what not. Whether Britain's policy was isolation, or alliances or collective security, it must be armed. That after all was the argument on which he and Baldwin had been insisting for years. But meanwhile, he said—in a phrase which rung in the ears of the world—to go on with sanctions against Italy would be the very *Midsummer of madness.*

Such was the speech which prepared the world for Eden's statement in the House of Commons on 19th June that the Government had decided to abolish sanctions, because to do so was in the interests of peace. Peace, he said, should rule, not chaos and catastrophe.

The argument was repeated once more at Geneva a few days later. The session was interrupted by a man shooting himself in the heart. It was a Czech press photographer who chose this tragic way to make his protest at the way Jews were being treated in Germany. He left a letter addressed to King Edward VIII.

Meanwhile there had been a change of government in France. It was felt that Sarraut and Flandin had not dissociated themselves sufficiently from the Eden policy of sanctions nor yet made it effective. There was also a series of strikes which reduced the country to chaos. So they resigned and on 4th June a more distinctly Socialist government took charge, under the leader of the Popular Front, M. Léon Blum, a Parisian Jew, who made M. Yvon Delbos his Foreign Minister.

The task before them was to balance the budget, and to calm the labour troubles.

The new government had a strong leaning towards the left. Their policy was to combine all leftist parties and push forward Socialist measures for the ease of the working man. In Foreign Affairs the link with Moscow was, of course, to be made closer, fitting in with the Moscow plan of combining with and using all the parties of the left. A week later Moscow itself drafted a new constitution. With it was announced a policy that meant an accord with every popular front, with the added promise that any left-wing leader who wanted it could find asylum in Russia.

So much in France. But in Central Europe also things were happening. Up to that time Austria had been at issue with Germany over the murder of her Chancellor by German agents. Now they announced that they had come to terms of agreement. As time went on, however, this was to prove that in the new Austrian Cabinet of Schuschnigg came in men who if not actually Nazis were prepared to support them. The chief of these was Guido Schmidt, the Vice-Director of the Cabinet.

CHAPTER XVII

THE following day a crime with immense repercussions was committed in Madrid: the Spanish Monarchist, José Calve Sotelo, who had been Finance Minister under Primo de Rivera was murdered. Investigations soon showed that the assassins were in government pay. In Spain the tradition had always been for the army to assert order when governments fail, as they had too often failed, to do so. Five days were enough for the army to decide that a government which had arranged for the murder of its political opponents was intolerable.

There had already been grave disorders in Spain, and a growing indignation. Now it spread and materialized in a military movement. On 18th July many a military garrison in Spanish Morocco rose to protest against the outrage. Three days later military forces stationed there had crossed from Ceuta to the coast of Andalusia; and almost at the same time town after town in Andalusia or Castile was found to be under the control of General Mola who had established his quarters at Burgos. The Spanish Civil War had commenced.

The King had been a naval officer: all naval officers felt a professional zeal in the Spanish affair because Spanish ratings had risen on certain ships, murdered their officers, and thrown the murdered bodies overboard. After this outrage on the laws of the sea, the Spanish warships were legally pirate ships which the navies of the world should sweep from the seas. That was the general feeling of British naval officers.

Here then in Spain was the third new, tense, fierce controversy which swept up among the nations of Europe in the first six months of the new reign. The sixteen years of comparative lull which had followed Versailles were over. The smouldering heaps of combustible rubbish had burst into new flame. The winds were rising.

What was the King to think, what to advise? Before he could make his opinion cogent he must have a thorough grasp of the essentials of the situation. But such a grasp required a careful knowledge of state papers, the sort of work he tells us he disliked. He himself writes that he has never had much zest for paper work. His attitude to his boxes was not what his father's had been. The forte of Lord Wigram was, like his own, more in easy personal relations than in attention to the machinery of government in the files. The result was that from the beginning the chief work of the boxes fell upon Major Hardinge who was responsible for seeing that all papers requiring the King's attention were regularly dealt with. It was for his office to maintain good relations between the King, the Prime Minister and the Cabinet. And the papers would go from Buckingham Palace to Fort Belvedere. But when later they came back there might be no sign whether His Majesty had worked on them or not, and special precautions were taken to check them. On the papers from the Foreign Office the King wrote no cogent comments, made no constructive suggestions. He seemed to think that his role was silently to assume a cynical mood. For it was certainly not without cynicism that he waited while his Government joined with those of France and Germany to speak yet again of their will for peace. Yes, Germany, too, for it was ever the way of Hitler to throw over his programme for armaments the profession of a reasonable desire for conciliation.

So just as the Spanish War began, the three powers of Britain, France and Belgium met for a day of compromise in London. This was on 23rd July. The three powers decided to invite Germany and Italy to join them in another conference as soon as possible. Nothing could be more sinister than to allow Europe to unite into opposing blocks. The declared aim of the conference was to consolidate peace by means of a general peaceful settlement. On 31st July the invitation was accepted in Rome and Berlin. But nothing had happened by 17th September when Eden again brought up the suggestion.

And meanwhile Italy had had time to consider what she had gained by her conquest of Abyssinia. Suppose she were to be successful in colonizing such portions of it as Italians could inhabit, could they do better than the British and Dutch had done in the Transvaal and Natal where there were six Europeans to the square mile? But in Abyssinia none could expect conditions to be half as profitable as they had been in South Africa. In this case, 200,000 square miles of territory could provide for 600,000 inhabitants,* and all the time Italy's population was increasing at the rate of 400,000 a year! It looked as though the Abyssinian affair which had caused such heart-burnings and which had so fatally betrayed the solidarity of Europe against the Hitler danger was not a real solution of Italy's real problem but the grandiosity of an opiate dream.

The difficulty all over Europe was that politicians talked sometimes to meetings, sometimes to crowds, sometimes to one another. But they did not arrive at solutions for the real difficulties which beset them. They wrestled with one another in terms of balance and prestige. They, neither at Geneva nor elsewhere, got so far as to use for the full ends of peace their mutual relations.

Few people cared to give much attention to such things but

* *Morning Post*, 15th September, 1935.

83

there were two other questions of far-reaching importance which came up for consideration in this reign. Each had to do with waterways opening on the Mediterranean. The first dealt with the Suez Canal, and therefore with the relations of Britain and Egypt: the second with the Dardanelles.

In 1935 the Egyptians had become restive in relation to the arrangements made before Sir Samuel Hoare resigned: there was a demand for more definite rights, from liberation from the presence of the British Army in their capital. To tell the truth, Egyptians complained of arbitrary interferences, and said the time had come for both King and people to express their will more freely. Then while the pressure from Egypt was at its height, King Fuad at the age of sixty-eight fell ill and suddenly died. He was succeeded by a son in his seventeenth year, Faruk, who was preparing to enter Sandhurst at the actual moment his father collapsed.

The change on the throne delayed but it could not obviate the need for reaching a settlement which would free Egypt from the dependence—sometimes driven as far as coercion—which had been her lot since Egyptians had murdered Sir Lee Stack in 1922. In later years the British Financial Adviser, as he was called, had assumed from inside a suzerainty over Egyptian administration and sometimes unscrupulously applied it. His post was now abolished and with it that of the Judicial Adviser. The British Forces were to leave Cairo and, limited to 10,000 men, were to take up their station close to the Canal. Egypt was to have a government almost entirely independent, able to enter the League of Nations and plead its case there. Meanwhile a band of astute advisers gathered around the boy King of Egypt to counteract the influence of the contrary party, the Wafd, who were in power when the Treaty was drafted, the British Government insisting however that it should be finally drafted by representatives of all parties. So did it look for a time as though Britain and Egypt were on terms of free association to ensure the function of the Suez Canal. The treaty was signed on 26th August.

The other waterway was the Dardanelles. Here important issues had come up. On the one side was the might of Russia with her perennial claim to a free outlet into the warm waters of the Mediterranean: on the other the new strength of Turkey under the ablest ruler she had known since the days of Amurath, the bold reforming organizer who had changed his name from Mustafa Kemal to one meaning Father-of-Turks: he naturally claimed the right to fortify the Dardanelles, for they were Turkish territory just as the borders of the Canal were Egyptian.

Between these two waterways there was an analogy. Both were international waterways while each had an international importance. The Egyptians had right on their side in reminding Britain that clause 10 of the Agreement of 1888 provided that the Canal should not be used to the detriment of Egypt or to impede her self-government while the British wanted security for a waterway which became yet more important to them as the oilfields on the Persian Gulf developed. The compromise reached was to allow the British to maintain their force of ten thousand men strong on the Canal with installations in the hands of appropriate technicians. As for the actual running of the Canal that as before was left to a personnel mostly French under a board of directors who met in Paris, and the majority of whom were French. Such then was the position fixed as summer ripened into autumn in 1936.

PART FOUR

The Pressure from America

CHAPTER XVIII

ON 20th June the period of court mourning had ended, or rather turned into half mourning. The period in which officials automatically remained in their former posts came to an end, and the King had to settle the question of who was to exercise the post most important constitutionally in the Court, the post of Private Secretary. In the six months which had already passed the work of dealing with boxes had become very formidable for the reason that the new King gave such vague attention to them. This had become a concern to every department of government. And so a heavy task had fallen upon Major Alexander Hardinge for the reason, as we have seen, that Lord Wigram's skill was less in dealing with papers than with men, and Hardinge had been trained under Lord Stamfordham in the solid Victorian tradition which went back to the masterly work of the Prince Consort. Although the King states that he had offered the post to another who refused it, the obvious choice was the man to whom he gave it, and on whom he could rely to deal effectually with the function and routine of all papers requiring the Royal signature. This means that for the rest of the reign, Major Hardinge had an immense amount of work which was essential to the working of the Constitution and which without his combination of training, energy and experience could hardly have been done.

As Prince of Wales, King Edward had combined his business gifts with a dislike of routine. What he could do easily, he had done well; uncongenial things he preferred to avoid. Now, when with the cessation of Court mourning, the ways of the Court and its duties became more obvious, all then who had to do with them must face the question of how far the King intended to go through with them. Often he would not begin his work on papers till the time when it was normal to lunch, for he ate almost nothing in the middle of the day. At such a time he would send an urgent message to his Private Secretary who had finally to expostulate that he could not arrange to be regularly interrupted as he was entertaining guests at lunch.

With mourning ended, it was time for ladies to be once more presented and a number of débutantes had gathered who were particularly interested to think that they would make their curtseys before a bachelor King.

After a number of young ladies had been presented, there was a storm; and before the débutantes could reach the marquee, their dresses had suffered from the downpour. At this point, the King gave orders for the file of advancing damsels to stop. The presentations were to be taken as made, though they were not made. The King left the marquee and hurried back through the rain into the Palace. The shower, as is the way with heavy showers in London, was soon over. But the King did not reappear.

Those who had not passed before him were disappointed. Criticism which was inevitable said not only that the King ran away from a duty but that he was "profoundly bored with the whole performance", as Lord Curzon had written of him some fifteen years before at the funeral of Bonar Law. Often at ceremonies and functions he had given that impression. Once when being shown over Durham Cathedral by the Bishop, Hensley Henson, he had followed glumly till at the approach to the tomb of the Venerable Bede, who was England's first historian, the aged Bishop, walking backwards and therefore not noticing that he had approached some steps that led to a lower level, tripped on them and fell on his back. As the old man fell the Prince's boredom vanished.

If there had been such a reaction it would not have been unnatural for, as both Prince and King, Edward VIII had been pursuing a course of action which none of his ghostly counsellors would have deemed likely to attract the heavenly favours which they so regularly invoked upon him.

Nevertheless, as the months wore on, he had to prepare the order of his Coronation and give formal instructions accordingly. It was noticed that whenever such an occasion arose he managed not to make any personal intervention. When he could, he handed his duties over to the Duke of York. This was so marked that in the Court a doubt arose as to whether he really intended to go through with it. What also seemed significant, he refused to sanction the name of *King Edward VIII* for a new battleship. He could not but remember that the Coronation was itself a rite inserted into the Celebration of Holy Communion, as Ordination was. The whole service was essentially religious, besides, he must himself swear that as Defender of the Faith he would maintain the laws of the Church of England.

There are many who will take their ease with the rules of the Church, but would at the same time be horrified at the idea that while doing so they are to receive its most sacred ministrations. The new King was one of these: this being so, he asked Lord Cromer, who as Lord Chamberlain was responsible for Court ceremonial, to enquire if it were not possible to have a Coronation without these intimate and sacred obligations. Were there no precedents for this ? The answer did not help. Edward V had not been crowned—poor boy, he had been murdered first. The other, the only other sovereigns who had not fulfilled the Coronation ceremonies were James II and the wicked John. All this was most embarrassing; because as he said "to go through the Coronation ceremony while harbouring in my heart a secret intention to marry contrary to the Church's tenets would have meant being crowned with a lie on my lips."

It was true: in the very service into which the rite of coronation was incorporated came the commandment which had thundered from Sinai: Thou shalt not covet thy neighbour's wife.

It was the more awkward because while he recoiled from sacrilege he had no intimate adviser on Church affairs; he knew that the Archbishop of Canterbury was a zealous Churchman who wished to make the Coronation a call to religion for the whole Empire. The Archbishop aimed that the Coronation should not only invoke graces upon the King but lead on to a consecration of the whole life of the people over whom he reigned.

But there was, as we know, one thing upon which more than any other the King's heart was set; he wanted to take to himself Ernest Simpson's wife. Other people had obtained divorces and started again. Mrs. Simpson had already done it once. Why should she not do it a second time ? If she was considered to be living a decent life with Simpson, why should she be blamed if she changed once more and settled down with himself ?

The battle in the King's mind was on a straight issue. It was the battle between his obligations as a Churchman and American standards inconsistent with his Church; and those standards were seeping swiftly into a certain strata of the society of Britain. Now it would have been logical if the King, accepting these standards from America, had defied the Church; but tradition was too strong for that. Therefore he was in the awkward fix of trying to work things without clashing with his Royal position while he intended to circumvent the Church; yet it, after all, was to crown him.

He must compromise; so his way of procedure was to get Mrs. Simpson accepted in London and in official society: already in his father's time he had had her invited to Court functions. Now he designed to put her name into the Court Circular. His object was not to model himself on the discreet King Carol in his secret intimacy with a Lupescu who, though known to all, was seen of none. That would not in the least have suited the project of either the King or Mrs. Simpson. What they wanted was to arrive at a strategic position where she could become the Queen of England and be openly hailed and honoured as Her Majesty.

He aimed at doing this in the teeth of the Court traditions; of his mother, the Queen; of a Government with strong Churchmen and Nonconformists in the principal posts; of the general moral sense of the masses of his subjects; and of the Church dignitaries of which, according to the phrase invented by Henry VIII, and adapted by Elizabeth,* he himself was the supreme governor. And such in temporal things he legally remained.

This was the paradoxical situation with which he now set out to cope till the Court and Society became clearly aware of his *penchant amoureux*—though the masses of the people remained entirely ignorant.

It was the tournament of his moves with the information given by American—but withheld by British—newspapers which now became one of the chief preoccupations of the Government as well as the Court. It was this which now distracted their attention from the crucial complication of European alignments.

In May he announced to Mrs. Simpson that he intended to marry her; but the only hint of his intentions to Government or Court was that one spring evening he had invited both his Private Secretaries with their wives to meet him with the Simpsons at Windsor, the evening of 28th March. They talked of George IV and Mrs. Fitzherbert, and the very subject seemed to hint at the possibility of something like a more or less equivalent situation. With the Simpsons came that other American lady, Madame Raffray, who talked to Mr. Simpson while his wife occupied the King. The name of George III was brought up and the 'King's Party' which had been formed for him; and then they went on to discuss Mrs. Fitzherbert in tones which, as the groups formed and reformed, bristled with unspoken hints and with half confidences. There are times when questions are less questions than admissions. And the way the point was pressed could not but betray the wishes, if not the thoughts, of certain members of the company. It was a startling thought—were the two friends planning marriage while one was married and actually, as she pressed her questions, in the presence of a husband with whom she seemed on friendly terms ? No, thought Mrs. Hardinge, who was present, one must not harbour suspicions so sensational. She knew that if the King was entertaining such a conjecture, the struggle within him must be sad and bitter, knowing that it meant living "in the darkness of secrecy, because it was the secrecy born of fear".†

And then talking of the discussions already current in the circles close to the Court, the narrative goes on: "All the world

* Queen Mary Tudor had her doubts whether Elizabeth was his daughter.
† Lady Hardinge of Penshurst: *The Path of Kings*.

knew of the predicament; too much so; and the King clung to his secret and private life with a sort of desperation. Only a selfless woman with no ambition could have made private life and public life possible for him at this point. But then a selfless woman with no ambition could hardly have been in such a situation. This one was not prepared to be a Mrs. Fitzherbert, nor was the King able to think of her so."* That was as far as the King's clearness about the situation extended. After that the confusion in his mind darkened his whole prospect.

On one move they agreed; she must move in Court Society and be announced as doing so. So in May invitations went out for a dinner at St. James's Palace. The guests were to include with the two Simpsons the Lindberghs and the Baldwins. With them came Lord and Lady Mountbatten, Sir Ernle and Lady Chatfield, the Duff Coopers, Lord and Lady Wigram.

What would the Baldwins think of this? The Prime Minister was not unresponsive to the sprightliness of the city man's lady, though his taste and style were for something less American and modern; to her in fact few men were unresponsive: she always succeeded in amusing them. The women felt differently and said so. And Mrs. Baldwin was no exception. Her sense of rightness was shocked. Though she could not be blind when she was in Canada to the way his flirtations developed, she had managed to envelope her Prince in romance, and she was loath to see the sheen wear away. But she felt now the advent of something which would smirch the unsullied pleasure with which she had admired him. She could not but see how her peach had lost its bloom.

When the announcement of this dinner party appeared in the Court Circular those who knew of the King's interest were aware of what the announcement implied. Gossip raced through London; it started comments in the American papers. And many guessed that the time could not be far off when Mrs. Simpson's husband would leave her and settle down in the Guards' Club. He was more and more often with the American lady, Madame Raffray, whom he afterwards married.

Not long afterwards Mrs. Simpson, who was then employing private detectives, wrote to her husband that she was about to bring a divorce case against him.

Then conjecture enquired into the point: what were now the financial resources of Mrs. Simpson? Did she expect to be maintained by her husband while she was suing him for misconduct, and if not who had rescued her from penury?

Of that her narrative says nothing, though she records that her life at this time was full. In London itself she had many engagements, many invitations. And weekend after weekend she

* Lady Hardinge of Penshurst: op. cit.

joined the King at Fort Belvedere where he entertained a little circle of those friends he then favoured most. They were a naval officer, Colin Buist; Evelyn Fitzgerald whose sister was a friend of Lord Beaverbrook. These with two equerries were now his particular set. With them as Lords-in-Waiting were Lord Sefton and Lord Brownlow, who could not but notice how different his taste was from the old Court and from the company of his relatives in general. These who came so often were prepared to accept, and had in fact long accepted, Mrs. Simpson as the favoured friend of the King.

It was just a year since on 10th July, 1935, he and she had both been guests at a great dinner at the German Embassy, for the Ambassador, Leo von Hoesch, who, as we saw, was his personal friend, had been aware that he would like Mrs. Simpson to be present, and cultivated her accordingly. It did not escape comment that she was *persona gratissima* in German circles; it even caught the attention of the secret police who were already beginning to keep a vigilant eye on all who seemed to have close German connections. Many Germans came to the country in ever increasing numbers, and established connections with all whom they opined could help them, or provide them with information.

Now as July came round again invitations were sent out for a great Royal dinner on 7th July—a dinner which would mark Mrs. Simpson's place in official society. The Duke and Duchess of York were invited: the First Lord of the Admiralty, Sir Samuel Hoare with Lady Maud his wife, the Chief Whip, Major Margesson, Lord and Lady Willingdon who had just been raised a step in the peerage, Lord and Lady Stanhope, Lady Oxford, Lady Diana Cooper and Lady Colefax, his new Private Secretary, Major Alec Hardinge and Mr. Winston Churchill. Such that night was the company who were summoned to greet and amuse his favourite lady.

It did not escape observation that *this time she came without her husband*. Among the guests there were enough who had accepted her to make it an evening free from awkwardness. Sir Samuel Hoare who then met her for the first time noted her as an attractive and intelligent American. He also noted that she knew little or nothing of English life. She knew England only from a small set, largely American, or from the few who were boon companions of the new King.

On the same day as the King gave this dinner party it was announced that Austria and Germany had agreed to restore friendly and normal relations. So closely were personal and diplomatic affairs connected at this time in the interest of those who were watching affairs.

On 16th July the King received the Guards in Hyde Park and

presented them with their colours. In doing so, he made a moving speech: "With all my heart," he said, "I hope and indeed I pray, that never again will our age and generation be called to face such stern and terrible days. Humanity cries out for peace and the assurance of peace, and you will find in peace opportunities of service as noble as any that bygone battlefields can show." On the way back from the impressive function at which he had made in true Churchillian tone this moving speech, a man threw at him a loaded revolver. What this gesture meant it would be hard to say. The King rode on undisturbed; and he received congratulations from many heads of states, including Hitler. But, as enquiries showed, he had not been in any real danger.

The King's next engagement was in France. In 1918, thousands of Canadians had fallen in the assault on Vimy Ridge: now 6,000 Canadians who had survived that bloody episode were to come back and see the monument raised to those who had fallen, and share in the tribute to their glory. These Canadians were received by the King. Once again he made an eloquent speech resonant with hope. "Around us this day is peace and the rebuilding of hope. And so, in dedicating this memorial to our fallen comrades our thoughts turn rather to the splendour of their sacrifice and to the consecration of our love for them than to the cannonade which beat upon this ridge a score of years ago." Then massed bands played Elgar's anthem:

> Land of Hope and Glory
> Mother of the free,
> How shall we requite thee
> Who are born of thee?

Seeing the record of the King in these ceremonials, surrounded by guards in uniform, with Ministers of the Crown and prominent citizens, the people as a whole accepted the idea that the new reign was carrying on the traditions of those preceding it; and that the Court was the focus of the Empire's most distinguished life. The central figure seemed still to satisfy the people's need to look upward and admire. As for the papers, they were occupied with the new war in Spain, the progress of the treaty with Egypt, the hopes of some better understanding with Germany; for on these the mind of Anthony Eden still was set.

Then the Great Officers of State, the Archbishop of Canterbury, the Lord Chancellor, the Lord Privy Seal came to York House to prepare for the Coronation. The King, however, did not receive them: he arranged rather that under the Duke of York should be made the adjustments required in order that this medieval ceremony with its hereditary officers should be in accordance with the fact that the throne was now centre not only for Great Britain but for wide dominions. These all had their right and their need to take their own prominent place in the act of Coronation.

In the Court Circular, mentions of the King's movements were few. On Sundays it was always related that there was Divine worship in the Chapel Royal, but of course no mention that the King was absent at Fort Belvedere. Thus there came to be an immense gulf in opinion between those who really knew the Court, and those who merely read the newspapers.

For who could see the slightest hint of irregularity in reading the Court Circular and seeing that the Earl of Sefton had succeeded Lord Brownlow as Lord-in-Waiting to His Majesty?

CHAPTER XIX

NOR was it known beyond a few that the King was now preparing an unconventional holiday. But he had determined to escape from ceremony to relaxation and the sun; he was to be bothered with none whom he found uncongenial, and enjoy every opportunity for the company of the woman who pleased him above every other.

The King's plan was to take, on the Cote d'Azur, near Juan-les-Pins, the smart villa of Miss Maxine Elliot. But the new Blum government had not succeeded in calming the angry mood of resentment which had led throughout France to strikes and riots. When these strikes had spread to the Riviera, it was found inadvisable for the King to settle there for a long visit. He decided he would gain his end if he hired a yacht to sail down the Adriatic, beginning at Venice.

His Foreign Secretary, however, made strong objections to his going through Italy so soon after Mussolini had won the Abyssinian war. Suppose the Italians made an unfriendly demonstration—well that must be avoided. But suppose on the other hand they were obviously friendly. That might indicate that they believed the King to agree with them about the League of Nations. The King was not pleased to have his movements thus dictated to him by his Foreign Secretary, but he did not press the point.

He cut out Venice and boarded a train which would take him through France and Austria to the realm ruled by Prince Paul, and so to Sibenik where with two destroyers he had ordered a yacht to be in readiness—this yacht was the *Nahlin* which he had arranged to charter from Lady Yule.

No more news about them appeared in the Court Circular. A photograph of him taken in the company of Mrs. Simpson at

Salzburg was printed in the *Daily Sketch*—and then the ban on British newspapers came down again. It was left to Americans to report on the tour from day to day.

The affair, however, was no secret on the Adriatic Coast. Wherever the Royal yacht went and the Royal party appeared, the crowds gazed at them and sang the praise of hearts melting into unity. They were mobbed at Dubrovnik: greeted with shouts that meant '*Vive l'amour!*' Mrs. Simpson gives the impression that this situation made her somewhat uncomfortable; but the King appeared pleased that all recognized the close relation in which he delighted.

Day after day, the American pressmen were dogging them close, for by now Mrs. Simpson had become the special sensation of the United States. There the papers, who had made her already the best known of American woman, decided they must make a sensation of this cruise. Imagination helped where eyes could not reach.

What, as they came through, did Prince Paul make of their much discussed affair? For he could not allow the King of England to pass near his summer palace without inviting him to a visit. He met them at Iesnice on the frontier and drove them out to his villa at Kranj nearby from which they returned to dine on the train. And so they rushed on through the night to Ljubljana and drove down to the sea at Sibenik.

The next royalty they visited was the King of Greece whom they found at Corfu: was it much better being King of that land of eternal summer and imperishable names than living in the modest elegance of Brown's Hotel in Albemarle Street? Very often when King George of Greece was receiving, his sister stood at his side as hostess. On the present occasion her place was taken by Mrs. Britten-Jones, a friend of King George who had of course no official position. There was no question of discourtesy actual or imagined. King George entertained King Edward at a very pleasant dinner, his other guests being two senior British officers who were staying with him.

But now the beautiful island of Corfu faded in the mist of evening. Its cypresses and cliffs, its island of the dead left but a slight impression upon the royal party as they sailed on to the picturesque gulf of Corinth with Missolonghi on its coast, Missolonghi where Byron died. Farther on was the Delphi where the oracle had spoken beneath the snows of Parnassus and where the Royal party drank of the Castalian spring. The King cared for none of these things. At last at the head of the gulf they entered a narrow canal, with high banks on either side, a canal so narrow that it scarcely gave room for the *Nahlin* to sail through. But it was known that the King—and his lady friend—were on the yacht, and just as in the Adriatic British tars, spying the yacht, rushed to the decks to catch the flavour of the affair, so here crowds lined the banks to see what they could.

Mrs. Simpson writes that what they saw was the King's quite bare torso. She says that he refused to wear anything above his shorts but the straps of his binoculars, and that none dared to tell him otherwise though his suite were pained and puzzled at his departing so far from Court convention. Others in his suite deny this story altogether. None admits to any impression that the King's clothing was too scant. The Duff Coopers had accepted his invitation with alacrity and having come they were impressed by the charm of their host as well as by the tact and good taste of Mrs. Simpson who could intervene effectively if the King's temper ever came in the way of a move which might cause complications.

The *Nahlin* having run through the assembled sightseers on the Corinth Canal emerged into the Aegean sea and sailed past the island of Hydra to the Piraeus. On landing His Majesty was met by the principal A.D.C. to the King of Greece and drove straight to the British Legation. After that he spent some time on the Acropolis. The next day he went for a long walk with the British Minister with whom also he dined that evening. One must not think that his main object in visiting Athens was, as Mrs. Simpson's narrative might suggest, to be entertained at a café by Lord Dudley.

They were now to go forward among the Isles of Greece to the coasts below Mount Ida and so to Gallipoli. Wherever they saw a lonely beach, they put down the dinghy and rowed out to bathe, as they had done a year before at Corsica and the Iles d'Hyeres. Then, as they approached Gallipoli, the King remembered the huge adventure sponsored by his friend Churchill some twenty years before in the days when the Anzacs (so did Birdwood coin a name from the initials of Australia New Zealand Army Corps) had landed at Suvla and Cape Helles. There they found the graves and monuments of the fallen; the King was given a reminder of the thoughts he had voiced at Vimy a few weeks before.

But now the cruise was nearing its end: the waters widened into the Sea of Marmora, and the *Nahlin* sailed up into the picturesqueness where Stamboul and Pera rise on either side of the Golden Horn, with its minarets, its mosques, its palaces and its cypresses.

They could not but be gratified by the arrangements made for them by the Turkish Ghazi. He had decided to offer Mrs. Simpson royal honours. At every turn they were greeted with sumptuous festival, and the whole visit was an unqualified success.

Here was a man who had attained to power by his own efforts. Finding himself master of Constantinople and of Turkey, his aim was to free them from the shackles of a tradition that impeded them from stepping forward to enjoy the natural exercise of life. Better to Americanize his country, or, at least, to make it more like the West! So the Turkey of Ataturk was a land of happy youth, eager for the heritage of freedom to live their lives with energy and joy. The harem and the yashmak had been abolished. The women of Turkey now walked breathing free air like other women in Europe, and voted as they would. Turkey marched forward, healthy and conscious of its strength. No *mufti* was its master. For it to be free was to be strong.

This discerning Dictator, after putting through his fortification of the Dardanelles, craved the support of an English ally; and so flattering was his welcome to the King, so *empressé* was he in his attentions to Mrs. Simpson, that the King went so far as to invite his host to pay a state visit to London. Sir Percy Loraine, his Ambassador, had well prepared the ground, winning the Ghazi's respect and confidence not only in convivial evenings, and in sport. For the Ambassador was these as well as a writer of despatches. But when the Foreign Office heard that the King, without consulting them, had in that year of 1936—the year of the Rhineland march, the Abyssinian campaign and the Spanish War —invited a ruthless dictator to London, they were by no means in accord. Whatever they thought of a King taking their business into his own hands, they had to judge public opinion. The resources of diplomacy were soon at work to dissuade Ataturk from taking the royal words of invitation as part of an official plan. Such is the story of certain diplomats; there is no reference to it in the diary of the cruise.

Before this had happened, however, the Ghazi had offered the Royal party his own train to take them to Vienna. In this they soon found themselves passing by Adrianople to the primitive towns and rough countryside of Bulgaria, one of the barest and most backward countries in Europe, except where in its capital German princes and Russian largesse made a new outpost of European elegance. Here it was clear that Czar Boris reigned, popular and astute, with the young Italian Queen who was awaiting their first child.*

Boris was one of the bravest and ablest of Kings, secure in the confidence he had gained from his people. Outside the *Petite Entente*, having lost territory to the resuscitated Greece at the end of the First War, and by no means eager for a Russia which was Bolshevized, he finally found his country drawn into the orbit of Italy. It was, however, his business to remain neutral in the blocs into which Europe was divided, and if anything to draw with Turkey into friendship with the Western Powers: but we have no word that such considerations occupied King Edward VIII

* He was to be christened Simeon, but many newspapers changed the E in this name to an S.

No spats. The Prince of Wales sets a new trend, 1924

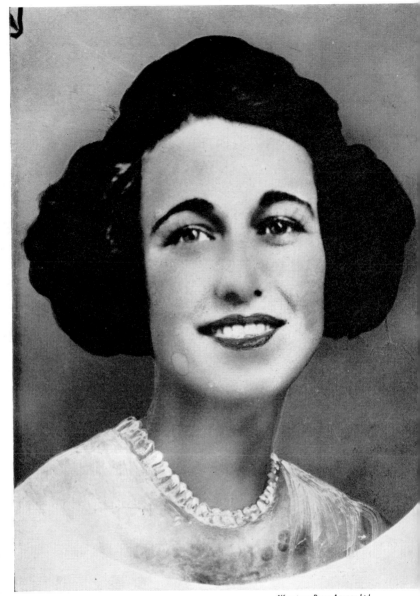

Mrs. Earl Winfield Spencer, *née* Wallis Warfield

The Prince inspects the British Legion, 1933

The Prince enters the
Adriatic

[Paul Popper Ltd.

The Prince of Wales comes a cropper at Bicester

The Prince and his
younger brother at
the Derby

[Keystone Press Agency Ltd.

The Prince with Mrs. Simpson at Ascot

Mrs. Dudley Ward

Thelma, Lady Furness

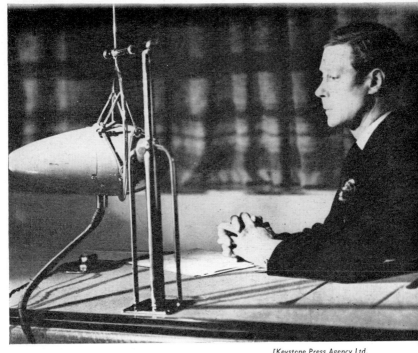

[Keystone Press Agency Ltd.

The King speaks to the nation

The Dean of
Westminster, the King
and the Archbishop of
Canterbury after the
distribution of Maundy
money (l. to r.)

[Paul Popper Ltd.

The King takes a jump at Belvoir

The King greets Queen Mary

"Le Roi enchaîné". The first official engagement at Windsor

The embarrassing garden party at Buckingham Palace

The King inspects the Yeomen of the Guard in the gardens of the Palace

The King, followed by his three brothers York, Gloucester and Kent,
at Trooping the Colour

[Paul Popper Ltd.

"The King is dead. Long live the King!"

The King and
Mrs. Simpson come
ashore on the
Dalmatian coast

[Paul Popper Ltd.

The King and Mrs. Simpson off the Dalmatian coast

The Prince of Wales on holiday in Biarritz

The Prince of Wales about to take a row with friends in Yugoslavia

in his swift passage through this Balkan country. He tells only that the Czar insisted on driving the engine of his train, allowing his brother of Britain to stand beside him and blow the whistle.

And yet relations with these countries were not without importance. Great efforts had been made to keep Belgrade within the orbit of the Western Powers; the special success in this direction was the close collaboration of Prince Paul, as Regent, with the British Minister, Sir Ronald Campbell. Though the Envoy endeavoured to keep it secret, he conferred several times a week with the Regent, and he believed he had countered the Nazi intrigues and was keeping Yugoslavia with Greece in the orbit of the Western Powers.

None of this does the King mention: he spoke only of Prince Paul's interest in private collections. This Prince was—and is— a man of unusual taste who shared Parisian interests with his wife, who, as we saw, is a sister of the Duchess of Kent.

And so the special train of Ataturk rolled onward with the Royal Party till it reached Vienna where Sir Walford Selby was waiting to receive and welcome the King. Here was an old friend who really admired him. As he drove with the Minister to his Legation, he was cheered and cheered by enthusiastic crowds. "Why?" he asked. "What have I done to earn this?" They liked him. They were flattered by his returns. They sympathized with his relaxations. And they were longing to express their old loyalty to a reigning sovereign as they had done in the days of their glory. So at Vienna the King received the last great ovation of his life—for both the Minister and the Viennese were enthusiastically on his side.

Here then he could enjoy for a few days of early autumn the Viennese atmosphere he loved—here take a Turkish bath, or see an ear-specialist: here renew his friendship with the Rothschilds at Schloss Enzesfeld: here receive the latest official news in the red boxes that met him from London. So five days passed. On 14th September he was back in London and dining with Queen Mary at Buckingham Palace. The Queen knew that there was ever more cause for concern with regard to her son's projects. But she had not come to speak plainly of them when he was Prince; her natural instinct to avoid all personal conflict kept her weighted heart silent now.

And the Prime Minister? Duff Cooper had returned to London some time before. Did he consider discussing with the Prime Minister what the cruise suggested? Baldwin was not unaware of the comments thickening in American newspapers. He had his press cuttings like the rest. But so far, they did not mention divorce, and, having been gratified by the King's courtesy it was hardly for him now to protest or play gooseberry. His personal impression of Mrs. Simpson was entirely favourable.

So the King had no special talk with Baldwin who, though he now knew a great deal from one source or another, decided with his knowledge of the King's headiness that the time had not come for him to speak. Furthermore, neither Duff Cooper nor any other on the cruise was aware of scandalous behaviour. All had enjoyed their trip; all approved of Mrs. Simpson's demeanour; she had been tactful and discreet, and her host agreeable. What had Baldwin to go on? Mainly cuttings from American newspapers which in detail were often inaccurate. He was a man who never acted precipitately. He decided the time was not yet ripe for him to curb the royal lion. He was right. He was to find a month later when events, which we shall follow, did at last force him to speak that his words were almost ignored. But from now on things moved with hastening pace.

The King on his return to London found himself among affairs that really pressed on his attention. On the one side was the rush of events in the Spanish War: on the other, the fact that the treaty with Egypt, signed a few days before, was now to come into force.

Such then were the chief European events of the first six months of the reign of Edward VIII. They meant already a new orientation in Europe which required energy and vigilance, for by upheaval the balance of forces had been shaken. What did it all portend? At the centre of information sat the new King of England looking with doubt on the policy his Foreign Secretary was pursuing, and wondering where England stood in the sharpening contest between Moscow and Berlin.

Both were harnessing their powers: both made the pretence that they were leaving the Spaniards to fight their own battles while they each attempted to gain control of the Iberian peninsula. Geography made it strategically paramount: it was the mouth of the Mediterranean. Could it be gained for a Russian block acting in unison with the friends of Moscow in France, all under the name of the Popular Front, it would leave the German nationalism with enemies all round it. Could it be gained for the other side, now called the Fascist Powers, it kept the Mediterranean open for Italy, and provided a second front on which to engage the French. For the Spanish Civil War was not merely a Spanish Civil War. It was a tussle between Russia and the Central Powers, who each found an opportunity to test their weapons. In this tussle the governments of London, Washington and Paris took no part—but furious arguments surged around them.

CHAPTER XX

THE papers, being still full of these affairs, made little of the sovereign's return. But he was to pay his annual visit to Balmoral, and the one guest who stayed there longest was Mrs. Simpson who arrived there with those who had been her hosts and supporters in Pekin, Mr. and Mrs. Herman L. Rogers.

The minute this was announced in the Court Circular it made a sensation in Scotland where talk travels quickly, in America where enterprising papers, as we have seen, had long been chronicling the moves of Mrs. Simpson, and in those circles in London which, whether official or unofficial, were well aware of what happened in the royal household.

At this time the American newspapers began to dominate the situation. Crossing freely into Canada, as they did, they disturbed that wide Dominion in its zeal to enrich the King's chronicle with praise. Percolating slowly into England, they passed among people of importance to string their minds to expectation and surmise.

Mrs. Simpson had gone from Vienna to the smartest of Paris hotels. There she was met by American newspapers, which showed her what effects her cruise with the King had had on her impressionable countrymen. That, added to the alleged unconventionality of his demeanour and dress, had aroused comments enough. And stories rushed to the extreme. That he had not overdone himself with dress on those sunswept days was true: he wore habitually shorts with a striped cotton jersey above them; from that rumour rushed the false report that he wore much less —and even nothing! His rows to lonely beaches, his supping in a cabaret, his walks with Mrs. Simpson, the honours done by the Turk Dictator to her, the resumption of late evenings in Vienna —all these had been observed, all reported to suggest an atmosphere of scandal. It has been already averred that no one on the cruise had detected this.

But now came the sensational additions which rushed her story into the most serious of American papers: *she was pressing on with her divorce.* On the day when she arrived at Balmoral, the King, having declined to go that day to open the wing of a hospital in Aberdeen was seen waiting to greet her at the railway station. The reason he gives for his refusal was that the Court was still in mourning. Finding his brother taking his place at Aberdeen, the Scots attached scant importance to the reasons, however valid, which the King gave; it was soon known everywhere in Scotland that on that very afternoon, going early to the railway station, he was waiting there to press his welcome on the lady who had been the companion of his tour in the Adriatic and the Balkans.

This occasioned a burst of indignation. Good Scottish Presbyterians took the severest view of what was happening, and gravely voiced the standards of the Kirk. Words not mincing such opinion were chalked upon the walls of certain places in Aberdeen and Edinburgh. The situation was becoming disagreeable, especially as servants dismissed from the Balmoral staff had also their tale to tell. Nor could any fail to notice the change of the kind of guests now being entertained. The King might still have the old Scottish aristocracy—the Buccleuchs, the Sutherlands, the Roseberys, and with these the Marlboroughs as his first guests at the Castle. At one time in a royal car there were five Duchesses; for the Duke and Duchess of York were as usual at Birkhall on the Balmoral estate, the Duke and Duchess of Gloucester at Abergeldie. These were both entertaining friends and relatives who were well aware of what Scotland was saying; and these Royal Duchesses were anxious not to be put in equivocal situations.

Their anticipations were not calmed by the event. The Duchess of York was a very religious woman and a very sweet nature. When she was invited to dinner she found that Mrs. Simpson received her. She left as soon as she conveniently could. To Scottish taste the long visit of Mrs. Simpson and the presence of her friends clashed with the Balmoral tradition and the standards of Queen Victoria, Queen Alexandra and Queen Mary.

From this much followed, and since all was done before the servants, the whole story soon ran through Scotland. To it was added chit-chat about late drinking at night. Such was the sort of backstairs gossip that at this time was diffused to the East winds of Scotland, and the Covenanters' Hills, carousal in a fastness where Victorian traditions had till then never ceased to rule. The story reached Queen Mary at Buckingham Palace. She could not restrain her dismay that such should now be the tenor of the place she had revered from the days of Queen Victoria as "Dear, sacred Balmoral". But even to those who gathered their chief impressions from the Court Circular, it was noticed that, if the Castle was not closed to Dukes and Earls, there were few members of the Government: the only two were Sir John Simon and Mr. Ormsby-Gore,* who came to discuss a project Major Hardinge had brought up in order to counteract what the newspapers had noted about his recent tour: a royal visit to the distressed areas in South Wales. Instead of the Prime Minister came Mr. Herman Rogers; instead of the Archbishop of Canterbury Mrs. Ernest Simpson.

* Now Lord Harlech.

Such names, published everywhere in the Court Circular, meant that the King intended to proclaim his personal predilections to the country. All informed people made their comments accordingly. To deal with his aim the King now took a definite step. He invited to Balmoral Lord Rothermere's son, Mr. Esmond Harmsworth, who was Chairman of the Newspaper Proprietors' Association. The idea was to discuss how the newspapers of Britain were to be managed. Up to now the newspapers had been in everything to do with the King excessively discreet. Even as Prince of Wales he had always escaped their criticism just when he needed it to help him. But no matter how reticent the British newspapers might be, the stay at Balmoral produced a fresh spate of items always sensational, not always correct, in the press of America. At the end of a fortnight at Balmoral it was not only deer which had been killed: the good report of the Crown of England had suffered, and those who were responsible for the well-being and unity of the Empire felt an anxiety that distracted their attention from the conduct of state business.

British subjects in the United States, and vast numbers of Canadians were now hard put to it to defend the honour of the Crown from the gossip occasioned by the American journalists' story that was now becoming more and more circumstantial. What had struck Mrs. Simpson's attention in Paris when she saw her mail from America now elbowed its way among the members of the Cabinet; it also strained the ostrich policy of the British newspapers; these had subjected all their immense possibilities, nay certainties, of profit from the publication of such items as appeared in the American Press to their loyalty to the good name of the King.

Apart from the Chairman of the Newspaper Proprietors' Association, there were the Proprietors themselves, those new but important peers, Lord Beaverbrook, Lord Rothermere, Lord Camrose, Lord Kemsley, Lord Astor—and Lord Astor's brother had the principal interest in *The Times*. These men controlled the policy of the principal newspapers, and they determined not to throw the searchlight of publicity on to predilections of the King any more than any newspapers had done thirty years before on the gallantries of King Edward VII.

They must maintain intact the credit of the Crown in spite of the fact that the Court Circular had mentioned Mrs. Simpson and her friends, as it could not do had the King been averse to that.

About this time, Mr. Attlee, the Leader of the Opposition, began to be aware of what was coming; he went therefore privately to the Prime Minister and asked for information. He added that he knew the temper of the industrial constituencies was much stricter than that of London, and made it clear that the Labour Party would have little sympathy with the King's favour towards Mrs. Simpson.

After the King's arrival at Balmoral, Englishmen who knew anything of American newspapers were bound to observe how strident their tone had become. Savoury items of gossip were exchanged for what a troubled Englishman who lived there was soon to call a "perfect avalanche of muck and slime". Even the *New York Times*, which up to that date had said nothing, began in the month of October to print columns about it. As for the others they were already making it the sensation of the day. In their statements they preferred sensation to silence; in their tone was no reserve.

With the items of information came many photographs; photographs of the pair during their tour on the *Nahlin*; photographs in bathing attire; photographs of them together in Vienna; photographs of them parading streets together; photographs of the arrival of Mrs. Simpson at the station on her way to Balmoral in the company of him who had come there to meet her; to which was added the telling detail that she was also with the King in the train on his way back to London.

Yes, it was said, the ubiquitous Mrs. Simpson is the companion of the King on every conceivable occasion. Now things were pushed further. For somehow the American press had got hold of the report that Queen Mary had contrasted her memories of Balmoral with what she heard had been happening there. So the papers said that while he, the son, was enjoying his jollities with his American friends, the widowed mother was spending her last days at Buckingham Palace.

Such was the sort of story now shouted by the street-boys of Chicago, now placarded on hoardings in the staid streets of Boston. Paper after paper boasted not only in headlines but on hoardings that it could give the inside story of the King's relations to Mrs. Simpson!! When distinguished persons arrived in New York from Britain, American journalists stampeded to get their views; hearing nothing the reporters made capital out of their very refusal to answer and mockery of their embarrassment.

Then the Hearst newspapers took up the affair with a biography of Mrs. Simpson as the most talked-of woman in the world. The Scripps-Howard syndicate which crossed the States from ocean to ocean put in monster headlines—what again was untrue—that the Archbishop of Canterbury had snubbed Mrs. Simpson and rebuked the King. *Liberty*, selling over two million copies, called Mrs. Simpson the most envied woman in the whole British Empire. *Time* talked of 'Queen Wally', while a monster headline bore the words, also untrue:

102

WALLY DINES WITH QUEEN

It was worse than this: American newspapers began to canvas the idea of Simpson divorcing his wife on the ground of adultery! As far back as 23rd September, that widely-read weekly the *New York Woman* had spoken of three speculations: (1) that Ernest Simpson would sue his wife for divorce in America; (2) that he would not divorce her because he enjoyed being in royal circles; (3) there cannot be a divorce case in England because there one cannot sue the King. With regard to (2), it is obvious that the *New York Woman* was a month or two behind the times as far as Simpson's frequentation of the Court was concerned.

On 21st October that still more widely-read paper *Time* came out with something yet stronger. *Time* was known for the general accuracy and inwardness of its information; and certainly the facts it printed on this occasion could hardly be denied—but for what the *New York Woman* had mentioned, that in England one cannot sue the King.

When the lady arrived in Paris from Vienna she had, as we saw, her opportunity to see what her countrymen had been saying about the trip she had been making. In the following weeks, as she went on to Balmoral, the American publicity became steadily more sensational, more blatant.

As for the King, he took no notice of it whatsoever. When he saw it—and he had to see it, for his Private Secretary felt bound to put it before him—he proclaimed that he was inured to gossip. Those who were closest to him were only too well acquainted with the fact that when he had wanted to pursue a certain course of action, there was no more to say. So the King hardly gave the papers his attention.

The Prime Minister, however, began to pay them a great deal of attention. He was in close touch with the loyal Dominion of Canada where, as we know, he had travelled in the company of Edward as Prince nine years before. He was now seeing the reactions of the Canadian newspapers: they showed alarm and anger. Baldwin, by now, fully shared their alarm. What steps was he to take?

His was a mind of many facets, many involutions. Reflection and instinct, astuteness and idealism, authority and pensiveness governed in turns the complexity of his powerful mind. He was compact of energy with leisure, of hard sense with ideal dream. He dealt with politics as a croquet player with his balls. For long he must remain inactive while another had his turn. And then it came to him to see how much he could by skilful shots do to advance his own game by taking advantage of his enemies' balls, to push on his own, and to place them at a distance when the next player must take his turn. The King had had his long turn with the game which had been to have Mrs. Simpson received first by society and then made known to the people as a whole through the papers. But as long as the British papers took no particular notice of the Court Circular, which they perforce printed, his game was for the time at an end. Baldwin knew therefore that it was now the turn of the Government to play— and it was for him to decide what their strokes would be.

For a fortnight after his return from Balmoral, the King was at Buckingham Palace which he was now taking over from the Queen. One of the first to call there was his Ambassador at Washington, Sir Ronald Lindsay. Later came the Prime Minister on 14th October. Still nothing was said by either. The papers were full of the dramatic events in and around Madrid on which Franco's troops were converging while terror marked the reign within the capital of the weakening set who had claimed to be a Parliamentary Government. On 4th October the Conservative Conference ended at Margate with Neville Chamberlain making one of his strong clear speeches on what he felt were the two great needs of the time: more solid defence forces and better physique among the masses of the people.

Was the King paying much attention to affairs? Had he done anything effective to show the way he intended to give a new impetus to the idea of monarchy? Had it not been noticed at Balmoral by the two Ministers who did go there that he paid practically no attention to State papers? Was it not frustrating to a Private Secretary trained under Lord Stamfordham to a meticulous attention to all the papers which came before the King to find how many of these were neglected? The King's attention to his functions as the person who was first to be informed, and then to advise, and to warn the Cabinet as to any course they were pursuing often seemed slight. The habits he had formed as Prince of Wales were every day proving more inadequate to the functions of the reigning sovereign.

CHAPTER XXI

THE Prime Minister, after seeing the King on Wednesday 14th October, had arrived on the following Friday to pass the weekend with Lord FitzAlan at Cumberland Lodge, another royal house on the Windsor estate and not far from Fort Belvedere; in this house Lord FitzAlan had entertained King George and Queen Mary to both of whom he was devoted.

At that time a great deal of the Government of England was carried on at weekend parties where a number of people would meet for a day or two in the amplitude of great houses; in the confidential atmosphere these created they would discuss the information received, and sketch a plan to deal with it. The week-end which Lord FitzAlan had then arranged was the most important he had ever had. He had invited to it not only his nephew, the Duke of Norfolk, who as hereditary Earl Marshal of England was in charge of the Coronation ceremony, as Lord FitzAlan himself had been in the minority of the Duke. He had also invited with the Prime Minister Lord Salisbury, who had been Leader of the House of Lords before Lord Halifax, and the competent press magnate, Lord Kemsley.

Within call was Major Hardinge, the King's Private Secretary. The subject that was foremost in his host's mind was the safety, honour and welfare of the Imperial Crown.

The immediate cause of his anxiety was what he had read in the American newspapers—that Mrs. Simpson was about to commence at Ipswich her divorce suit against her husband. As long as she was the legal wife of another, it might occasion gossip for the King to associate with her, but if the thing were kept out of the newspapers one might hope that nothing very serious to the prestige of the Crown would result. But now there was the implication that he intended to marry her.

On that subject all at the party felt very much alike. The Prime Minister took Lord Kemsley aside to sound him about public opinion. He received an answer which accorded with what he had heard from the Leader of the Opposition that 'the Nonconformist conscience' was still a thing of might in the country.

The strong feeling of the house party was that the Prime Minister must at once warn the King accordingly. So Baldwin at last agreed to act. So it was that Major Hardinge sent his telephone message to Sandringham.

What had driven Baldwin at last to decide on the need to speak? What was it that the party at Cumberland Lodge had learnt and what had they decided? What was the fresh information before him and the Private Secretary?

He knew definitely now that the American papers were this time handling solid fact. Major Hardinge talking things over with his friend Mr. Walter Monckton, had learnt definitely that Mrs. Simpson had filed a suit against her husband, and mean-while had taken a house at Felixstowe in order that on a country circuit the thing might go through more quickly. But the American journalists soon noticed that the judge on the Ipswich circuit was Sir Anthony Hawke who was well known to the King because he had been predecessor to Mr. Monckton as Legal Adviser to the Duchy of Cornwall. And they tried even to make capital out of that—for which they had no ground at all. The traditions of British law had not fallen *so* low! What the lawyers had been asked to consider was the date of the Coronation in the following May and how they could best hasten the case to suit it.

It was late on the evening of Saturday, 20th October, that at Cumberland Lodge Baldwin decided that he must see the King as soon as he could. Next morning telephone messages were sent first to Fort Belvedere to make the appointment, then, since the King had already left, to Sandringham. But all through the day he failed to arrive there, where his brother-in-law Lord Lascelles and Sir Samuel Hoare were to join him on the Monday evening at a shooting party. Evening turned to night and still there was no news of his whereabouts: it was already turning to the morning hours when he arrived. The truth was that he had been with Mrs. Simpson at Felixstowe. His arrival at Sandringham came too late to make the appointment till the following morning. He then fixed to be at Fort Belvedere at 11.30 the morning after that, the 22nd.

While the journalists were asking why the Ipswich Court had been chosen by Mrs. Simpson and why she had accordingly transferred her domicile to this dreary little town on the Suffolk shore, they noticed that the King's own private detective was generally with her, as it was the King's own chauffeur who drove her big new Buick. And behind the pointed observations of the journalists on these affairs came the whole question of Canadian opinion. Canada, being the one Dominion in which many saw the American newspapers, was the most disturbed part of the Empire. The subject was brought before the Cabinet with the more insistency because that moment saw the arrival in London of Mackenzie King, the Canadian Prime Minister.

That was why at the time when the King was on his way to Felixstowe, Sandringham and back again that Baldwin was waiting to speak at the earliest hour that could be arranged. That was why the King hurried back to Fort Belvedere while his guests wondered why he had left them in the lurch.

The King has given his account of the talk, and the Prime Minister gave his to the House of Commons a few weeks later. The King stresses the nervousness of the Prime Minister to whom he seems in retrospect to have felt a strong antipathy of which at the time Baldwin was completely unaware. For it was certainly not made evident at the time. It was with complete sincerity that Baldwin spoke of the good will being mutual. The King does not contest what the Prime Minister told of his argument: that there was the Crown, which though it had lost many of its prerogatives had gained in compensation a value greater than ever before (after the death of George V the point had been made by Attlee) in being a point of union, a focus of loyalty for all parties in the country, as for all constituent parts of the Empire. To it flowed great tides of allegiance.

Baldwin had hoped that the new King with his popularity, his energy, his intimate touch with the masses of the people would make the Crown a yet greater glory, a more cogent chain of union. But, said the Prime Minister, there is a point beyond which loyalty would not go. There were certain things the people would not stand; they demanded that the throne should be above the noise of scandal.

At this point the King, he himself tells us, was on the point of losing his temper; but, after all, he had said to the Prime Minister that he should speak to him with frankness on every subject. So Baldwin had asked if that held good when the subject in debate was a woman. Well now, he had to report that there was great noise in the newspapers not only of the United States but of Canada on the subject of the divorce case. "I pointed out," said Baldwin, "the danger of the divorce proceedings. That if a verdict was given that left the matter in suspense for some time, that period of suspense might be dangerous because then everyone would be talking and when once the Press began as it must begin some time, in England a most difficult situation would arise for him, for me, with sides and factions being taken where no faction ought to exist." "Must the case really go on?" he asked. It was the gentlest, the kindest, the most tactful way of suggesting to the King what Baldwin had already said to Ministers—that "he hoped the young man would see sense".

This was a state of affairs which the King had not wanted to face and so it was an issue which his mind had refused to envisage. There is in each of us a tendency not to recognize a fact that will be extremely inconvenient for us. All the processes of the human mind are subject to the play of instincts, tendencies and feelings. As Burke said, "Our passions instruct our Reason". So the King was for the first time facing a mastering fact which was extremely inconvenient. He and his friend had drifted on, enjoying each opportunity as it came, and thinking that they could continue to manage the crisis of each succeeding hour. They had drifted, as we know, into the idea that if Mrs. Simpson was divorced, and was therefore legally free to marry, then American ideas would overrule traditional morals and they could work the situation.

Mrs. Simpson was so ignorant of England that the idea of any standard but that which was socially acceptable to the majority of American opinion found no abiding place in her mind. The King, who after all was not an American but who was in the habit of having his own way, had been won over to her way of thinking. He had simply refused to consider the questions raised by the proposal to marry a lady who was putting through a divorce case, and he did not want to face them now. He had been heart and soul with the idea of the divorce so that it would give him the means legally to marry. He was therefore very much annoyed with what Baldwin had said. But, governing his temper, he found an answer that turned the issue aside. He pretended none had the right to interfere with a case between two private individuals. He refused still to consider what facts had already made abundantly clear that the mere talk of the divorce had already opened the floodgates of discussion and of scandal. What he said was: It would be wrong merely to attempt to influence Mrs. Simpson just because she happens to be a friend of the King!

In other words he refused even at this late day to open his ear in any way whatever to the arguments and counsels of his Prime Minister. He simply closed his eyes to what was happening. Just as he had ignored the newspapers and mailbag which his Private Secretary had been obliged to put before him, so he now neglected all that their words meant in relation to the function of the Crown and its consecrated prestige. Sensitive, highly strung, affectionate and sympathetic, Baldwin had found it a great nervous strain to put a case which meant so much to the Royal Figure before him, the slim figure who had enjoyed unparalleled prestige and who could see nothing around him but through the mist of a passion which was the deepest experience of his life. Baldwin asked for a whisky and soda. As he poured it, he received a cold rejoinder that his host did not drink at that hour and could not join him. This no doubt accentuated the moral stand that the King thought that he was making; it nevertheless came a little oddly from one who at later hours normally imbibed. Nevertheless to Baldwin the King kept up his cordial tone. After all, the warning given had to be voiced and it had been given with tact and sympathy. His Majesty was constrained to meet his Prime Minister's effort with courtesy.

Nevertheless it made his mind a battleground. On the one side was the Minister who voiced the claims of his state—on the other the woman who ruled his mind because she ruled his heart. Up to that time he had silenced the voice of his Kingship. Now it could be silenced no longer. He had to face square the fact that his reputation counted as a real and insurmountable concern of his Government; he began at last to realize that his good name was really a huge stake in world affairs. Like the stridency of Hitler, the cruel war in Spain with Russia supporting one side and Central Europe the other, the question of rearmament, the balance of power, the now manifest inadequacy of the League of Nations, or the duty to find work or sustenance for 1,500,000 men and women living on a scanty dole—like all these, *he, in the fulfilment of his duty, was to his Government a paramount political concern*. That meant in turn that the debate that he was causing distracted attention from affairs of state so pressing that upon them the fate of Europe was already hanging.

It was now but a week till the divorce case was due to come up at Ipswich. He could not ignore the need to come to some sort of decision with regard to the point on which the Prime Minister had so firmly—if tactfully—insisted. He should, of course, have consulted his Private Secretary. But he felt instinctively that from Major Hardinge he would find a directness which was the one thing he was anxious to avoid—he wanted a compromise which would gloss over the dilemma he had tried so hard not to face. He turned, therefore, to two men beyond his immediate entourage, two men of very different stamp and experience, men whom he hoped to find accommodating to the designs and devices of his own heart.

To both he had already spoken. One was the Canadian to whom King George had been so loath to give a peerage. The other to whom the King spoke had succeeded Mr. Justice Hawke as Legal Adviser to the Duchy of Cornwall. This was a man of his own age, Walter Monckton, who had been President of the Union in those Oxford days before the war when the Prince of Wales lived his quiet and happy life at Magdalen, finding as many a young naval officer has found that a College at Oxford or Cambridge can be just as pleasant as a cruiser or a battleship.

Monckton was a special help not only because of his urbane manners and sympathetic and conciliatory quality of his mind but still more because he was an Harrovian. With Baldwin he had been a governor of Harrow School. While at school he had been a close friend of Major Hardinge in that chivalrous relationship of English school life where between an elder and a younger boy there is an interplay of protection and admiration, and which often outlasts the years of maturity. He had been, furthermore, in the confidence of King George V who relied upon his friendship and influence as Legal Adviser to the Duchy of Cornwall. He had already recommended in Allen and Overy, and in Goddard, firms useful to help Mrs. Simpson in her divorce action. To Monckton the King explained his doubt whether he could ever comply with what the Government were evidently demanding: for he recognized that, though he wanted Mrs. Simpson to share in all he had, if it were put to the test her hold on him was stronger than the apanage and prerogative of the throne. With Lord Beaverbrook he had another point to make, it was not to allow the divorce case to bring the glare of publicity on the life and personality of Mrs. Simpson. And here he suggested that he ought to have support from Esmond Harmsworth who had been his guest at Balmoral the month before.

So the days passed until 27th October, the day fixed for the divorce case at Ipswich. On the plaintiff's arrival at the tribunal she found that her case had not attracted the public. She saw no one in the court but the wife of the Judge and a friend. But journalists were able to report the case word for word, and it appeared fully in the next issue of the *New York Times*, which, of course, was available in London a day or two later.

Her case had been carefully prepared by one of the ablest counsel of the day, Mr. Norman Birkett, who guided her through her evidence word for word as she related how she had gradually broken with her husband and finally come to the knowledge of his spending a night in the Hotel de Paris at Bray near Maidenhead with an American (not Madame Raffray) whose name he wanted kept out of the newspapers. Waiters were subpoenaed to give their evidence of bringing in breakfast to a pair in bed of which Mrs. Simpson they could swear was not one. Mr. Birkett cross-examined Mrs. Simpson, and when the evidence was completed after some twenty minutes he asked for a decree. The case was uncontested. The judge evidently did not like it. He asked why it had come to that circuit. He seemed uncomfortable as Mrs. Simpson was being cross-examined by her advocate. But in the end when pressed for the decree he grunted out the words permitting it. From that moment, in the words of Lord Brownlow, *Mrs. Simpson had become political dynamite.*

All around the courthouse were posted police; they allowed none to pass the doors while she issued from a side entrance to the building, hurried into her car and drove off rapidly to London. Those who tried to follow her found that, immediately after her car had passed, a police van was slung across the road and that it was therefore impossible to follow her as she drove on to London where she had arranged to dine that evening with the King.

He reports that he was waiting in tense anxiety for the verdict. He held a council at eleven-thirty in which his Private Secretary was made a Privy Councillor, with Mr. Ramsay MacDonald as Lord President waiting upon him before the Council and Mr. Mackenzie King, the Canadian Prime Minister, after it. But the Canadian did not speak, as Baldwin had done, of the way newspapers from the United States were troubling Canadian opinion: he spoke rather of the popularity the King had enjoyed in former years. Baldwin and his friends felt afterwards that an opportunity had been missed. For while the Canadian who was called King was talking to the man who was King about the enthusiasm of the Canadians, these were undoubtedly to be swiftly and more deeply disturbed by the rumour and innuendo which swept into the Dominion from the United States as soon as the evidence was published and the decree announced.

These details were at the disposal of a score of American journalists who in spite of the police precautions had obtained tickets to enter the court. All of them published word for word what the witnesses had said. From that time on the *New York Times*, which a month before declared that the King's interest in Mrs. Simpson was Platonic, now spoke openly of the probability that she would marry him. Enlarging on the fact that she was driven by the King's chauffeur and accompanied by his detective, it went on to say that the silence of the British newspapers was foolish and futile.

The silence in Britain did not in fact extend to *Cavalcade* or *The Week*.

In America the Hearst Press now in fact announced that the King's friends were stating that he was deeply and sincerely enamoured of Mrs. Simpson, that his love for her was a righteous affection, and that almost immediately after the Coronation, he would take her as his Consort.

It is plain that this is what the King wanted to do; but how was he to surmount the barrier of public opinion of which Baldwin had so precisely spoken? There was another difficulty of which his Private Secretary was made sharply aware by a number of communications, and it was mentioned afterwards by the Bishop of Durham. It was the suspicion of collusion. The Bishop, with many others, pressed it on the Government.

The King announced that he felt great relief when the news was telephoned through to him. None of his Ministers shared in that relief.

The reason for both of these statements is plain. The King was, as we have seen, convinced that he could expect the country to tolerate him marrying a divorced woman, as it was some fifteen years later to tolerate remarriage after divorce in the case of both the Prime Minister and the Leader of the Opposition. The country—he might well argue—did not really mind about divorce, nor therefore about remarriage after it. He was therefore convinced that he could give the lady the full advantage of standards which, first in America and now in Britain, had become elastic. But the Cabinet saw very clearly that to which he resolutely closed both ear and eye: the amount of scandal he was causing, and the harm it was doing to the prestige and function of his eminent and central role.

But meanwhile there were certain outward affairs of state which took his mind in other directions. One of his duties was to receive a number of new Ambassadors. And here again he showed his disregard for constitutional arrangements. These demanded that when he was receiving Foreign Envoys, a representative of the Foreign Secretary should be present. Sir Victor Wellesley came with the South Americans to present them. After he had introduced them to the royal presence, the King asked him to retire, and Sir Victor did so, for he did not see that he could insist on remaining against the King's pleasure. The King's object was probably only to use his Spanish with the Ambassadors. But the Foreign Office was aware that its rights had been infringed.

The other Ambassador now to be received was no other than Ribbentrop. It was already six months since the King's friend, Leo von Hoesch, had suddenly died on 18th April, and now Hitler had decided to send for his vacant place a man very close to his own designs, very high in his own esteem. The object was to draw Britain and Germany closer together, and both the Government and the newspapers gave Ribbentrop a welcome. Was it not the avowed policy of the Government to make with France an *entente* to put both on good terms with Germany? Here, it seemed, was the chance to do it.

The new Ambassador presented his credentials on 30th October. His tall form, his finely moulded features, his quiet bearing bore witness to the fact that though he had travelled in England for German wines, he had been other than a crude upstart like Hitler. At the head of the staff that accompanied him was Prince Bismarck, a grandson of the Iron Chancellor.

But this time the King did not ask the representative of the Foreign Office to withdraw. This time that representative was Anthony Eden himself. Fully conscious of the invitation to Ataturk, and of the King being closeted alone with the South American Ambassadors, he was determined that his policy should not be in any way compromised now.

The message Ribbentrop brought was one of peace—peace was the word which Hitler used to beguile Germans into accepting his risky ventures, and to soften the resentment they aroused in other governments—and who knows that at times he did not fall himself under the spell of the vision he invoked? Ribbentrop's first speech in London was on the encroachment of Moscow's moves on the Continent. As the Conservatives did not like these, and peace was the primary aim of Great Britain, it did not seem as though there was much disagreement. Nevertheless the stridency and push of Hitler had already caused public strain. Was the Foreign Secretary ever to make up the ground which had been lost in the three months before? How few weeks had passed since the same Minister had warned the King that if he was going down the Adriatic he must not embark at Venice! It was still the fatal year of the Rhineland March, and Abyssinia.

On the last Friday in October the King was again occupied with Foreign Affairs and giving a dinner—his only official dinner at Buckingham Palace—in honour of the Argentine Minister of

Foreign Affairs who had come to Europe to receive a Nobel prize. With him and the Argentine Ambassador came a most interesting company, for the King wanted to seize the occasion to further the ends of trade which were always dear to his heart. His other guests were Anthony Eden, Walter Runciman, Montagu Norman, Sir Malcolm Robertson, Sir Herbert Lawrence, Sir Robert Vansittart, Sir Edward Peacock, Sir Follett Holt, Philip Guedalla, William Rootes, Sir Hill Child and Major Hardinge. During the dinner a kilted Highlander came in playing the bagpipes to a screeching tune which His Majesty announced to his Spanish American guests as "*Mi composición*". Quietly, modestly and with the social charm in which he excelled, the King pressed forward the object he had in view: the preparation for a trade agreement. He had not lost his knack of getting together businessmen and officials to put through practical plans for getting things done. This was the last occasion on which he was to exercise it. And none who watched him at a congenial task in which he expended the highest talent could have guessed how at the same time routine could be neglected.

So October ended: and the last golden leaves were falling on the park that surrounded the great Palace where, although on a restricted scale, the King was playing his London part. But now the weather changed: and the sky was dark with rain, as the air was charged with question and surmise, as on 4th November the King rose to open his first Parliament.

Whether it was wet or fine, he was to drive along the Mall in his state coach, attended by a Sovereign's escort of cavalry. And for this eager crowds waited in a downpour. They waited in vain. For the King said he would refuse to have his cavalcade bedraggled. Just as he had stopped the presentations when the rain began, refusing to return when it was over, so now he decided to drive to the House of Lords in his car. The crowds which had held their places through the drenching rain were deprived of the pageant for which they had gallantly gathered. Once again there was intense disappointment; and it might have been avoided if he had learnt from the disappointment of the débutantes some months before. And this time there was among those waiting a large group of ex-servicemen who were anxious to show their loyalty. Men had spoken of the Royal weather which had so often greeted the functions of his parents; it was already being noticed how on him the sun was more likely *not* to shine.

Once arrived at Westminster he met the full panoply of royal state. He donned his robes in the robing room, and placed himself in the midst of the waiting procession. With Great Officers of State walking backwards before him, and followed by pages in the royal livery carrying his train, he walked in state through the Royal Gallery and the Princes Chamber, preceded by the heralds in scarlet and gold, until in due time he entered the House of Lords, and with beating heart took his seat on the Throne.

The central figure in this gorgeous scene knew that he was on his mettle. Everyone of the persons gathered there in robes which witnessed their high function in the country and their knowledge of affairs looked at him with the question whether his conduct was to square with the honour which was given him as King. There could not have been a soul here who did not know that, exactly a week before, Mr. Norman Birkett had been pleading in the little courtroom at Ipswich the divorce case of Mrs. Simpson for whom that central figure showed so manifest a predilection.

And now what was to happen?

This was the question which occupied them much more than the morning's news that Franklin D. Roosevelt had the day before been elected for a second term; or the letter they read in the morning's *Times* from Lord Dawson about the way to improve the health and physique of the people, or indeed than any point which the King was to mention in the Most Gracious Speech he was to read to them.

The Lord Privy Seal, Lord Halifax, knelt before him to present him with a scroll from which he was to read "I am a faithful Protestant", a declaration which he would rather not have made. Then the Lord Chancellor stepped over from the Woolsack to hand him the speech he was to deliver. It was the Government's declaration of its policy.

The reports of the ceremony paid so full a tribute to the King's demeanour that again no outsider could have guessed how slippery was the ground he had chosen to tread as on the edge of a sharp declivity he walked his narrow path.

And only a day or two before an experienced observer of affairs had published an article on the crisis in international democracy. It was Alfred Zimmern who had pointed out how up to then it had been argued that if the people were left to decide for themselves, they would work for one another's good. But by now it had become clear that democracy was not—as Woodrow Wilson had thought it was—a movement tending towards universal brotherhood. It had proved just the contrary. The masses of the people think almost always of what they understand, the interests most immediate to them, the social claims, the national ambitions which are within their own range and understanding. What gratify the masses are local and national privileges, or patriotic ambition. They respond to chauvinistic leaders.

The year 1936 had proved in the case of Italy that a people

could be selfish and aggressive, because they were hungry. It proved that in the countries of the League the people intended to make no sacrifices for a general principle; but to leave each country to fight for itself. Such was the lesson of Abyssinia. At a time when France was no longer powerful enough to enforce Versailles, intellectuals talked of collective security, but peoples as a whole cared not a jot for what it implied. Shrewd men therefore no longer looked towards Geneva to ensure peace.

What made nations and alliances effective was not ideal dream; it was common interests. The way to secure peace therefore was to bind certain nations together in the strength of a common and mutual economic advantage.

That this was the trend of the King's thinking—whenever he approached the process of thinking—there can be little doubt; it is even more clear, alas, that he did nothing precise to bring Europe to face the problem of adjustment that it might turn away from the rivalry of arms which was stalking on it, like a hunter on his prey, to that interdependence of commerce and work which was both the significance and the safeguard of peace. How much of his time did the King really give to the danger that was gathering over Europe?

On 9th November Baldwin was at the Guildhall. "Today," he said, echoing his speech at Vimy Ridge, "while we are still finding and burying the bodies of the men who fell in the war, the whole of Europe is arming—an inconceivable folly for those who have the responsibility of governing the great countries of Europe. What good can come of it? . . . There is no one today who does not know what war in the long run means. It means all over Europe—degradation in the life of the people. It means in the end anarchy and world revolution. Knowing that, what can our duty be but to come together to save Europe?

"What is our position? In this island home of ours we are looking to our defences and quite right too. I am prepared to devote all our efforts, whatever it may cost in men and money to do what is necessary. But I am conscious all the time of the folly for all of us."

At the time that Baldwin was speaking so, day after day told of the miseries and murders in beleaguered Madrid, as the tottering Cabinet attempted to maintain its hold over people who were welcoming the forces of Franco which surrounded them. But any effort that Baldwin, or his government, might have made for peace was paralysed by the preoccupation with the dire conflict of loyalties in the Court of St. James.

CHAPTER XXII

On the very day before the divorce, Geoffrey Dawson, the Editor of *The Times*, found the scandal was crystallized in a single document now sent spontaneously to him from a man of position in America, and which he now forwarded to both the Prime Minister and to the Private Secretary at Buckingham Palace. It had been written in the United States on 15th October and must therefore have arrived in London a few days later—that is to say, before the divorce case had commenced. It gave a full and cogent account of the reference to the King in the American Press and the resulting effect, as seen by a British subject who had been living for some years in the United States and working for good relations between the two countries.

His first theme was "the poisonous publicity attending the King's friendship with Mrs. Simpson". The letter went on: "I am one of those who had a deep admiration for the monarch when he was Prince of Wales: and looked forward to the time when he would bring new vision and inspiration to the task of kingship. In common, I fear, with a great many others, I have been bitterly disappointed. The doings of the King, as reported in the American Press, have in the course of a few months transformed Great Britain, as envisaged by the average American, from a sober and dignified realm into a dizzy Balkan musical comedy attuned to the rhythm of jazz. It must be remembered that the American man in the street sees other countries through the medium of some outstanding personality who is 'played up' by the Press. To him Italy is Mussolini, Germany is Hitler, Russia is Stalin. For many years Great Britain was George V. I believe that when the throne is filled by a King like his late Majesty, a democratic monarchy has many advantages over a democratic republic. It serves as a convenient device for providing the nation with a colourful figurehead, escaping on the one hand the disadvantages of a personal dictatorship and on the other the drabness of a republic. There is no doubt that France, for instance, has failed to make much impression on American public opinion through the lack of an outstanding personality." But, as the letter went on to say, every American knows the name of the King of Great Britain. George V had been respected, even admired by Americans, even if they were, as citizens of a republic, strongly opposed politically to the principle of Kingship. What had Baldwin said of George V? "He earned the loyalty and respect of all parties in the State, new and old. He hands down in turn to his son the throne received from his father, and he hands it down with its foundations strengthened, its moral authority, its honour and its dignity enhanced. It is an incomparable and awe-inspiring inheritance."

But what had happened in those nine months of the reign of Edward VIII ? Where was now the moral authority of the Crown, where its dignity, where its honour ? "The prevailing American opinion," said the letter, "is that the foundations of the throne are undermined."

This was not due to the sensational proclivities of the American press: for that had never brought the glare of scandal upon the life of other sovereigns. "No," said the letter bluntly, "George V was an incomparable asset to British prestige abroad: Edward VIII has proved himself an incalculable liability . . . under the impact of the recent avalanche, I have given him up as a hopeless case. Before one can expect to persuade others to respect the British Crown, one must at least expect the example of respect for the Crown to be set by its chief custodian."

The writer viewed the affair as less personal than political. He saw a serious, a tragic aspect of the case in the effect it would have upon international relations. It was a year in which Britain's international prestige had fallen. Her attitude towards Abyssinia had given that country no effectual help, yet encouraged the vanity of the Negus to resist; Britain's reliance on the League of Nations which, in the event, had proved ineffectual had given the impression that Britain's grip was weakening. And now, went on the letter, with all nostrils dilating to the whiff of these odours of unsavoury gossip, this same ineffectual Britain had in a few months "usurped the pre-eminent place in the realm of sordid intrigue formerly tenanted by some such place as Rumania".

It was true. That Carol was interested in Madame Lupescu was well known; but none could cite an incident or show a photograph. The King of Rumania was the paragon of discretion. The King of England drove prudence to despair.

The plain fact was that on one side he wanted his affair to be known so that public opinion would be prepared for his choice as he gradually moved towards making it manifest with all the *éclat* that his royalty could give; but at the back of his mind there had always been the commonsense considerations that what he wanted to do was really beyond the capacity of any man on earth to compass; and also that Mrs. Simpson's position as well as the sadder episodes of her past must be saved from any close scrutiny. The paradox was plain—after all he enjoyed the highest social privilege, the most imperial rank and honour of any man living. The question was whether he could keep them if he set out to share them with an American woman who had seen dark days, and was *still* legally another's wife.

On that point the best brains in England were just as clear as his was clouded. So when a theme so melodramatic was crystallized in a single letter which summed up in nine cogent pages the burden of hundreds of letters pouring in on Fleet Street and Printing House Square, on Downing Street and Lambeth Palace—letters joined to an ever-plashing cascade of pained or piquant gossip, it was clear to the Editor of *The Times* that, in view of his position as the leading journalist of London, high in the confidence of both the Government and the Court, he must take counsel of both the Prime Minister and the King's Private Secretary. He knew them both well. So he handed copies of the letter to each of them on 25th October—two days before Mrs. Simpson succeeded in obtaining her decree *nisi* from Mr. Justice Hawke at Ipswich. The momentum of this letter made itself felt in the days that were to come.

Meanwhile it might have been expected that the divorce case would put a certain barrier of prudence between Mrs. Simpson and the King. It was *imperative* that before the decree was made absolute six months later nothing should occur to compromise her case of the faithful wife aggrieved. Should that occur, the law might contend that it could not connive with her in weakening that bond of marriage which, from time immemorial English law had regarded as a bond for life. The law considered that bond to be a safeguard of the social order which the law exists to preserve.

This being the case, Mrs. Simpson's solicitor now had the responsibility of warning her. He could not be unaware of suspicion about the case, and about its transference to Ipswich. He was also very angry, for he had undertaken the case on the express condition that she should leave England as soon as the case had gone through. On the contrary she had driven straight to the King. The last thing his legal conscience would permit was to put a client in a position that would be dangerous to the work he was doing for her, and which at the same time would both compromise the integrity of the law and harm the position of the Crown. As the case produced a flood of correspondence, this responsibility became more pressing with the passing of the days.

To the Government also this correspondence became a preoccupation centring, as we saw, on the word *collusion*. That could mean two things: either that Mrs. Simpson had made a bargain with her husband that he should provide her with the evidence on which to sue him, or that she herself was guilty of misconduct. The Attorney-General who had the King's Proctor at his command was therefore compelled to enquire into these two questions, especially as they were pressed by the Bishop of Durham. It was soon found that legally they could not for a moment be sustained: Mr. Ernest Simpson afterwards threatened to take legal action against George Cornwallis West who made allegations about Simpson's motives. As for Mrs. Simpson enquiries failed to produce cogent evidence of her misconduct. The most that could be proved was that she had often travelled with the King and joined the parties that he gave for his guests. She now did so with her aunt as chaperone.

And still the King said nothing either to his Prime Minister, or to his closest friends in the Court of any intention of marrying Mrs. Simpson.

CHAPTER XXIII

IF we now turn back to the personal case of the King, we see that in the week following the divorce, an immense weight of responsibility began to fall on the Prime Minister and on him who was the constitutional link between the Prime Minister and the King. It was the first duty of the Private Secretary to keep the King informed of any important move in the Government: it was not less his duty to inform the King of anything in public opinion which could affect the Crown.

Throughout the whole autumn, the position of Major Hardinge had become more and more difficult. He had found that the King ignored every hint and warning that had been given, pretending that none could interfere in his private affairs. It was only at that point that his life became a definite constitutional issue that anyone was actually obliged to mention it; the King's constitutional adviser was the Prime Minister; and this task had, as we saw, been thrust upon him when the talks at Cumberland Lodge had added to the gathering weight of protest from all parts of the Empire proof of a danger of which Baldwin had at last seen that there was no option but to speak.

Now with the divorce case finished, the responsibilities of both the Prime Minister and the Private Secretary had heavily increased. "By the first week in November," writes Major Alexander Hardinge, "there was scarcely a leading figure in the political or religious life of the country whose postbag was not flooded by protests from British subjects in every corner of the globe, asking why no denial was given to the outspoken Press forecasts of the coming marriage of the King with Mrs. Simpson. In order that the King should be under no illusion about public opinion overseas, I saw that he was kept aware of those that came to Buckingham Palace. In the dominions, the political leaders were becoming increasingly concerned;" while in Britain there was little doubt what the opinion of the people could be (once they were allowed to know the facts) when even the ex-servicemen, in spite of their devotion to the King, let it be known what they thought of Mrs. Simpson stepping into the shoes of Queen Mary. The silence of the British press could not be continued indefinitely, and at any moment the floodwaters might burst the dam. Mrs. Simpson was the incessant subject of conversation in both social and official circles: the American papers were arriving regularly in England.

At this point the King was due to leave London to pay a visit to the Fleet at Portland Bill. He had not been present when Baldwin spoke at the Guildhall on the 9th November; but on the 11th, which was Armistice Day, he must come in uniform with ceremonial to the cenotaph in Whitehall and lay his wreath in honour of those who had given up their lives for their country twenty years before when he was young. Those who were still serving in the forces, placing with their service the offer of their lives, were soon to be asking in great numbers what some were asking already, what he would give up for them. Sometimes, they were to say, one must at the call of duty offer one's life, sometimes one's wife, or at least another's wife.

But in the meantime the King's programme was to spend the two days of 12th and 13th November with the Fleet. Sir Samuel Hoare, as First Lord of the Admiralty, went with him to Portland, and on arriving was more than ever struck with his flair to delight and mix with the crowd.

He succeeded in everything—he seemed to know everyone. Wherever he passed mirth and liveliness followed. He did well in the Officers' mess but he was at his best when leaving the officers he came to the men, who had organized a concert. He elbowed his way through the throng, and from one end of the party to the other there was a thrill. They, like the rest, had heard the gossip. But all they cared for was that their King was among them and mixing with them as one of themselves. The crowd vibrated with enthusiasm.

While this was happening on the Dorset coast, the Prime Minister sent for Major Hardinge to ask if after the divorce there had been any change in the amount of time the King was spending with Mrs. Simpson. The answer was that all was going on as before. That meant two big worries for the Prime Minister —first the scandal and danger of the King being with a woman whose decree could yet be made null and void; secondly the evidence it brought that the King had decided not to act on the advice which his chief constitutional adviser had given him. This meant that the Prime Minister must be prepared for stronger action and he decided, therefore, to call for a meeting of senior Ministers to discuss the affairs, and consider a plan of action.

Such a communication thrust a new responsibility upon the

Private Secretary: he was bound to inform the King of every important step the Government was taking. So he must give the King this new information, and warn him of the great danger of Mrs. Simpson remaining at his side. For no sooner had the King finished his visit to the Fleet than he was to meet her once more at Fort Belvedere and spend the weekend in her company. Revolving the endless complications of the tangle, Major Hardinge spent a sleepless night thinking out the phrases in which he would convey his message to the King.

It would have to be in writing, for the King was absent and the message must meet him at the earliest opportunity. This was not the only reason for putting it in writing. A letter would be a permanent document which the King must read, while, if his temper was high, he could always say "Be damned to you!" to anyone who brought up a subject he had every reason not to discuss.

In the morning Hardinge put down the essentials of the situation as he saw them. He had hardly done so when he received a call from the Editor of *The Times* who wanted to show a leading article he had prepared in the light of the letter from Canada of which he had already sent a copy to Hardinge. In return the Private Secretary himself brought out the draft of the letter he had just composed. Geoffrey Dawson was an ideal censor of phrases: to experience and integrity he added an infinite discretion: he knew what must be said and what one was not to say. He gave his entire approval to what he now read.

Before going further, Hardinge went again to 10 Downing Street to make sure first that the Ministers would meet as Baldwin had arranged, then to have the authority of the Prime Minister to hand on the information which had been given, and finally to ask if the Prime Minister would care to postpone the meeting till he heard of the King's reaction to the letter. Baldwin decided that he could postpone that talk no longer: the pressure of the last few days upon him had been overwhelming—the pressure was not only in print from overseas. It was equally strong among all who had discussed affairs from the inside. Geoffrey Dawson had reinforced the general impression. On 2nd November he had lunched with Lord Dawson, the King's Physician, who referred to the King's state of mind as obsession: in the evening he dined with a literary society where two prominent men had left the subject of letters on one side to ask if there was no one in the Brigade of Guards who could influence the King. It was too plain that there was no one else to whom he would listen.

But alas! even among Guards officers there was none. Clarendon writing in the reign of Charles I had said: "His single misfortune which indeed was productive of many others was that he never made a noble and worthy friendship with a man so near his equal that would frankly advise him for his honour and true interest against the current, or rather the torrent, of his impetuous passions." Here, too, the words were only too apposite. The higher the responsibility of the persons the deeper was their concern. Central among these was the Archbishop of Canterbury who knew all, though he said nothing. He remembered how King George had discharged his heart on this perilous subject. He had talked more lately with the Queen. With all these Major Hardinge was in touch: he knew furthermore of the quandary in which newspaper men were finding themselves when they considered what line they were to take in reporting the King's visit to the Fleet. They did not want again to write in the tone of enthusiasm—as in fact they had done at the opening of Parliament—if a day or two later they were to be voicing the disquietude of the papers they were reading from abroad.

But it was the special obligation of the Private Secretary now to report to the King the concern which every day's predicament augmented, and the action the Prime Minister felt obliged to take. He had drafted the letter he showed to Geoffrey Dawson and which Geoffrey Dawson approved. It ran as follows:

> "As your Majesty's Private Secretary I feel it my duty to bring to your notice the following facts which I *know* to be accurate.
> "The silence of the British Press on the subject of your Majesty's friendship with Mrs. Simpson is not going to be maintained; judging from the letters from British subjects in foreign countries, the effect will be calamitous . . .
> "The Prime Minister and senior members of the Government are meeting today to discuss what action should be taken to deal with the serious situation which is developing."

The letter went on to say that the Government might not improbably resign and that it was clear from members of all parties in the House of Commons that no other party was prepared to take its place. "The only alternative remaining is a dissolution and a general election in which your Majesty's personal affairs would be the chief issue—and I cannot help feeling that even those who would sympathize with Your Majesty as an individual would deeply resent the damage done to the Crown, the cornerstone on which the whole Empire rests."

The latter proceeded to say that the matter was one of great urgency in view of the growing impatience of the press. Finally it stated: "There is only one step which holds out any prospect of avoiding the dangerous situation which is developing, and that is for Mrs. Simpson to go abroad *without further delay*."

Such were the terms of the letter which the Private Secretary wrote and placed in its Red Box for despatch from Buckingham Palace to Fort Belvedere. He marked the Red Box URGENT AND CONFIDENTIAL and when it arrived this notice was duly brought to the attention of the Butler so that the King might be informed as soon as he arrived back through the wintry air from his visit to the Fleet.

He had been hoping to relax with Mrs. Simpson. Hardly had he greeted her on his arrival than his attention was called to the Red Box. Feeling cold and tired he drew the key from his pocket and opened the Box. And then, he tells us he was confronted with the greatest crisis of his life!

Yes, infuriating as it was, this time there was no escape—he had to face the facts at last. The letter told the grim truth. The people would not put up with Mrs. Simpson, and the Government must decide accordingly.

Major Hardinge has said that neither then nor afterwards did he ever receive the slightest reference or response to this letter either in writing or by word of mouth. The King explains why. He was shocked that such a crisis should come on him before he had prepared himself. Goodness knows he had been given warnings enough. But here at last was one which told him plainly and urgently to what extent he was endangering the throne. He pretended that the thing had been thrust on him suddenly because every time the warning drew nearer he had done all he could to thrust it from his attention. Furthermore he was hurt that this time the warning had been formal, and weighted with political authority—as though he would have allowed anyone who came in the guise of an unofficial friend to speak at all.

But above all he was furiously angry that anyone should suggest that he should part from Mrs. Simpson. What? Was he to send out of his kingdom, and at once, the one person he wanted in it, the woman he intended to marry? So, pretending that he had been improperly treated, he refused all discussion of the affair with his Secretary, and complains that he could not understand.

It would surely have been proper for the King, as the crisis developed, to have taken into his confidence the man—an old friend of his own age—whom he had so lately appointed as his personal political adviser. On the contrary, he had studiously avoided any mention of the information which Major Hardinge had put before him and of the difficulties that information implied. This being so, the writer must needs state in no indefinite terms that the most serious crisis was at hand. The letter was not an ultimatum, not a challenge, but intended as a friendly warning to a master who seemed to be heading for the rocks "in a state of blissful if unaccountable ignorance". Writing later, the recipient of the letter said he failed to understand the motives which had inspired it. "A simple way out of the difficulty," answers Hardinge, "would have been to ask me, for on the following Tuesday I spent two days with him in South Wales. I continued to see the King for the conduct of ordinary government business right up to 3rd December" and yet during all this time the King never once made the slightest sign that he had received the letter, written on 13th November.

It is obvious that if the King had sent Mrs. Simpson abroad, he would have cut the ground from under the feet of his many critics at home and abroad, "especially those", adds Hardinge, "who were showing an embarrassing interest in the explosive subject of collusion", and the problem could have been dealt with more peacefully and calmly. "As it was, the same suggestion had to be adopted three weeks later, as the crisis rose to its peak —in humiliating haste and at dead of night."

But these vindicating words are carrying us on too quickly. Much was to happen before Mrs. Simpson had to be rushed away. We must trace the course of those three weeks.

When we observe the way the King treated the crucial letter of his Private Secretary, we cannot wonder that people spoke of obtuseness, of infatuation, of obsession; in the intervening days since the Prime Minister had so clearly warned him of the constitutional difficulties he had done nothing but indulge the dream of his approaching marriage with Mrs. Simpson, closing his eyes completely to the grave dangers of which the Prime Minister had warned him. Was it any wonder that those who had to speak to him had postponed their duty till they had something to say which would be *overwhelming*?

So there he was back at Fort Belvedere on 13th November, the visit to the Fleet over, Mrs. Simpson his guest, and in his hand the letter from his Private Secretary, telling him that he had reached an impasse. "There was very little sleep for me that night," he wrote. His pugnacity and pride were aroused: he was challenged at last.

What the King did on the following day was to turn to the supple mind of another friend, less constitutionally engaged. He had, as we have seen, already after the talk with Baldwin consulted Mr. Walter Monckton, Legal Adviser to the Duchy of Cornwall, who had also been counselling Mrs. Simpson about her choice of solicitor and barrister. The King turned to Monckton again now, and found in him the man he was wanting to help with counsel, and control. Monckton while humouring him could act as go-between with the Government in the crisis which the King had forced upon it; furthermore he had his special Harrovian connection with both Baldwin and Hardinge in the zeal and comradeship of their great school.

The King intended to fight; and he persuaded himself that

he could win. So he opened his mind to Monckton whom he planned to meet on the Sunday afternoon at Windsor. They talked till he was told that Mrs. Simpson had arrived to be driven over to pay a visit to the Duke and Duchess of Kent at Iver.

So far she could only have guessed what was distressing him. Not till the following evening did the King hand the letter to Mrs. Simpson. She was stunned; for she had shrewdness enough to see that Major Hardinge had been right. She, after all, had been watching for weeks the gradual accumulation in the papers of references to herself: she was not without an inkling of the scandal the affair had been causing. Acute and practical she saw that such a letter would not have been written without a great deal behind it; and that to save the King's position, if not for her own comfort, it would be best for her to leave the country at once.

Far from Baldwin manoeuvring as foe, he had refrained from saying any word at all till the talk at Cumberland Lodge had shown how close was the pressure of a grave constitutional crisis. Even then he had spoken reluctantly and with great effort. Now, with a mixture of worldly wisdom and fatherly solicitude, he was exercising his tact, his judgment, and his patience to do all that he could to help a younger man whom he was to see under the spell of the biggest emotional experience of his life—and who had somehow persuaded himself that the call of personal attraction was the supreme duty. Baldwin understood all that: he was ready to go to any extreme rather than to drive his young friend from the throne. But he was bound to preserve the Crown from being the subject of a controversy which would do infinite harm.

He looked at every mention of the facts of the case as the act of an enemy who had broken the rules of honourable encounter. Yet he had to acknowledge that this so-called challenge which came through his Private Secretary, was really from the Government. They were the people who had broken in on his opium dream of carrying on as King at the same time as he prepared to marry a woman not free to marry. So he must come at once to grips with the Prime Minister and "the nebulous figures behind him". "Once David was in the grip of an idea," the lady writes, "wild horses would not hold him." Her literary mentor leaves it to us to explain her meaning which was a mingling of two different ideas: first that he was a wild horse none could hold, and that once he had taken a certain stand he would allow no reasonable considerations to temper his choice. She was, of course, quite right.

While his mind was in confusion, brooking neither remonstrance nor refusal, his will was uncompromising. His was the mind of a man who rather late in life had found a woman who so fitted his mentality and instincts that he believed that nothing was beyond her, nothing too good for her: it was lastly the mind of a Prince who had been taken as the leader of a new and revolutionary age which set at naught the standards and rules of the past.

Such was the stormswept mind which men of ability, wisdom and experience had to bring into relation with what the mass of the inhabitants of the British Commonwealth and Empire thought was sound and right. They who wished him well, those who were most faithful and resolute to help him had to deal with one whose thought no longer followed in the normal tracks of a mind, whose psychology was governed by the fact that he was at war with anyone who thought Mrs. Simpson could not be the Queen of England. Such was the drama of the succeeding weeks, a drama which was extremely trying for all who had to take a leading part in it.

Of course the King could argue that he based his stand on what the law permitted. The contest was over the point whether a King could take advantage of the law when the Christian tradition was at issue with the law. The Government were aware that even if they wished—and very few of them could wish it—they could not override the Church's ordinance when it came to the reverence which was given to the King. So the Government had to take its stand on higher ground than the actual law, and base their policy at this time on the principle that marriage is meant to be a sacred bond, a lasting obligation. They knew that large sections of the people would not tolerate the idea that the King in his coronation year was to flout the Church that was to consecrate him.

Apart from the Established Church there was still that 'nonconformist conscience' of which Lord Kemsley had spoken at Cumberland Lodge to Baldwin. This was, in point of fact, strongly represented in the Cabinet. None who cared about the Bible could ignore the words of the Redeemer Himself: "Those whom God hath joined together let no man put asunder." So apart from the fact that the Established Church of which the King was supreme governor forbade the remarriage of divorced persons, there was a general feeling among the Christian bodies: some recalled furthermore that in certain parts of the King's Dominions there was a majority of Catholics who argued that the indissolubility of marriage was not only binding on themselves but salutary for society.

All this was plain to the leading Ministers of the Government. These were not only personal friends and supporters of the Archbishops of Canterbury and of York. They were also men with an instinct for the welfare of the Empire which loyalty to the Crown held together. Their own fealty was lifelong, deep, and unquestioned; they were men with personal knowledge of and feeling for the Royal Family—men who had centred hope as well as devotion, on the King.

Of these none was truer than the Prime Minister. He was a man of the world, but, as we saw, not a Puritan. He was a very religious and conscientious man but not one who was every Sunday in Church. Anxious not to interfere in the affairs of another man's heart, he had taken the least possible notice of the gossip that in London was gradually accumulating to a roar. He was verging on seventy now and feeling tired, the more so as that autumn he had been prevented from going to Aix-les-Bains for his usual holiday there. He had fresh worries in the drama of faction in and around Madrid because all that was connected with the armament drive in Germany portended: the madness of war drawing nearer. Besides all that the plight of the poor had now for fifteen years been with him day and night, and he knew how little had yet been done for the million and a half who hung on the side of misery clamouring in vain for work to occupy and sustain them.

Yes, although Stanley Baldwin had shown himself extremely skilful in manoeuvre: although he was worldly wise: although he had swum long in the muddy waters of politics, he had never lost the habits gained when he was brought up with personal responsibility of the 300 workmen in the family factory; that responsibility now embraced his country and his King. Behind his mingling of cleverness and evasions—for he had always preferred to leave things to settle themselves—he had proved himself one who in the exercise of power and the management of men had not lost warmth of feeling or zeal for the betterment of nations. Two things came first in his view of his work as Prime Minister: to deal with the enmity of Hitler, and to guide the new King into his reign. But in both these matters doubts were already staining the texture of his hope.

No, he did not want to interfere with any other man in the affairs of his heart. But he could not ignore his responsibility: to maintain the honour and integrity of the King's Majesty as the luminary round which the planets of Empire revolved, to preserve it from the anger and alarm which the press and people of Canada had for weeks been expressing. First of all he had spoken about stopping a divorce which must make disquiet insistent. Now things were worse: he saw no alternative but to insist once more that a crisis would soon arise unless Mrs. Simpson were quickly to leave England. Events were soon to prove how, even for her own sake, Hardinge had been right.

Baldwin could not but be aware that when the King had received this warning in writing, he did not even acknowledge the letter! But the Prime Minister had not long to wait. Monckton, as soon as he read that letter from Hardinge, saw that one point was clear: that there was pressure from the Government and that the King must again see the Prime Minister without delay. It occurred to the King that he might find some sympathy in two Ministers who had been with him—in Hoare who had been with him at Sandringham and Portland, in Duff Cooper who had been Minister in Attendance on the *Nahlin* in August on the Adriatic. But as Monckton pointed out, before consulting these he must say a word to the Prime Minister—a sovereign must not secretly concert with any Minister against the head of the Government.

The King on the other hand had at this time become aggrieved to the point of fury. Declaring to the woman he loved that rather than give her up he would abdicate, he was yet determined not to hand over the Crown till forced to do so. And she! Only two days previously she had arrived at Fort Belvedere with her decree nisi three weeks old, with the King accordingly indulging his dream of marrying her. And now here was this abominable letter—here was the King disclosing to her that far from making her Queen, his love of her was to lose him the Throne!

She tells us that before the drama of that dilemma, she burst into tears and told him he was mad to think of it. But we shall see later that this was not her only reaction.

So when the weekend had ended on Monday, 16th November, the Prime Minister received in the morning a summons to meet His Majesty at six-thirty in the evening at Buckingham Palace. As soon as he entered the King came straight to the point of the Hardinge letter: he asked if the Cabinet was facing a constitutional crisis over his friendship with Mrs. Simpson.

"Yes," said the Prime Minister, "that is correct." "I told him," said Baldwin later, "that I did not think a particular marriage was one that would receive the approbation of the country. That marriage would have involved the lady becoming Queen. I did tell His Majesty that I might be a remnant of the old Victorians, but that my worst enemy would not say of me that I did not know what the reaction of the English people would be to any course of action, and I told him so far as they went, it would be impracticable." His actual words were: "I believe I know what the people would tolerate and what they would not." The claim was not exaggerated—the accusation against Baldwin was that he guessed—and followed—public opinion only too well. "I pointed out to him," says the Prime Minister, "that the position of the King's wife was different from the position of the wife of any other citizen in the country: it was part of the price a King has to pay: his wife becomes Queen: the Queen becomes the Queen of the country, and therefore in the choice of a Queen the voice of the people

"Lest we forget." A wreath at the Cenotaph

[Paul Popper Ltd.

The King among his Welsh miners

[Paul Popper Ltd.

"Something must be done." The King in Wales

[Central Press Photos Ltd.

Mr. Baldwin and Sir John Simon leave to do their duty

Display of loyalty outside the Palace

[Mirrorpic

Hot news at Charing Cross Station

[Radio Times Hulton Picture Library

The lunch editions

The lady who speaks for
herself

HANDS OFF
OUR
KING
ABDICATION
MEANS
REVOLUTION

Feeling mounts

"Read all about it!"

The Archbishop of Canterbury comes down the steps

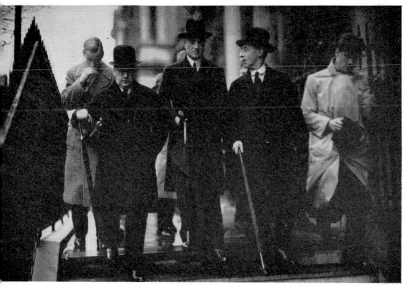

The Crisis: Sir Kingsley Wood, Sir Samuel Hoare and Lord Zetland
leaving Downing Street

INSTRUMENT OF ABDICATION

         I, Edward the Eighth, of Great
Britain, Ireland, and the British Dominions
beyond the Seas, King, Emperor of India, do
hereby declare My irrevocable determination
to renounce the Throne for Myself and for
My descendants, and My desire that effect
should be given to this Instrument of
Abdication immediately.

         In token whereof I have hereunto set
My hand this tenth day of December, nineteen
hundred and thirty six, in the presence of
the witnesses whose signatures are subscribed.

SIGNED AT
FORT BELVEDERE
IN THE PRESENCE
OF

Edward R I

Albert

Henry.

George.

Instrument of Abdication

Enter the Prelates: the Archbishops of Canterbury and York

The nation listens

Mr. Winston Churchill and Lord Samuel leave the Accession Council

The Bishop of London arrives at St. James's Palace

The King and Mrs. Simpson

The Duke of Windsor and Mrs. Simpson just before the marriage

The Duke and Duchess with Mr. Herman Rogers and Major "Fruity" Metcalfe

"It happened like this."
On board the *Queen
Elizabeth* returning
from America

The Duke and Duchess revisit the scene in 1961

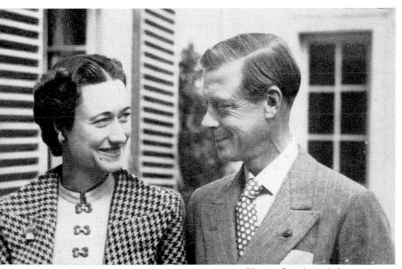

The Duke and Duchess

Fort Belvedere

The Duchess of
Windsor leaves
hospital without her
appendix

must be heard." Simon, when helping to prepare Baldwin's speech for the House of Commons, quoted from Shakespeare the words:

His will is not his own
For he himself is subject to his birth.
He may not, as unvalued persons do, carve for himself.
For on his choice depends
The safety and health of the whole state.

That was precisely the argument Baldwin now put forward: it was, of course, a perfectly sound one. The answer to it was that the King now considered marriage a state he could not forgo: it had become the dominant aim of his life. "I intend to marry Mrs. Simpson as soon as she is free to marry." He would, he thought, make a better King if he were married to her, but if the Government opposed the marriage then he was prepared to go.

Baldwin's answer was: "Sir, that is most grievous news." And those who knew him best were sure that the words were sincere. The King writes as though Baldwin were trying to manoeuvre the King into abdication. On the contrary his design was to do all possible to keep him on the throne.

The truth was that not only did the King believe in both his prerogatives and his popularity; but his psychology was so unusual, so abnormal that few could even guess at it. He complains that Baldwin, although a sound Churchman, was apparently prepared not to cavil at a mistress in the Lupescu style; that would have seemed to many a man of the world a situation to which court history was no stranger. But at the mere hint of such a thing, this by no means Puritan Prince—who was at that moment scandalizing thousands—appeared *shocked*. "Mrs. Simpson is a lady," he said in the severest tone. It was plain that his scruples were outraged; he looked as though sacrilege had been committed with regard to a vestal virgin.

Generous as Baldwin felt towards the attractiveness of the divorcing lady, yet having cognizance of the dossier which the Secret Service as a matter of routine had been preparing, he was somewhat taken aback. But, as he looked again at the figure of the King, he observed the expression of a devotee enraptured by a vision. And he was deeply touched. None had really understood the King, none had realized his difficulties, his desires, his loneliness, his need for a soothing and calming potion until, when he was nearing forty, he met this American with something of the South about her and a reminiscence of the Far East: like other Americans who had attracted him, yet so different: wiry, witty, sympathetic, surprising, experienced, and endowed with an insight into the inmost needs of men; a woman who amused and understood him as Theodora had understood and amused Justinian—a woman at his own level of taste, intelligence, feeling—a woman who could appeal to men with wit and ease, with sympathy and sparkle and with a drive of personality that subjugated one who, in spite of headstrong temper, lacked steadiness of aim.

So the Prince had come to feel safe with Mrs. Simpson. Many who knew them best deemed his interest Platonic, and she herself was wont to announce that her ambition was to use the royal favour for herself and for a husband with whom she seemed to be on excellent terms and who was obviously gratified by her sensational success. For this reason some deemed her increasing influence propitious rather than otherwise: she appeared both to calm and to control the Prince. As for her, she was enthralled both by its glamour and his confidence. In breathless appreciation of a huge, cloudy, high romance, not least when he defied the Fates with his rich anger, she was fascinated by the King's command of resources, personages, and opportunities. His name was central in a galaxy of names—he stood apart and touching, a man seeking not glitter and power but relief from these and finding the relief in her company.

Those who knew her best say that hers were the normal interests of a woman of the world: clothes, food, ornaments, society and money. Who could gratify those interests like the King of England? She was fascinated by both his position and his imperiousness. So, though she had Monckton, Allen and Goddard to give her ablest advice, she ignored them all. "It is tragic," writes Lord Brownlow, "to consider the high quality of wisdom available to her, but the secrecy of the King's attentions forbade her to make use of it, and thus it was the King himself who became her only counsellor."

As for herself, able as she was, she remained, as Lord Brownlow adds, "wholly and blindly ignorant of British constitutional practice, the Statute of Westminster, morganatic marriage, the limited powers of the Sovereign, and likewise she was largely ignorant of the implications and dangers of her own position." The King's judgment was slave to his passion—but to her it seemed endowed with sacrosanct authority.

CHAPTER XXIV

WE have seen the King was loath to let passion openly transgress the actual law of his land. He was determined to vindicate both his own character and the lady's reputation by conformity to what American custom and contemporary legality condoned.

Determined, nevertheless, still to enjoy her society, he therefore brushed aside the warning that she should leave the country. That would be to accept what he found so odious: the recommendation forwarded by his Private Secretary. Besides, he felt he needed her—and that too was a deep psychological truth. The greater the strain in any situation the more he depended on her company and support.

But above all they each believed in both his prerogatives and his popularity. Everywhere men deferred to his personal desires; everywhere they praised his qualities; everywhere he met with loyal acclaim and never with a word of criticism. So, surely, as they saw it, this claim of Baldwin to assess the people's reactions must be unjustified. Was the old Minister so much a clairvoyant that he had in himself the power to register the trend of feeling as those polls and ballots that were being imported into England from America to test opinion on any given subject.

The idea that Baldwin was right was one which both the King and Mrs. Simpson deemed impossible. Besides this they were swayed by the supreme fact that he was madly in love, and she passionately interested in the stake. To record this the lady allows her literary adviser to depart from the accustomed skill with which her story is told. It drops into an hyperbole of liquid metaphor, saying she was "prepared to go through rivers of woe, seas of despair, oceans of agony".

But meanwhile the dramatic weekend was drawing to its close. At Fort Belvedere she was to enter her car with her aunt and drive back to her new big house in Cumberland Terrace, a house now well guarded by police. He was to meet his Prime Minister at Buckingham Palace at six-thirty in the evening and announce that whatever happened he would not give up the idea of marriage with this lady as soon as her decree *nisi* was made absolute.

After she had returned with her aunt to London, she could read from the imported papers something more of what the world was saying about her. She was bewildered and, to tell the truth, by this time a little frightened. She could not but see that not only was her own character attacked but that she had been the occasion of Canada's loyalty towards the King turning into disgust. This proffered a warning of what would be the indignation of the British people once they were allowed to know the facts.

Baldwin after his talk with the King at Buckingham Palace was more and more perturbed. What could he do with a man who was the prey of such an obsession? Those who saw him later in the evening found him unusually depressed and worried.

His talk with the Prime Minister over, the King went over to Marlborough House to dine with the Queen, his Mother, and disclose to her in turn the state of his mind. Much as she always sought to avoid a personal clash she did not forbear to remind him of his duty. But to him, of course, one duty was supreme over every other: to marry Mrs. Simpson. He had waited long to find the woman he wanted—now he had found her he was not going to give her up.

The Queen did not argue: she never argued. So she said no more. But when he asked her to receive Mrs. Simpson she declined. She had no wish to compromise herself or her own position. *Her* duty was not to accept, but to reject Mrs. Simpson.

The following evening, 15th November, the King left for the tour in South Wales which the Private Secretary had arranged with the Government in order to bolster up his reputation. He had in attendance two Ministers, Sir Kingsley Wood and Ernest Brown, and two officials from the Palace, Commander Lambe and Major Hardinge.

Sixty per cent of the men and women in that area were unemployed. At Dowlais he found an enormous steel works unused. "These people were brought here by these works," he said. "Some kind of employment must be found for them." Before he left he telegraphed a message to the Lord Lieutenant of Glamorganshire and Monmouthshire: "I am greatly touched by the warmth of welcome accorded to me wherever I went, and I shall be glad if you will let it be known how deeply I appreciated it. On leaving after these two days' tour my first feeling is one of admiration for the spirit in which the people in these special areas of South Wales are facing the ordeal of prolonged unemployment. I have been encouraged by seeing the fine efforts, both governmental and voluntary which are being made to help them until, as I sincerely hope, some revival of industrial activity may bring back the prosperity which is their due.

"In the meantime I would urge them not to lose heart and to rest assured that their troubles are not forgotten."

"His visit", said *The Times*, "has cheered the population as nothing else could have done, and tonight there is a new-found faith that the solution which has so long eluded those stricken areas cannot be much longer delayed."

While the King went off on a tour of South Wales, Mrs. Simpson went to Claridge's to lunch with Mr. Esmond Harmsworth; he had been charged by the King to keep out of the papers any gossip which might be occasioned by the Ipswich divorce. He was Chairman of the Newspaper Proprietors' Association. Mr. Harmsworth now told Mrs. Simpson of a special proposal he had to make, a proposal which many thought came from Mr. Winston Churchill but which was really the idea of the then Lord Rothermere. It was to face the fact that the country would not accept Mrs. Simpson as Queen and to suggest instead that following the Continental idea which Queen Mary's grandfather had used, the King should make a morganatic marriage with Mrs. Simpson. Mr. Harmsworth proposed for her the title of Duchess of Lancaster.

Knowing that to put this idea through they must enlist popular support against the Cabinet, Lord Rothermere and his son arranged that the *Daily Mail* should say of the King: "He went to see for himself, personal investigation being the basis for every job of work the King touches. . . . Surely those who have recently confessed that they did not tell the people the truth will realize the gulf between their conduct and the King's methods in Wales." Such was the comment of Lord Rothermere's paper; for it knew nothing of how and why the tour had been really arranged; those who were occupied with the crisis knew that while it spoke of the King knowing better than his Ministers about distressed areas it meant that he could also do better than they in the choice of a wife.

So there must be a quick and conclusive reply in London's leading newspaper. "To write in that way," countered *The Times* next morning, "is to strike at the very root of the monarchy: for if the monarchy is to be dissociated for the purposes of political argument from some actions of his Ministers, then by inference he must bear a more direct responsibility for the rest. The King's constitutional position is above and apart from party politics and those who cherish the institution of the monarchy will always strive to keep it so."

The Times pushed its point further. The following day it had a leader on the appointment of Sir Patrick Duncan as the Governor-General of South Africa. Although enlarging on the rightness of appointing a man living in South Africa to be Governor-General, the article contained this sentence: "It is the position—the position of the King's deputy no less than that of the King himself—that must be kept high above reproach or ridicule, and that is incomparably more important than the person who fills it. . . . The King's deputy, like the King himself, should be invested with a certain detachment and dignity." The significance of these words coming at such a time did not escape comment in America, comment which must soon have reached Mrs. Simpson. She did not forget it.

As for the suggestion made in the *Daily Mail* that while the King sympathized with the sufferings of the wretched, his Ministers felt no concern, it was the opposite of the truth. The Ministers were indignant, not least Neville Chamberlain, who had the most advanced ideas of what should be done.

All that week a chilly fog lay deep on England. The country's attention had been arrested first by the shooting of hostages in Spain and then by the announcement of the German pact with

Japan. The Coronation Court of Claims met in the Privy Council Office under Lord Hewart. Then Lord Halifax, speaking at Edinburgh, said: "How bitter was the contrast between the ideals of 1919 of which the League of Nations was the outcome and the state of the world as they now saw it. From insecurity came rearmament with its dangers, possibilities and repercussions. What a change, what a danger in economic stress if the national spirit were over-emphasized, above all when the world had not called to its aid clearly enough the old cardinal virtues on which human life was based." Next day Mr. Eden and Mynheer van Zeeland spoke in the same sense in London.

Hardly had they settled down at Fort Belvedere for that third weekend of November—it was Saturday, the 19th—than Mrs. Simpson brought up what Mr. Esmond Harmsworth had repeated to her of his father's ill-considered project for a morganatic marriage. The King answered that he wanted to make her Queen. But he had seen, and she had seen, and to the Harmsworths it was clear, that Baldwin was perfectly right when he had said, on the preceding Monday evening, that this was an idea no government would accept. On the face of it, the morganatic proposal seemed to offer a compromise which would satisfy the King's prime need which was to marry Mrs. Simpson: and at the same time it would obviate the obvious difficulty of setting her up as Queen. It was a solution that she was disposed to accept.

Although, then, the King regarded the idea as unsatisfactory, he agreed to discuss it as soon as possible with the Prime Minister and arranged a meeting for the following Wednesday, the 25th.

Over that weekend the icy fog which had fallen on England and Wales some days before seemed to freeze the hearts of men: it was in this atmosphere, obscure and chill, that the King and his Minister prepared to discuss the new proposal. But when asked by the King if he thought it would be an acceptable solution, Baldwin said No; it would not. But it was his policy, on the other hand, to leave no stone unturned in dealing with the problem which so far the newspapers were still holding back from discussion. It was, therefore, still possible to sound opinion confidentially. Baldwin characteristically did not try to impose a plan, but to find one that public opinion would accept. He saw at once that though with a morganatic marriage the people would not have to accept Mrs. Simpson as Queen, they would still have to swallow the fact that defying the order of the Church, the King had married her. How would the country, how would the Dominions, respond to *that*?

One must repeat that as soon as Baldwin heard of the proposal he determined honestly to examine it, taking the unfettered opinion of all concerned, especially of the Home Secretary and the Attorney-General. Immediately the proposal was put before the Secretary of State for the Dominions that his office might draft the enquiry in such terms that it could be set before each Dominion Government without a hint of prejudice.

Lord Beaverbrook afterwards suggested to the King that by leaving it to the Prime Minister to draft the question put to the Dominion governments the King had lost a move, that it would be framed in such a way as to elicit an unfavourable reply. He turned out to have misjudged both Baldwin's character and his sagacity. Not only was Baldwin a man scrupulously loyal in meeting every indication of his Sovereign, not only was he personally friendly and sympathetic to a human problem, not only was he free from any narrowness of outlook, but a man who never interfered in the administration of departments. He naturally left it to his colleagues and their staff to find the precise official phrases in which such a question could be best couched along constitutional lines so as to make it plain to each government that *no pressure was being put upon them from London with regard to a matter which according to the Statute of Westminster they must decide for themselves.*

Such in the days following 25th November was the preoccupation of the Government departments involved. Such then was soon the question which in turn occupied the Dominion governments. They all faced an identical problem for, again by the Statute of Westminster, they would all have to introduce a principle hitherto unknown in their law.

It took a very short time for each of these governments to decide that they could not entertain the idea of putting forward any such proposal. The idea struck them, whether in Ottawa or Canberra, in Wellington or Capetown, as repugnant and impracticable. They saw at once that such a proposal would be most embarrassing to debate; everywhere it would provoke disagreeable questions. Foremost among them were those which would touch the conduct, honour and wisdom of the King, and the past of Mrs. Simpson. If such legislation were introduced therefore, what effect would it have on that prestige of the Crown which because of remoteness was a thing yet more abstract and mysterious than in Great Britain, so that the Sovereign was exalted in the imagination of the people as a yet more august and unarguable being? Such considerations, apparently, had been overlooked by Lord Rothermere and his son.

Even had the country looked back to the time of Mrs. Fitzherbert and Madame St. Laurent, neither of those had been through a divorce court. Both had lived lives unassailable by gossip. And they each, after all, had been in the background with no attempt being made to give them legal status. What arose now was a problem really without precedent, and placed before an empire which kept hard to a traditional morality.

In Britain also, as soon as the idea was mooted, opinion was formed quickly. The Leader of the Opposition was again apprised of affairs and his opinion sought by the Prime Minister. "I said," writes Lord Attlee, "that while Labour people had no objection to an American becoming Queen, I was certain they would not approve of Mrs. Simpson for that position and would object to a morganatic marriage. I told him it was important not to think that London was typical of the country as a whole and that opinion in the Commonwealth was likely to coincide with that of the provinces rather than with that of the metropolis. I found that I had correctly gauged the party's attitude." He had in fact been already warned by members of his party that the provinces were much stricter than London on such questions; the working class opinion in the North was quite as dogmatic ethically as that of the middle classes. He knew enough of the Dominions to be assured that their governments would be even more uncompromising.

On the subject of the morganatic marriage the Labour Party took a view particularly strong, as was soon to be shown by an article by Miss Ellen Wilkinson in the *Daily Herald*. She said that such a proposal was a slur on the status of woman. It meant asking a woman to sign away the immemorial right which gave her the status of her husband: it was therefore an outrage against the dignity and independence of a human person. For it would force a woman to deny to possible offspring their birthright as their father's children. It cut deep at something essential to socialist principles—the inherent dignity of the individual.

Very definite therefore was the opinion which the Leader of the Opposition swiftly conveyed to the Prime Minister.

Although *A King's Story* says that Lord Beaverbrook was suspicious of Baldwin putting the question in such terms as to prejudice the judgment of the Dominion governments, it admits at the same time that Beaverbrook knew what the answer would be. This leaves us to decide whether the King or Beaverbrook was at that time the more muddled in his estimates. Which was the more likely to be confused? After all Lord Beaverbrook was a Canadian, and furthermore he had only just crossed the Atlantic. Shrewd Canadian as he was, he could not be blind to the indignation in his own Dominion.

Besides he was hardly likely to be ignorant that something like it was spreading in London. During that week Mrs. Simpson was aware of hostile eyes being fixed upon her. Then the windows of her house were broken. Anonymous letters delivered in her post gave her a pretty good idea of public opinion. And with her since just after the divorce was her shrewd aunt from

Baltimore, Mrs. Buchanan Merryman, who was already known in Court circles as 'Aunt Bessie'. Aunt Bessie was no fool and she had had months in Baltimore to see the tide of gossip rising there, as American newspapers week by week accumulated their highly flavoured items.

Finally a letter came to the King threatening that Mrs. Simpson's house might be blown up. He took it seriously. He heard of vitriol being thrown by someone near her. It was intended to sear her flesh. Driving through the fog to that house on 28th November he took her into his car to give her asylum at Fort Belvedere. But did it not dawn on them that indignation was now spreading through the whole Empire? They must all have been aware that though the papers still said nothing, these were straining at the leash so hard that a crisis was at hand.

PART FIVE

The Final Crisis

CHAPTER XXV

THE King did not return to Fort Belvedere before he had put through his project of seeing those two Ministers who he thought would be sympathetic both to him personally and to what he had most at heart.

Here again Baldwin proved as ready as possible to meet his wishes. Indeed, the day after he had seen the King, Baldwin happened to run into Duff Cooper at the House of Commons and at once gave the message that the King would like to see him, adding (what so far Baldwin had not divulged to his Cabinet) that the King wanted to abdicate and marry.

Duff Cooper therefore arranged to have an audience at Buckingham Palace the following day. He began it by asking the King to change his mind and received a very firm answer. As far as Duff Cooper could see the only sensible proposal he could make was that the King should wait and see if his passion cooled —as, after all, passion is wont to do. He estimated that if the lovers would arrange not to meet for a year, the King enjoying his state would certainly value it more—and perhaps even meet another woman he could love.

The King's answer was that it would be wrong to allow himself to be hallowed and crowned in Westminster Abbey unless at the same time he avowed that he intended to marry the lady of his choice. This indicates exactly where we shall come upon the chief confusion in his mind and conscience: an undue sense of his prerogatives in relation to the Church. The religious phase through which he had passed in earlier years had not been quite without effect: in his own way he believed in God, but it must be a God who suited himself . . . and Mrs. Simpson. Secondly he would not allow the Archbishop to give him his blessing for the work of King unless the Church would so far amend its rules as to allow him to marry a woman who had already two husbands living.

The comment of Duff Cooper is also characteristic of the mentality of the sort of adviser the King liked: "I could not argue against such principles but only respect them." The scruples the Minister felt he must respect betrayed either that the King intended to have Mrs. Simpson crowned, or that the Church must conform to the King's demands, not he to those of the Church. It was the mentality of Henry VIII! Both intended to guide and rule the Church on the subject of divorce.

As for Sir Samuel Hoare, he could only confirm the fact that it would be impossible to pass a bill for morganatic marriage. Though Baldwin left it to others to form their own decision he still had his own personal scruples. "Is this," he asked his confidential adviser, Tom Jones, "is this the sort of thing I've stood for in public life?"

While debating how far his conscience could go in meeting the King, he saw that the pressure on the newspapers was such that he could no longer delay in seeking the opinion of the Cabinet. So he called for a full meeting of it to be held on Friday, 27th November. For this two Ministers were actually recalled from engagements in the provinces. When it met, the Cabinet sat all morning.

A hint was given in the Lobbies of the House that a new crisis had occurred over the turn of events in Spain where the so-called government was leaving Madrid for Valencia, while the fact of foreign intervention—Russian on the one side, German and Italian on the other—was becoming too strong to disguise.

But the *New York Times*, like the *Manchester Guardian*, knew that the reason why the whole Cabinet had been called together in such haste that Friday morning was to discuss the possibility of abdication.

That was the problem the Cabinet was at last discussing while the newspapers printed their headlines about Spain, and the Dominion governments sent in their answers on the question of a morganatic marriage.

At the Cabinet meeting all were in agreement except Duff Cooper. But Duff Cooper's attitude was not so plainly expressed as to prevent Baldwin from claiming that he had them all with him; the Prime Minister now decided that it would be kindest for all if he let Beaverbrook know the state of affairs so that the newspapers and Government might unite to accept a situation in which the King would go quietly, and save the honour of the Crown.

But there was one thing on which they had not counted: the ebullience of Mrs. Simpson. She no longer claimed that she wanted to disappear from the scene. On the contrary she entered the fray with a real American *élan*. As soon as she arrived at Fort Belvedere from the dangers of Cumberland Terrace she put before the King a daring and extreme proposal. It was founded on the success of the fireside chats of Franklin D.

Roosevelt. It was that the King should make a broadcast appeal to the nation. Having on the Friday prepared to retire, he now suited his mood to her adjurations and started to prepare a broadcast which he could submit to the Prime Minister. Such was the position on 30th November.

CHAPTER XXVI

So far had the arrangements for the Coronation been now advanced that in various parts of England the ceremonies were already the occasion of formal discussion.

The Bishop of Birmingham had long been a thorn in the side of the Archbishop of Canterbury because of his insistence that the sacramental beliefs which the Archbishop shared with the Catholics were akin to mediaeval sorcery. Knowing that a Coronation Court had been sitting in London, the Bishop now came forward to urge revolutionary changes in the Coronation service: he wanted it to be separated from the administration of Holy Communion. Those who agreed with him in this were very few indeed, and the King hardly cared to assert at this point that he was among them.

On Tuesday, 1st December, the Bishop of Bradford in his Diocesan Conference answered the bold proposal of his tiresome brother of Birmingham. That, he said, might well suit those who regarded sacramental ordinances as effete superstition, but he strongly disagreed, asserting, "I believe that such a severance would infallibly go a long way towards weakening the religious significance of the Coronation ceremony itself and reducing it to the level of a mere piece of national 'Pageantics' like a review, or a state opening of Parliament, and I should be loath to believe that the English people would really welcome such an evaporation of religious meaning from the ceremony."

No, the Bishop urged, "The Coronation must be a recall of the state to religion at a moment critical in history. There never was a clearer need than there is at present for a great rally to religion. The world is torn by conflicting tendencies some of which are overtly and others covertly anti-religious. No Christian man can really be comfortable about the attitude towards religion being taken by the rulers of various European states. And the threat of national or international disturbance never seems to grow less pressing. Our civilization is in a tottering and unstable position which forces us to wonder whether it may not even yet perish of internal combustion."

Such was the main burden, such the conclusion of the Bishop of Bradford's long address. Like many another spiritual leader of the time, he felt the need for the Christian religion, and above all for the Church of England, to be a reality. So, argued the Bishop, when men considered the Coronation they must hold it to be a religious occasion: none can receive grace from a sacrament, he pointed out, unless disposed by good and firm intentions to receive it with faith. In the Coronation, the nation acknowledges that the King needs the grace of God to perform his office. To receive it, both they and he must be disposed by faith and good intentions. He holds a representative position, he stands for the people's idea of kingship. The Coronation means the dedication of the British monarchy to the care of God in whose rule and governance are the heart of Kings.

Such was the contention of the Bishop of Bradford, voicing the belief of practically every Bishop in England against the errant prelate of Birmingham. And in his speech he must perforce insert a reference to the consecration of the King himself. When he wrote his speech he had never heard of Mrs. Simpson: like millions of his fellow countrymen he was remote from the gossip of London and the American press. He had never read the headlines:

CUTIE SIMPSON CUTS OUT BLOODLESS BRITISH BLONDES
IN ROYAL CHOICE

He knew nothing of the sheaf of press cuttings which on the preceding Friday Baldwin had taken to the Cabinet meeting so as to inform it how opinion was moving. But he was one of those who were sufficiently discerning to see that, in spite of the King's popularity, there had been a decline from the standard of his parents, and something dubious in his ways. Edward VIII was not leading the life which the Prayer Book forms urged he should live—endowed plenteously with heavenly gifts, inclined to God's will and walking in His way.

So, in the course of his address, Bishop Blunt spoke these words:

"The benefit of the King's coronation depends under God upon two elements: first on the faith, prayer, self-education of the King himself, and on that it would be improper for me to say anything but to commend him, and ask you to commend him, to God's grace which he will so abundantly need, as we all need it—for the King is a man like ourselves—if he is to do his duty faithfully. We hope that he is aware of his need. Some of us wish that he had given more positive signs of his awareness."

Such was the tenor of the discourse which Bishop Blunt—and some were afterwards to remark that he was not inaptly named—put in that busy grimy industrial town of South Yorkshire before his Diocesan Conference. It countered the Bishop of Birmingham. At the same time it guilelessly lit a match beside the hidden but accumulated gunpowder which the newspaper-men knew that one spark would explode.

The reason was that by now there was a good deal more known than what appeared in the American newspapers, for it was impossible that the Government should be forced so far by events and yet confide nothing to the leading journalists, or compare what was known officially with what was being said and thought by informed people. Men cannot know one another intimately and yet mislead one another when confidential words are pressing for utterance. So it was that the Archbishop of Canterbury was necessarily apprised of the King's intention; and being so had taken counsel of other bishops who had unanimously supported his decision that he must not crown a King who avowed his intention to marry a woman who was yet another's wife. This in turn had become known to Geoffrey Dawson and among other leaders in Journalism to Arthur Mann, the Editor of the *Yorkshire Post*. When therefore he read what the Bishop of Bradford had said he never for a moment doubted that the authorities had chosen this way to prepare the country for the threat of abdication, and to enforce their own warnings to the headstrong sovereign. He was therefore the first to break the pent reticence of the press, instructing Charles Tower to write the leading article which follows.

THE KING AND HIS PEOPLE

"The Bishop of Bradford said yesterday that the benefit derived by the people from the King's Coronation would depend in the first instance on 'the faith, prayer and self-dedication of the King himself.' Referring to the moral and spiritual side of that self-dedication, the Bishop said the King would abundantly need Divine grace if he were to do his duty faithfully, and he added: 'We hope that he is aware of his need. Some of us wish that he gave more positive signs of such awareness.'

"Dr. Blunt must have had good reason for so pointed a remark. Most people, by this time, are aware that a great deal of rumour regarding the King has been published of late in the more sensational American newspapers. It is proper to treat with contempt mere gossip such as is frequently associated with the names of European royal persons. The Bishop of Bradford would certainly not have condescended to recognize it. But certain statements which have appeared in reputable United States journals, and even, we believe, in some Dominion newspapers, cannot be treated with quite so much indifference. They are too circumstantial and have plainly a foundation in fact. For this reason, an increasing number of responsible people is led to fear lest the King may not yet have perceived how complete in our day must be that self-dedication of which Dr. Blunt spoke if the Coronation is to bring a blessing to all the peoples of the Empire, and is not, on the contrary, to prove a stumbling block.

"When King Edward succeeded King George 'the well-beloved' the nation acclaimed him with the glad conviction that he would indeed, as he himself promised, follow in his father's footsteps. Deep disappointment must necessarily result if, instead of this continuity of example, there should develop a dispute between the King and his Ministers such as must almost inevitably raise a constitutional issue of the gravest character. There is no man or woman in any rank of life who has not some conception of the very high demands which are made on the King-Emperor, demands which many men might well shun. But the demands carry with them today the greatest opportunity, perhaps, that could be given to any one man. The King, by manifesting his own grave sense of responsibility, can do more than any other man to ensure that his subjects likewise will be of one mind to walk warily in very dangerous days."

At the same time the *Bradford Telegraph and Argus* circulated the Bishop's address to the Press Association; so it was that the result of this combination with Mann's article broke the floodgates at last.

The truth was that, only a day or two before, there had been a conference at which editors in the North had considered whether they should maintain silence much longer. Now therefore not only in York, but in Leeds and Bradford, as in Manchester and Birmingham, as well as Nottingham and Darlington attention was drawn to the importance of the Bishop's allocution. The *Manchester Guardian* now went so far as to disclose that the recent meeting of the Cabinet had been concerned not with the troubled state of Europe but with a domestic problem involving a constitutional issue, since it bore on the relation of the King to his Ministers, and his readiness to be guided in all matters which might affect the welfare of the British Commonwealth by the advice Ministers saw fit to offer.

It was plain that opinion in the North of England was aroused. The urgent warning given a week or two before by the King's Private Secretary was now seen to be an exact prognostic of the truth. Up to now the London papers had maintained their silence. The only hint had been from *The Times* which on 2nd December carried an article on the attendance of the Duke and Duchess of York at a Masonic banquet in Edinburgh Castle. That castle it caustically reminded its readers had been used by the Covenanters for the burning of witches. But this custom had ceased at the Accession of Charles II, for the Merry Monarch did not mind being bewitched. The object of the article was to turn admiration towards the Duke and Duchess of York who worthily maintained the traditions of the Royal House.

But it was, of course, an anomaly when the papers of the North anticipated those of London in making any disclosure of what all responsible men were thinking and saying. It remained for Geoffrey Dawson, the Editor of *The Times*, to consider how he would follow the lead given by the *Manchester Guardian* and the *Yorkshire Post*. There had already been a responsive stir in the House of Commons where there had been for weeks little ignorance of what was happening. There, as in the offices of Fleet Street, the eagles had gathered together. Members of Parliament could say nothing official. Certain members gave notice of things they had at heart:

Lord Apsley called attention to the weather.
Mr. Daggar spoke of the condition of the distressed areas.
Mr. C. Gibson said he would speak of the suffering caused by hard times in the Highlands and Islands of Scotland.
Mr. Gallacher, the Communist, urged a discussion of a subject overdue for discussion, the need of hot baths at the head of the Coal Pits.

But now a tremendous pressure of opinion and responsibility was brought to bear on the Prime Minister. At his house in Downing Street the telephone rang all day. His Secretary, J. C. C. Davidson, kept in constant touch with Lord Camrose and the leaders of the press. The publicity agent, George Steward, exercised infinite tact in calming and soothing the lobby correspondents. Everything was being done to avoid anything in the way of a sordid situation and to present the case with tact and dignity.

The Government found at this point that the discourse of the Bishop of Bradford was a godsend. It was the peg on which full reference could hang, and yet be tactfully and respectfully introduced; it obviated any reference to the tone and disclosures of the papers of America, and the bad odour into which the Crown had come both there and in France. While Baldwin's staff was thus busy in giving a guide to the London press, he himself received an urgent message making an appointment that evening with the King who had decided to drive in to Buckingham Palace. To keep the affair as quiet as possible the appointment had been arranged direct by Bateman, the King's wireless operator, and the King did not arrive till long after dark in the hope that his arrival would escape detection by the reporters. They, however, had arranged magnesium wire at the gates and were able to take a flashlight photograph as soon as he arrived.

Baldwin also did his best to escape detection. He went in an old ramshackle car from which he alighted for a time to have a walk in the park.

The King's object was to get news of the answer to his proposal of a morganatic marriage.

Later, in his story in the House of Commons, Baldwin was so anxious to save the reputation of the King that he gave of his talk an account more conventional than revealing. "I had intended," he then said, "asking for an audience later that week, because such enquiries as I thought proper to make I had not completed. The enquiries had gone far enough to show that neither in the Dominions nor here would there be any prospect of such legislation being accepted. So when the King asked about the morganatic marriage I gave him the reply," said Baldwin, "that I was afraid it was impracticable for these reasons. I do want the House to realize this: His Majesty said he was not surprised at the answer. He took my answer without question and never referred to it again. I want the House to realize—because if you can put yourself in His Majesty's place and you know what His Majesty's feelings are, and you know how glad you would have been had this been possible—that he behaved as a great gentleman. He said no more about it." So Baldwin saw fit to relate the story to the House of Commons. But the King himself admits that he pressed his case and that the Prime Minister tersely put the alternatives: either give up the thought of marriage or marry against the advice of his Ministers and therefore abdicate.

Baldwin admitted to his staff at the time that he had found the thwarted King fractious and irresponsible. He had spoken of the King's disappointing the people in whose esteem he stood so high and affecting the loyalty of the Dominions who looked on the Crown as the supreme emblem of Imperial unity. "To all arguments based on responsibility towards his people," Baldwin had to say "the King did not react, not feeling any responsibility which should dictate or influence his conduct." "There are very few people in Canada, Australia and the Colonies," he said. His whole thought was with and for Mrs. Simpson, dwelling on the delight it would be for her to be Queen, thinking of the things he could give her as Queen. He went back to his favourite phrase: "Wallis is the most wonderful woman in the world," and this he kept repeating. Sarcasm and sympathy joined in Baldwin's manner as he said: "Well, Sir, I hope that you may find her so."

The King had been difficult and spoke bitterly of the Blunt speech which he suspected had been inspired by Baldwin.

To all this Baldwin had to answer as though he were trying to soothe a fractious invalid. He put everything as gently as he could, but he stuck to the points he had to make. He had to deal with Mrs. Simpson's pressure on the subject of the broadcast: there again he avoided a blank refusal. Finding at the end that his arguments were unavailing he said, out of warm human sympathy: "Well, Sir, whatever happens, I hope you will be happy." That seemed to dissolve the suspicion and stubbornness with which a woman thwarted had impregnated the Sovereign who was at her feet.

It was the enterprise of Mrs. Simpson that Baldwin suspected through this and other interviews. Both in the Court and in the actual family of the King her influence, and the ability with which she worked upon the King, had awoken a furious resentment. And much as Baldwin sympathized, his feeling was still more of pity for a man whose strength of character he found inadequate to the demands his rank made upon it. The attitude of the Prime Minister was that of a father wanting to help a spoilt, difficult, petulant and headstrong son, the magnitude of whose decision was too vast for him to grasp and whose burden was too heavy for his slight stature to shoulder. Gradually the invalid was soothed by the imperturbability of his devoted Minister. The impression of Baldwin was that he was fighting a duel with Mrs. Simpson over the person of the King.

He felt also a real concern whether the King might not have a breakdown. And such there might have been had not the King found so generous and warm a friend as Monckton, who listened with sympathy and always tried to help, but who remained a friend of Baldwin and therefore could put to the King the difficulties which Baldwin would raise or face. They agreed that there must be no sacrifice of dignity and honour. But any adviser's task was a burden. Baldwin has written of the King's rapturous dream, but this was at times exchanged for a fighting mood with which it was yet more difficult to deal. Baldwin who was given information about his various reactions and who always wished to save him from himself redoubled his solicitude, feeling more and more anxiety.

If this was a trial to Baldwin, what was it to Monckton who must appear to carry out instructions which any practical man knew would meet with strong resistance from a Government which he knew was both benevolent and wise? Nothing would have been more fatal than for the King to think that Monckton was in agreement with Baldwin. Monckton therefore had to be constantly ascribing to Baldwin the obstacles which any sane man could foresee. The immediate subject at issue at this

146

point was the broadcast which Mrs. Simpson was still urging; the King's object was to persuade the country to what he had tried to persuade his mother—to share his admiration for the lady under whose mesmerism he was at this point both living and thinking. "The feeling mounted within me," he wrote, "that if I could only speak directly to the people, explaining what was in my mind, the confusion would be greatly dissipated, the tension relieved, and the atmosphere cleared for the exercise of justice and reason ... the more I thought about the idea, the more a broadcast appealed to me as the only possible way in which I might be able to mobilize the support of the whole Commonwealth."

How did the King arrive at so naïve a view? Let us repeat the four explanations. First that newspapers all voiced his praise: he was always presented as a paragon whom all adored. It seemed indeed as though he could do no wrong. The second point was that his intention was not crude immorality, but legal marriage. Thirdly he was entirely unable to estimate how public opinion, being solid with the old immemorial standards, must therefore disapprove his intention to marry a favourite divorced once, but not yet freed by a second divorce. Fourthly he was, partly by innate habit of command, and partly by the hypnotic quality of his lady's hold upon him, blinded to the Blunt case put so cogently by Mann, the case representing the best opinion in the Empire. For what the Empire wanted was a King with a hallowing and a Crown.

The poor man! He spoke of the exercise of justice and reason: he could no more apply these to Arthur Mann's article than to the case put so loyally by his devoted Prime Minister, so gently by his mother, the Queen. Even when, fifteen years later, he brought out his book he still seemed to think that he had all the right on his side and so had been the victim of an intrigue contrived and led by three cunning old men determined to down him. These, of course, were the Editor of *The Times*, the Archbishop of Canterbury, and the Prime Minister. Why did he think this when they were doing all they could for his safety and welfare? All that was the matter with them was that they identified loyalty to the Empire with the moral law which was, in any case, one with the opinion of a vast number; they could no more change that than they could promulgate another law for the hearts of men.

At times the King seemed gay and amusing, and when out dining could give the impression of not having a care in the world. It was said of him by those who knew him best that he had a wonderful way of 'turning on charm', and when charming he was certainly irresistible. But at other times he was in a highly nervous state.

147

His fear, not unfounded, for the physical safety of Mrs. Simpson now mingled with concern for her reputation. He and she had somehow conceived the idea that Geoffrey Dawson of *The Times* had a personal feeling against her which would lead him to print an attack on her character. Dawson had no personal antipathy towards her: he had met her once with Lady Oxford and thought her quiet and sensible: he knew that Lady Oxford regarded her influence as good.

Although *The Times* had now and again published cryptic sentences which to the initiated might raise a smile at Mrs. Simpson's expense, it would have been very far from the style and judgment of Geoffrey Dawson to hint a word against the character of one who was so often with the King. Everything that *The Times* published in connection with the affair was based on constitutional considerations: never did it carry a word of the references to Mrs. Simpson's past which were common enough in American journals. What Geoffrey Dawson had prepared for any sudden need—and yet kept holding back —was a weighty judicial statement on the function of the Crown.

Nothing, however, could free the mind of either the King or his constant companion of the anticipation that *The Times* had prepared a personal onslaught on Mrs. Simpson's character, and he now begged Baldwin to have it stopped. Baldwin tried to explain to him that a Prime Minister cannot dictate to a free press. But the King insisted that Baldwin should demand to see what Dawson was intending to print. When therefore the Prime Minister returned to Downing Street, he did actually telephone to Geoffrey Dawson about the King's insistence that nothing should be published without his supervision. He did this with the greatest embarrassment and innumerable apologies. "You know, Geoffrey," he said finally, "the trouble is that the little man hasn't the faintest notion of the way this country is governed." This meant, of course, at this juncture that Mrs. Simpson lacked the knowledge. For it was she who was behind the King's nervousness about English papers repeating what American ones had said.

On Wednesday, 2nd December, Lord Beaverbrook, aware that the storm was about to break, invited to dinner Allen, the King's solicitor, Monckton and Lord Brownlow. They decided that Mrs. Simpson should be at once advised not to linger in England. But before any of these could act both she and the King had heard the cannon's opening roar.

For the next morning, 3rd December, the long awaited article of *The Times* did at last appear.

'This is what it said:

'His present Majesty, who is known at first hand to far

more than any of his predecessors, came to the throne for this reason with all the greater opportunity for perpetuating and strengthening the tradition to the immense advantage of the two great English-speaking democracies. That opportunity has lately been fast disappearing in the picture which has lately been drawn in scores of American newspapers—much of it exaggerated, some of it sheer invention but displaying sufficient basis of fact to make it plausible. It has even gone to the length in the last fortnight of predicting a marriage incompatible with the throne and of announcing Queen Mary's approval of it— suggestions which may well seem startling to most of the King's subjects in England but which are doing infinite harm in the United States and the British Dominions. The reaction of the public to this spate of gossip is by no means what might have been expected by those whose whole impression of Americans is derived from the popular press. It is neither light-hearted nor indifferent and certainly not sympathetic. On the contrary, there is clearly the most profound and widespread sense of bewilderment extending far beyond the individual monarch to the admired and envied institutions of the British Monarchy itself. . . .

"Even a King is entitled to his relaxations and the companionship of his chosen friends. What the nation cannot afford is that the influence of the great office which he holds should be weakened if ever private inclinations were to come into open conflict with public duty, and be allowed to prevail. It is a curious paradox that in an age which is supposed to be laxer and more tolerant than its predecessors, and in countries which pride themselves on the obliteration of social distinctions there survives more universally than ever before the sense that the kingship must be kept above public criticism.

"The wave of gossip and rumour from across the Atlantic has spread in ever-widening circles throughout this country—the cumulative effect of this campaign of scandal will be serious damage to the monarchy. This is what matters to the nation. The high office which His Majesty holds is no man's personal possession; it is a sacred trust handed down from generation to generation, and maintained for the last century with growing strength by the willing allegiance of the whole people to Sovereigns who were secure because they were respected. . . . The constitutional growth of the British Empire has lately placed upon it a far heavier burden of responsibilities. The Crown is the symbol of the Dominions' unity . . . and events in the world outside have imposed as never before on the British monarchy the duty to stand as a rock amid the seething tides of Communism and Dictatorship; but the public need reassurance."

That was the line taken by *The Times*: that was as far as it went in a personal onslaught on the character of Mrs. Simpson! The day before, far away in South Africa, *The Friend*, at Bloemfontein, had written: "the moment there is the slightest indication that kingship is merely a formality of state, not an exemplar of conduct and righteousness, the foundations of the monarchy are shaken."

The *Birmingham Post*, however, had been pretty precise: "The gossip and rumour and highly circumstantial tale-telling as to one particular phase of His Majesty's private life is not without its basis in solid truth . . . in the eyes of the people of this country, as in the eyes of subjects of the Crown overseas, the private and public life of the King-Emperor are inseparable."

Such were the views from provinces and Empire which now percolated into the London papers which for the most part were strongly in agreement. At the first it is true that there was some support in the *News Chronicle* for the idea of a morganatic marriage, but this was dropped when it was seen that it would satisfy only a fraction of opinion. Otherwise the only exceptions to the general view were the *Daily Mail* under Lord Rothermere, and the *Daily Express* under Lord Beaverbrook. This peer, while taking the stance of an Imperialist, now resolutely put aside the decisions of each and all of the Dominion governments.

In the British press as a whole there was on the morning of 3rd December a note of disapproval so distinct, so unmistakable that the King and Mrs. Simpson as they read the papers at Fort Belvedere were taken wholly aback. Theirs was now the "anger and alarm" which had characterized the mood of Canada when it first realized what of their story had appeared through the unfolding months in the papers of the United States. The more important the paper, the more definite was its pronouncement on the obligations of the Crown. It was all turning exactly as his Private Secretary had warned him in that essential letter written three weeks before that it must. But still he refused to believe in public opinion: he seemed to think that Baldwin had been working the papers. "The bitter unanimity with which they lashed out," he writes, "could only reflect the definiteness of the Cabinet." "Could this be the King," he asked, "or was I some common felon?" And yet how plainly his kindly advisers had warned him! How often he had deliberately closed his ears to every inkling of the truth! Gradually his mind had become incapable of dealing with fact because he had so forcibly subjected it to the fancies which flattered his obsession: that is why the balance of his mind was now imperilled. He was going to fight against fact to the end, but it was a losing battle which obliged him to take up one after another desperate and unsafe positions of defence while he gradually became aware of the advancing and relentless force of his one overwhelming enemy, which was truth.

It is plain that as they read those morning papers at Fort Belvedere, both concerned lost their nerve. At last the King was forced to acknowledge that he had put his favourite in a position vulnerable to the artillery of his people's opinion. As for her, she saw still more clearly than when she read the Hardinge letter that his devotion to her was not only unable to raise her to the coveted throne but was certain to drive him from it; she knew well that if it did so his position and resources would be much diminished.

Besides, if her windows at Cumberland Place had been broken before a word appeared in the papers, what would happen to her now? Now all London was loud with voices which implied reprobation, now in the hearts of the people the storm of general indignation was rising like a hurricane in the forest where a chance match might set fire to resinous timber heated by the sun. A people whose religion had been devotion to their royal idol could thrill with the wrath of the Moroccan who hears an insult to the name of Allah. Opinion made no allowance either for Mrs. Simpson's good influence on the King, her personal gifts, or her unparalleled temptation. They regarded her as one who had desecrated the shrine—she had made their hero unfit for their honour and admiration. An outraged fanaticism swept beyond suspicion and resentment to a fury which pictured her as witch, as demon, as traitor. Advice reached the King that there were the strongest reasons why she should leave England, reasons so strong that even if he had not shared something of her panic, he would have been unable to dispute them.

Those whose minds echoed with classics and history might have recalled a line from the *Henry IV* of Shakespeare:

King Edward: Away with her and waft her hence to France.

He now echoed that order. He arranged that she should leave his house under cover of the dark, drive to the Channel, and seek a shelter on the Riviera. There, as she had quickly ascertained by telephone, the Herman Rogers for whom she had secured three months before that invitation to Balmoral would open the doors of their villa at Cannes, the quiet Provençal shelter which had the name of "Lou Viei".

Almost like a conspirator planning to evade arrest, the King set to work to arrange the flight of Mrs. Simpson in such secrecy as he could devise while she left him alone to meet the situation they had together forced on the astounded masses of his people.

No sooner had Mrs. Simpson departed than the King faced her Aunt Bessie, who was no fool, and who had had ample opportunity to gauge the spate of talk in her native Baltimore. She did not want to have her niece in danger or her royal friend to fall from the lofty state which had been so flattering to her. Knowing that Mrs. Merryman was worried too, he told her he was terribly sorry. She spoke words of prudence. He answered them by telling her that he still intended both to marry and to carry on his work as King. But, he said to her, as he had said to Baldwin, that if there had to be a choice, he put the marriage first. Here Mrs. Merryman warned him what her niece had already had to face, adding that as a result she was frightened and bewildered. Mrs. Merryman, aware of her recoil and trepidation, argued that if he remained on the throne it would be better for them all.

How could either of the American ladies desire that their benefactor should forfeit his power and affluence?

CHAPTER XXVII

THAT day was the most complex and dramatic of the whole situation. Not only did it mean that for the first time the King had no option but to engage with the hosts of fact and truth, not only did it mean that he had to cope with the danger to Mrs. Simpson and the fear that she could not fight off. But it was also a day in which he decided to push on with her project of a broadcast appeal against his Government. The papers had given him a shock which rivalled that when he received the Hardinge letter, but they had not purged his mind of the temptation which a countrywoman of Roosevelt had set before him: to win the people to him by a fireside chat.

On the preparation of this proposal he now engaged the forensic skill of Walter Monckton. The broadcast was to say that he had found the woman he loved and was determined to marry her, that he did not ask that she should be Queen if she were accorded a proper title and dignity. In order that his people might reflect calmly and quietly he would go away till they decided.

It did not occur to him to consider a recent parallel to this proposal. When King Alfonso of Spain had found himself up against a clamour from the masses he also had said he would go away to leave his people an unembarrassed decision. That departure had proved fatal.

The first thing to do was to go to Buckingham Palace to show the proposed broadcast to the Prime Minister. Here again

152

the King put the gifts of Baldwin to the test. Tact, joined with endless sympathy for a man suffering from the delusion that he was the victim of intrigue, had to be tempered to steel by sagacity. When Baldwin had heard the proposed broadcast he was obliged to point out that to make any such appeal was unconstitutional.

The King's answer was touching if confused: "You want me to go, don't you? And before I go, I think it is right for her sake and mine that I should speak."

"What I want, Sir," said the Prime Minister, "is what you told me you wanted: to go with dignity, not dividing the country—and making things as smooth as possible for your successor. To broadcast would be to go over the heads of your Ministers and speak to the people. You will be telling millions throughout the world—among them a vast number of women—that you are determined to marry one who has a husband living. They will want to know all about her, and the Press will ring with gossip, the very thing you want to avoid. You may by speaking divide opinion, but you will certainly harden it."

But in the mind of the King what weight could these recommendations of moral and constitutional sagacity have against the recommendations of "the most wonderful woman in the world"? Baldwin knew how he could best safeguard the prestige of the Crown and shield the reputation of him who wore it. But still he avoided a head-on collision with the careering passion with which he had to deal. He would not yet say a definite NO to a royal lover impelled by an idealized urge to put a case, which would be welcome to many, that the passionate drive of the heart should overrule the lifelong vows of marriage.

It was not an hallucination that this idea was gaining ground. The two lovers both believed that as in the United States, so already in Great Britain, it represented the freer standards of a new and enlightened age against the stuffy respectabilities of Victorianism. It was to emancipate from holy deadlock those whose bond had degenerated from ardour to incompatibility: it was to bring satisfaction to those who, leaving youth behind, felt impelled to renew in maturer strength the wonder of a new discovery in wedded union.

This is indeed an immense issue; but it is often complicated by a preliminary breach in the loyalty without which no personal relation can be expected to endure. Could it now be maintained, for instance, that the circumstances of Mrs. Simpson's transference of her heart from Mr. Simpson to the King must win the approval of those who recognized that a marriage contract—whether indissoluble or not—meant *something*? It is surely the duty of a wife not to try too much the patience and generosity of a husband, especially if he had rescued her from penury. Must it not be admitted that she had put Mr. Simpson in a difficult position which he had long accepted with extreme forbearance? Had she not led him into temptation? As for the King, it was his duty to keep the Crown untarnished by the murk of scandal, and uphold the dignity of the Court. For him there was some truth in the formula of confession he had in boyhood so often used: "We have followed too much the devices and desires of our own hearts."

A moment's consideration shows that the King's project was something more than unconstitutional: it must strike any experienced man of affairs as an indiscretion which would fix on the Court the scarlet spotlight of scandal. But yet so excessively accommodating was Baldwin to the royalty he pitied that he agreed not only to put the question of the broadcast to the Cabinet but also agreed that the King should consult Churchill as to the form it should take.

As soon, therefore, as Baldwin left the Palace, the King told Monckton to get in touch with Churchill, who then arranged to go over the draft later in the evening with Beaverbrook, to whom a copy was also sent.

The two concerned were not the only ones who had read their morning papers with a sense of personal and dramatic strain. Those papers had brought horror and anguish to Queen Mary. Here, blazoned to London and to the world, was the protest and warning of opinion on the conduct of her son. Through all those anxious days, she had had no word from him. She knew only from Baldwin that the constitutional crisis had become acute. From the beginning she had seen that the situation was becoming impossible. "This is a nice kettle of fish, Mr. Baldwin," she had said to him after her son had announced at dinner his determination to marry as he chose, in defiance of constitutional recommendations. And then stricken to the heart by all that was implied of discredit to the Crown which had been the lodestar of her conscience and her destiny she found that her reserves of physical strength had failed her and she had been forced to rest in bed.

Hardly had she recovered from this prostration than she had to face the thunder of the newspapers and all that it implied. Her son had not wanted to discuss with her his challenge to Baldwin. Since he had dined with her he had not sent her a single word. He had, in fact, been so brooding over his various dilemmas that he had forgotten her. But, if she insisted on seeing him, she, who was his mother and the Queen, how could he refuse? That morning she had sent him a message begging him to go at once and see her at Marlborough House. It was already late in that harassing day, and his nerves gave evidence of his strain. He told her now that he was not prepared to listen to advice and must act alone. Did he mention the broadcast? If so, she could not have approved it. She saw but too clearly that the point had been reached when duty demanded that he should go.

When he drove back from Marlborough House to the Palace, he found that Monckton had returned from his interview with Beaverbrook and Churchill. Did they advise the broadcast? Both had seen what of course was anything but surprising to Monckton—that it was highly questionable whether constitutionally the King could appeal to the country to support him against his Government. Secondly, they saw that if he left the country he would find what King Alphonso had found when he embarked from Spain five years before: those who remained in the saddle would fix the course. It would not take long for the Cabinet to come to agreement with any Council of State appointed when both had before them the refusal of the Dominions to consider passing a law permitting morganatic marriage. Although both Beaverbrook and Churchill went to the extreme in humouring the King, they made it nevertheless pretty clear that the broadcast must be abandoned.

It was late at night when Monckton met the King with this fresh warning, but, late as it was, a crowd still lingered around the Palace. This caused another wild fancy to play on the King's overwrought mind: he thought for a moment of actually appearing on the balcony and making a speech to the crowd.

But that was Mussolini's way. Was he to vie with that? He must not descend to that level, not make his affair into a national melodrama. Stepping out of Buckingham Palace for the last time he met Walter Monckton without any hint of the temptation he had rejected. He was glad to leave London for Fort Belvedere where he always lived in a certain privacy apart from the Palace secretaries.

CHAPTER XXVIII

How had that day of dramatic disclosure passed among the people? How did the Dominions react to the plainer speaking of London?

There is no doubt that the people in their mass were dismayed. Their general impression was summed in short words: "It isn't right."

But, of course, as the King had felt, there was, there must be, another current, another view: the people who delighted in a love affair, and wanted nothing to come in the way of strong attraction. And apart from them there were those who were—

one might almost say on principle—opposed to the Church. Some, like Mr. A. L. Rowse at All Souls in Oxford, even saw an opportunity to make political capital out of it, others saw in it money for their newspapers. So there were half-a-dozen leading men who approved Mrs. Simpson's bold blow on the wedge, and persuaded him she was right in the idea that if he could appeal direct to the people they would rally to his cause.

Already on that morning of Thursday, 3rd December, members had noticed that in the House of Commons Colonel Josiah Wedgwood had placed on the order paper the following motion:

"In the opinion of the House, the oath of allegiance which they have already taken to King Edward VIII is unaffected by the form of Coronation ceremony, or by the presence thereat or by the absence therefrom of any personage whatsoever. Nor will they substitute any other for the King of England."

This motion was supposed to refer to the current talk that the Archbishop of Canterbury had been much concerned about the whole affair, that he must be reluctant to perform the rites of hallowing and anointing a King who not only showed little awareness of his obligations to the Church, but, as it was now becoming clear, meant openly to flout them. But though the secret thought of the Archbishop had been confided to his diary and some Bishops, he had so far maintained discreet silence. It was plain, however, that he must be opposed to all who took the line of Colonel Josiah Wedgwood. The chief of these were Lord Beaverbrook, Mr. Winston Churchill, Sir Oswald Mosley, Lord Rothermere and his son. To these must be added the redoubtable vigour of Lady Houston, a woman of wealth who expressed downright views in a weekly paper which she owned. This with the papers of Lord Rothermere now became known to both government and the newspaper world as 'the Simpson Press'. Mr. Churchill did not write for these papers—his articles, which were far the ablest of current journalism, appeared regularly in the *Daily Telegraph*. But Lord Camrose, its owner, was the last man who would allow his paper to be used for such a purpose as Churchill now cherished. He and his brother Lord Kemsley had very pronounced views on the other side.

Before the Prime Minister met the King to discuss the question of the broadcast, he had had in the House of Commons to answer a question which he expected from the Leader of the Opposition about constitutional difficulties. So towards four in the afternoon Mr. Attlee put his question as to whether on such a point the Prime Minister had any statement to make.

"I have no statement today," Baldwin answered. "But while

there does not at present exist any constitutional difficulty, the situation is of such a nature as to make it inexpedient that I should be questioned about it at this stage."

"May I ask the Right Honourable Gentleman," continued Attlee, "whether in view of the anxiety that these reports are causing in the minds of many people, he can assure the House that he will make a statement at the earliest possible time that a statement can be made?"

"I can assure the Right Honourable Gentleman," was the answer, "that all that he says I have very much in mind."

Then Churchill rose to ask: "Will my Right Honourable friend give us an assurance that no irrevocable step will be taken before a formal statement is made to Parliament?"

Baldwin said he would consider and examine the question, but that at the moment he could add nothing to the statement he had made.

This discussion had taken place some hours before Mrs. Simpson set out for the Sussex shore. On the following morning, Friday, 4th December, the Government had to come to a decision on the question of the broadcast. While they were doing so, the King's mind was distracted by anxiety as to how Mrs. Simpson was faring on her journey. And no wonder.

CHAPTER XXIX

IT is hardly part of the history of the reign of King Edward VIII to trace the adventures of Mrs. Simpson on her way from Fort Belvedere to Cannes. But, as the King felt so much concern for her welfare, and the papers catered for the people's inevitable curiosity, one may perhaps give a sketch of the journey which both he and she have related, and to which others can add details they did not relate.

When her aunt had said she was bewildered and frightened, it was true. In *A King's Story* he writes of the strain it was "for a sensitive woman like Wallis" to see her portrait in all the newspapers. A penetrating analyst of the story has pointed out that this sensitive woman, having seen the American and French papers, had been facing that particular kind of strain for a good long time! But it added a strain of another sort when she might be assailed by insult, stones and even vitriol.

Her features were distinctive and fine, and by now they were portrayed in newspapers all over England and France. It was only to be expected that, wherever she went, she would be recognized at once. So the King sent with her that chauffeur and that detective who had for weeks been assigned to safeguarding her journey from place to place. It could hardly be said that these two revelled in their privilege—they had no more fallen under Mrs. Simpson's spell than other members of the King's staff. But this time they were not to work without special supervision. For the King had appointed as the lady's companion and aide his own Lord-in-Waiting, Lord Brownlow. He and she were to travel together under the joint pseudonym of 'Mr. and Mrs. Harris'. But any advantage of disguise this might have lent them was at once discounted by the fact that the car was registered in the name of Mrs. Simpson. It was recognized as soon as it went on board and also by the Customs officials on the other side. But otherwise she passed on to and off the boat without attracting notice.

She had not arrived at the coast without a question. As they were driving thither it occurred to Lord Brownlow that once she was gone the King would give up and follow her. He put before her three points: (1) if she left the country her great influence would be weakened by distance and poor communications. (2) That if she went abroad the King would inevitably follow her. (3) Lastly, that his departure, at that juncture, encompassed speedy and inevitable Abdication.

Mrs. Simpson, he adds, hopelessly trapped by circumstances, great devotion, and overwhelming pressures, did not wish to add to his troubles by a sudden change of plan. "You know what David's like when he's crossed," she urged. "Any change in his plan in the state he is in would drive him wild."

The answer was that no matter how furious the King would be, it was the surer way to keep him on the throne.

She too was anxious to keep him on the throne. But, she tells us, she calculated that if she turned back she would be accused of putting ambition before his good, and evidently they had come on communications which made her sensitive to that sort of accusation. Then she would be blamed even more bitterly. "In the back of every Englishman's mind," she writes acidly, "is a kind of Domesday body of moral principles that continually sits in judgment on the affairs of others." Certainly many passed judgment in her case, But was this thought for her reputation her strongest motive, or had her nerve broken at the prospect of meeting censorious and angry eyes? Whatever her argument, Lord Brownlow did not press his point. The King was left to cope with his situation without her personal presence.

Since, as we saw, the name of Simpson was on the car papers, no sooner had 'Mr. and Mrs. Harris' landed at Dieppe than all France began to buzz with the news that the lady was in that country, and the enterprise of journalism, which through the whole affair had been so strong an ingredient of the situation, was whipped to the extremest efforts. How their movements were traced it would be hard to tell: but traced they were from point to point. At Rouen the car was recognized, and a girl approached with a camera which the detective knocked out of her hand. They escaped through Evreux to Blois where the reporters soon found them out, greyhounds with the flying hare in sight. For this wave of fevered curiosity had its own piquancy. Her sensitiveness to the interest she had awakened in France made her mind a tournament between the fears which had prompted her departure from England and practical concern for the situation. But whenever she stopped to use the telephone, using the King's private number at Fort Belvedere to make her frantic appeals for patience and restraint, she had to make them at the porter's desk which generally had the only receiver. Thus her secret thoughts were scattered to the winds of France.

But naturally Lord Brownlow was anxious for sensation to be avoided, not only to eliminate any risk to her safety but also because he was most anxious to keep cheap publicity from his Sovereign, and to see that the Crown was not compromised by the sensations made by journalists. At Blois, therefore, he gave instructions for a start at three in the morning so that he might elude the journalists while they slept, and so get off on the quiet road up the Loire valley to Moulins. But no matter how early the start or how quiet the road, the passage of the car was noticed, and when they had driven from Moulins down to meet the Rhône at Lyons she found that as soon as they pulled up to ask the way she was recognized with the shrill cry "*Voilà la Dame!*" and this cry, she said, echoed in her ears as they drove on. The greyhounds had gained on the fearful flight once more.

So from Lyons a procession of cars followed them to Vienne where they arrived at three in the afternoon, the reporters now triumphant and ready to regale themselves accordingly in a famous restaurant. But while they were thus enjoying the fruits of victory, the enterprise of Lord Brownlow gave them the slip. Mrs. Simpson was led down backstairs to the kitchen, squeezed through a scullery window above the sink, and from here she did a jump into the arms of the detective who had been posted in a narrow alley below. Lord Brownlow wriggled after her. In a moment they were out of the town by back streets and drove down the Rhône valley through a storm of sleet, till, as evening fell, they reached Avignon. There again they seized some food and then took the Riviera road to Brignolles, from which Lord Brownlow, much of his patience gone, telephoned to Herman Rogers to expect them in the small hours of the following morning, Friday, 5th December.

Rogers had given warning that the villa was surrounded

by a regiment of reporters. Mrs. Simpson elected not to face these. Elastic in her moods as she was gymnastic in her movements, she slipped now from her seat on to the floor of the car, where she crouched beneath the rug, to emerge only at her friends' door after the gates had been closed behind her, a trifle dishevelled perhaps and not without signs of an exhausting journey, but safe in her chosen shelter at last.

But, as she was soon to find, it was both day and night beleaguered by reporters. These could not be fobbed off indefinitely—they must give some impression to the waiting world. After a day or two, therefore, a photographer was given instructions to come and take a picture of the group at the villa of 'Lou Viei'. Mrs. Simpson was not too exhausted to smile at the camera. Her face wears in that snapshot a subtle expression in which shyness is at issue with a knowledge of the power she has exerted. But she was hardly in a position to settle the King by her long-distance calls. Over her mind, says Lord Brownlow, was a film of ignorance, confusion and panic. A further difficulty arose from the fact that her calls were tapped and their secrets sold to the journalists till special operators were sent down to Cannes from the Quai d'Orsay.

Meanwhile, in the circle of Baldwin, her writing had been taken to a graphologist that they might have a further insight into a character who might yet play a determining part in the situation. For many believed that without her personal mesmerism over the King he would act from other motives than when she was at hand. What the graphologist wrote was that she was:

"A woman with a strong male inclination in the sense of activity, vitality, initiative. She *must* dominate, she *must* have authority, and without sufficient scope for her powers can become disagreeable. In a narrow circle without big tasks to perform she would be impatient, irritable. She needs a large field of organization, of influence. She is very subjective and so set in her personal colour as to make it impossible for her to take an objective view. The whole personality has an inclination to be great, and in spite of her temperament, she is inwardly aloof from her surroundings. She is extremely temperamental, but it is more emotional impulse than real feeling. Her capacity for sacrifice is not great, but in playing her part, good might come of it, though primarily all she does comes from her wish to be important. In the pursuit of her aim, she can be inconsiderate and can hurt—but on the whole she is not without some instinct of nobility and generosity. She is ruled by contradictory impulses; there is a certain restlessness in the writing, a sign that the satisfaction she gets is not strong enough to harmonize her life. She is ambitious and demands above all that her undertakings should be noted and valued."

This, for what it is worth, was the diagnosis of the graphologist; accurate or not, it reflected very much the impression of the Royal Dukes. They acknowledged her talents but resented the way in which she had separated the King from the influence and intimacy of his family. This feeling was particularly strong in the Duke of Kent. He at this time related his resentment at being told by her a few months before: "You're all right. I've put you both on the list to come to Balmoral."

And all the time her presence tended to keep the brothers from being alone with the King. The Duke of Kent had found that his confidential relation to his brother had vanished in the growing distance between them.

What, they asked, was now to happen with the whole world's attention fixed on the affair? They must be ready for changes. The Prime Minister had already approached the Duke of York to tell him to be in readiness for the result of a probable abdication.

Yet a question still remained whether it must come to that. There was a doubt on the side of the Government that now the King might make an independent choice—on the part of the King whether he could not manage opinion to indulge his will. He could not think that he had forfeited the hero-worship which had made him the personification of all that contemporary youth admired, nor that it would oppose his choice.

Meanwhile the attention of the whole country was riveted in excited curiosity. Shopping was reduced to a minimum. The stock market began to weaken. There was a question whether the cohesion of the Empire itself was not endangered. The Government, responsible, as it was, for the welfare of all, was put to the severest strain, while meanwhile its legal authorities had also to concentrate on another nice constitutional point. A number of Privy Councillors had already proposed to register their dissent from the King's choice. The Privy Council does not vote on Royal marriages, or indeed on any subject. Nevertheless King Edward VIII could hardly have ignored the precedent of his great-grandmother, Queen Victoria, who announced to her Privy Council her engagement to Prince Albert.

By the famous Act of 1772, Royal Marriages are not valid unless the Consent of the Sovereign is declared in Council, and signified under the Great Seal. If the King had now declared in Council his intention to marry Mrs. Simpson, obviously he would have had to face a situation!

Nevertheless the King himself was not bound by the Royal Marriages Act of 1772. Baldwin himself was soon to make this clear when he spoke on the 9th December in the House of Commons. The difficulty was that no Government would countenance the risk to the Throne involved in such a questionable choice. But, as Baldwin said: "The Royal Marriage Act of 1772 has no application to the Sovereign himself. Its only effect is that the Marriage of any other member of the Royal Family is null and void unless the Sovereign's consent declared under the Great Seal is first obtained. This act, therefore, has nothing to do with the present case. The King requires no consent from any other authority to make his marriage legal, but, as I have said, the lady he marries, by the fact of her marriage to the King necessarily becomes Queen."

This statement was drafted for the Prime Minister by a legal authority of the first rank, Sir John Simon.

("It is true," adds the present Lord Chancellor, "that Section I of the Royal Marriages Act provides that the necessary consent must be given under the Great Seal and passed in Council. It is also true that Edward VIII was a 'Descendant of George II' within the same section. On the other hand the preamble to the statute makes it clear, in my view, beyond any possible doubt that Parliament was only intending to cover the case of other members of the Royal Family. It is, of course, a well established principle of the Common Law that the King is not bound by a Statute unless he is expressly referred to in it. I am therefore in the fortunate position of being able to agree entirely with what I know to have been Simon's views.")

CHAPTER XXX

IF the legal authorities had been intently occupied, and if Mrs. Simpson had passed a day of agitation, what of the King? When he woke up next morning, the prey of moods, it was still with the intention of carrying on the fight. He was at one moment excitedly combative; at another unnerved; and with all this Monckton had to cope from hour to hour, counselling and calming the King, never running counter to his instructions, and doing what he could to keep the relation equable between the King and the Prime Minister. The first thing to do was to assess the state of opinion in the papers. He wanted to indulge the King with any word in his favour; seeing that the Rothermere and Beaverbrook papers were running counter to the Government, Monckton could refer to this as opening fire.

Their argument was that abdication was unthinkable because it had had a bad effect on the Empire; this was of course in itself a phantasy, which only ignorance of the Dominion governments could indulge. The *Express* went so far as to say that the King could override the Government if he wanted to do so.

Very different was the actual tone of the newspapers printed overseas. Their tone was expressed with force by *The Dominion*, the leading paper of Wellington in New Zealand, in the words which follow: "It is almost incredible that in less than a year from King George's death, the throne should be shaken to its foundations by indiscretions which age, experience, and cognizance of the obligations attached to his exalted office should have warned King Edward to avoid: it is a tragedy that he appears to have failed to realize what this may mean to the idea of Kingship throughout the British Commonwealth and the Colonial Empire." Perhaps the King would have answered to that that there were well below two million people in New Zealand.

Then it was noticed that, curiously enough, two weeklies extremely opposed to each other came out with views opposed to the Government. One was the Catholic *Tablet*, then edited by a convert from Methodism formerly in the wine trade. It refused to recognize that the Register Office could solemnize a marriage according to the law of the land, insisted on speaking of Mrs. Simpson as Mrs. Spencer. The other, free from that nonsense, was on the extreme left, the *New Statesman*. Both of these argued that the King, without consulting his Ministers, could choose his own wife. Both pushed on one side the fact that if a choice were made that lowered the prestige of the Crown, or weakened the cohesion of the Empire, it became an affair of the greatest import to the Government. On this point none of the Labour leaders hesitated for an instant. Not one of them would give any support to Colonel Wedgwood.

The personal sympathy for the King came mostly from young people of the educated and middle classes: the blackshirts, under Sir Oswald Mosley, would fight for him tooth and nail. Among the masses, however, disapproval was almost universal: in the villages judgment on Mrs. Simpson was particularly severe. One who was then an undergraduate at Cambridge thought that whereas his landlady said "Why not let him marry as we do?" the young members of the University were united in reprobation.

The Cabinet had to meet that morning to discuss the two separate issues of the broadcast and the morganatic marriage. The unanimous answers from the Dominions had come in. With those before them the Cabinet had no choice but to dismiss the idea without more ado. But they had also the judicial opinion of Sir John Simon who had drafted with extreme care a statement for the Prime Minister to make. When therefore in the afternoon Mr. Attlee repeated his question of the day before, the Prime Minister said he did think it advisable now to make some statement.

"Suggestions have appeared in certain organs of the Press yesterday," he said, "and again today that, if the King desired to marry, his wife need not become Queen. These ideas are without foundation. There is no such thing as what is called morganatic marriage known to our law. ... The lady whom the King marries by the fact of her marriage to him necessarily becomes Queen. She therefore enjoys all the status, rights and privileges which both by positive law and by custom attach to that position. ... The only way in which this result could be avoided would be by legislation dealing with a particular case. Neither the Prime Ministers of the Dominions nor the Opposition would consider such a possibility." This statement, which had been carefully drafted by Simon, disposed for ever of Lord Rothermere's suggestion.

Since the Cabinet had been equally clear that a broadcast would be unconstitutional, Baldwin after his speech in the House of Commons drove out to Fort Belvedere to make it clear to the King that there was really nothing more to say. He had wanted to help, but he saw very clearly that since people were feeling as they were the King must decide on the plain alternative: to give up Mrs. Simpson or abdicate.

Baldwin's tone was at once so firm and so friendly that at the time he seemed to carry conviction. Baldwin said to one of his confidants that he was sad at heart for the little man—despising him, loving him, and pitying him all at the same time, but hating the woman who had goaded him on to the fray. But restless and unnerved as the King was, the combination of firmness with warm sympathy again had its effect. This—who could deny?—was the tone of a true friend who was doing all he could to help. How could the King continue to see him and then the moment afterwards encourage a contrary policy? "The more I pondered the situation," he writes, "the more I became convinced that immediate abdication was now the only decision if the dignity of the Crown was to be preserved and the unity of the Empire maintained."

Between them Baldwin and Monckton had done their work. But all three that Friday evening were tired, harassed and sad. They showed the strain in different ways. Baldwin had the weariness of an old man who had had a great disappointment; Monckton the exhaustion of a competent brain kept continually on the stretch in trying to compass the impossible; the King the volatility of an excitable nature on the verge of breakdown.

But hardly on that Friday evening had Baldwin left Fort Belvedere when another guest arrived to dine and spend the evening. Who but Mr. Winston Churchill?

Mr. Churchill had always been—and was long to remain—a

man of great fertility of invention. Hour after hour he startled
and delighted his hearers with the variety of his brilliant hypo-
theses and proposals, poured out one after another with vivid
imagery, powerful eloquence, genial enthusiasm, and equally
genial irresponsibility. Like a cascade in sunlight, these gleaming,
glinting ideas sparkled melodiously forth to amaze, to dazzle,
sometimes to beguile. There were times also, as when he meant

> To quail and shake the orb
> He was as rattling thunder.

Now he said that all this talk in papers and Parliament about a
constitutional issue could be condemned as a distempered
dream. If the King were about to marry, then the Government
might speak; but the King should not think of marrying till the
decree was made absolute—and these politicians who always
trim their doctrine to the varying hour (Mr. Churchill was
himself a politician) must wait while the battalions marched—
marched, he meant, to the trumpet and command of Winston
Churchill. He then outlined to his royal host the appeal he
would furnish to the press. He based his argument on the
dramatic fiction that the Cabinet had demanded abdication from
the King. From this false premise he built up his picturesque
case.

What had the King done? Why had the Cabinet consulted
the Opposition? (So he put it.) Why could not time be granted?
Then came the appeals to sentiment, to imagination, to fair
play, to religion—yes, to religion. It went like this:

"The King has been for many weeks under the greatest
strain, moral and mental, that can fall upon a man. Not only
has he been subjected to the extreme stress of public duty, but
also to the agony of his own personal feelings.

"Surely if he asks for time to consider the advice of his
Ministers now that at length matters have been brought to this
dire culmination, he should not be denied.

"Howsoever this matter may turn, it is pregnant with calamity
and inseparable from inconvenience. But all the evil aspects
will be aggravated beyond measure if the utmost chivalry and
compassion are not shown, both by Ministers and by the British
nation, towards a gifted and beloved King torn between private
and public obligations of love and duty.

"The Churches stand for charity. They believe in the efficacy
of prayer. Surely their influence must not oppose a period of
reflection. I plead, I pray that time and tolerance will not be
denied."

Here then prepared for print was the Churchillian eloquence
which diverted the tired monarch at his dinner-table, and
attempted to persuade his legal friend to forget the effect of

the late disclosure of public opinion. Then, with a last touch of picturesqueness, Mr. Churchill counselled the King to retire to Windsor Castle and close the gates, with his physicians to keep watch and ward against intruders on his august exhaustion.

So, saying the Churches stood for charity, Mr. Churchill displayed to the Sovereign the wizardry in charm and chatter. But when this was published next day as a discourse, ending with words about the outrage of hastily extorting an abdication, admiration for the eloquence was smothered in scorn for the manipulation of the facts. The result was soon to shock him.

On the same day, Bernard Shaw, now eighty years of age, brought out a typical article called 'The King, the Constitution and the Lady'. Published first in the *Evening Standard* of Lord Beaverbrook, it was republished in the *Sunday Referee*, and the *Daily Mirror* as 'A Fictitious Dialogue'.

It pretended that a King wanted to marry an American, called Miss Daisy Bell (not divorced); that his Archbishop and his Prime Minister had 'shrieked' to him that it was impossible, that the King in return had asked "What will happen to the foundations of the Church if it tries to force me to contract a loveless marriage and to live in adultery with the woman I love?"

Yet none knew better than the author of *The Apple Cart* that "A demagogue may steal a horse where a King dare not look over a hedge".

Lord Beaverbrook could not vie with such efforts as these, but he persisted in similar contentions. Mr. Driberg, who wrote an unauthorized life of Lord Beaverbrook, admits that Baldwin had the support throughout the crisis of both Liberal and Labour parties as well as almost all the Conservatives, and of the overwhelming majority of the national and the provincial newspapers. Of this there can really be no question. Churchill himself freely admitted it in his book. But for Beaverbrook that was not the point. He was managing a great newspaper stunt—he was in his element according to Mr. Driberg, and not losing money either. "I would not have missed it for anything," he said afterwards. "I never had such fun in my life."[*]

While Mr. Churchill was launching his broadside, however, it was countered by the Archbishop of Canterbury. Here too was a master of eloquence, though certainly of a less flamboyant kind. He had preached the Coronation sermon for King George V in two minutes of classic phrase and golden oratory; alike at banquets, at memorial services, in pulpits and at the House

* The authority is again Driberg.

of Lords he aroused perpetual admiration for his command of phrases apt and fine. Taking by ancient right precedence of every peer of the realm except the Princes of the Blood, he was never unequal to the demands of his eminent role. Nurtured in simplicity, he had learnt in Oxford the ways, and attained in his cures of souls the aspect, of a supreme ecclesiastical aristocrat. He delighted day after day in the dignities proper to the Primate. A Frenchman said that "*Il assiste à sa vie comme à un spectacle*". It was also said that in his complex personality there were seven Archbishops and that one could hear almost with a click when one of these passed out for another to come in: for in one personage he was peer, prelate, hierophant, friend, counsellor, statesman or seer. Authority, urbanity, learning, experience, worldliness, wisdom, simplicity, and zeal in endless permutations, combinations and exchanges were at his command as occasion required.

His features were fine; he was a handsome man with a presence worthy of prelacy exalted.

In him gratified ambition and a polished knowledge of the world went with sincere goodness of heart, while vanity occasionally so mixed with his generosity as to array opinion against his judgment. This had once led to a ghastly shock breaking in on the imposing procession of his successes. In 1914 he dared to recall that, when thirteen years before the German Kaiser had knelt at the deathbed of Queen Victoria, he had seen him there. When, with the good object of tempering an orgy of fanatical fury, he called this "a very sacred personal memory," he had fanned the flame to such a degree that it scorched himself, and one might even say sizzled his hair. For the result was an attack of nervous trouble which upset his capillary glands and made him suddenly bald. Such can be the grim result of saying the right thing at the wrong time. It was a lesson not easy to forget —and the Archbishop was not prepared to hazard words at this juncture, though as one who had been long the adviser and confidant of King George and Queen Mary, their friend and their welcomed guest, he knew from them what other sources amply confirmed—that there was much that was dubious and difficult in him who had now become the supreme governor of the Church.

After one talk at Buckingham Palace with the new King just after his accession he had, of course, seen very plainly that he could not push his counsel further. That would have aggravated obstinacy and met with a rebuff. Any tentative feeler he had sent in that direction had warned him to be wary. The talk, frequently appearing in certain American newspapers, that he had refused to dine in the company of Mrs. Simpson was of course unscrupulous invention for the two simple reasons first, that the King had no inclination to invite him, and second, that he knew that neither personally nor officially could the Archbishop be won over to approving the Simpson project.

Archbishop Lang from boyhood in the streets of Glasgow and Mrs. Simpson from girlhood in those of Baltimore had so employed their talents as to have now become great luminaries in London. But though they moved there in hostile orbits it was at a distance which precluded personal collision. All that could be related was a moment at a London party when "The Bishop of Kensington and Mrs. Simpson" were announced, a moment very piquant, for not all remembered the Bishop's family name. But the Primate was deeply troubled. How much he regretted that so short had been the period when the jazz-boy Prince had undergone a sort of conversion, become High Church and sought a father confessor to give him absolution!

Walking warily, as the Archbishop was now doing, he was extremely annoyed when he read what Bishop Blunt had said at Bradford. It might have been a convenience to the Government, but it was not what he himself wanted. All the more because he agreed with every word of it, he feared that people would say that an impulse had been given—or at least that gossip had emanated—from Lambeth; and the last thing this episcopal courtier wanted was to lead a campaign on territory so slippery and ungaugeable.

As Colonel Wedgwood's motion in the House of Commons has suggested, the Archbishop was already in quandary enough with regard to the Coronation. He was not prepared to refuse to perform his part; he had no intention of resigning a role he loved, yet how repugnant it would be to administer a holy rite in circumstances that would make it a mockery near to sacrilege! What he wrote in his diary was "the thought of having to consecrate *him* as King weighed on me like a heavy burden". He was constantly being urged to do something, but he had hazarded no conclusion till the last moment when it hardly mattered.

On that Friday, 4th December, he lunched at the Swedish Legation to meet the Crown Prince of Sweden, who in a long talk spoke of his distress and his fears that the prestige of monarchy was being lowered in every country—as indeed it was. From the Swedish Legation the Archbishop went on to a talk with certain leaders of the Free Churches. Their view was that the mass of people would continue to support the Government, though a large proportion would sympathize with the man in love. "He is doing the honourable thing," they would say, "he wants to marry the woman he loves. Why not?" How many are those for whom sentiment rules decisions. And to how many, especially of the younger generation, the King was the paragon of men, the admired of all admirers as exemplar and mercury of a freer age, retaining even as he passed the age of forty the freshness, and the defiance, of youth!

But now after the Churchill broadcast the Archbishop decided that the time had come for him to break the complete silence of his caution and to give some hint to both the Court and to the nation of what in the eyes of a Primate the crisis asked. So he began:

"At this moment of deep anxiety and bewilderment in the public mind I venture to express two earnest hopes." His first hope was that those who had to speak over the weekend or on the Sunday would refrain from discoursing on the crisis that distracted them: the second that prayers would be offered not only in Churches but continually in the hearts of all Christian people that God might overrule in a momentous hour the decisions of both King and Government to the lasting good of the Realm and Empire. Between these sounding, yet very safe phrases, the Archbishop inserted a warning not less cautious. "Words spoken without knowledge of an extremely difficult situation can give no helpful guidance, and may instead only confuse thought and feeling."

Those were wise words. For London, even more than the world beyond it, was in tense excitement. The flight and whereabouts of Mrs. Simpson, the outpourings of Mr. Churchill and his allies (Lord Rothermere and Lady Houston, Bernard Shaw and Sir Oswald Mosley), the comings and goings of the great, with many details of the development of the whole affair and of the past of its protagonists were brought out by the news-papers in huge editions with enormous headlines. The whole of Britain, nay the wide world, was concentrated on the sensation. Gossip, comment and surmise, like the result of some porten-tous seismic convulsion, broiled through the country as from a chain of volcanoes which erupted from the bowels of the globe.

A day or two later this gossip, as we shall see, was to reach its most fantastic, because of a press report from four corres-pondents, a report to which the lady concerned herself gives prominence in her memoirs:

"Mrs. Simpson's solicitor Mr. Goddard, the well-known legal authority, has arrived in Cannes. With him is a well-known gynaecologist, and an anaesthetist."

CHAPTER XXXI

WHEN Mr. Churchill had finished at Fort Belvedere the presen-tation of his alluring phantasy, the King was left alone to cope with the gleaming prospects which had been so boldly depicted before his excited yet tired eyes.

He went up to his room to weigh once more those eloquent words which advised him to defy his Ministers. But, as he walked to and fro, his inner ear caught the echoes of another voice, the inner voice from on high, the voice in which a mighty angel counsels the hearts of kings.

It was, he tells us, a night of soul-searching. Here Churchill had been urging him to wait and manoeuvre, here were the young people ready to hold firm to the object of their admiration, here were the two Press Lords with their popular papers, backed too by Lady Houston, and by Sir Oswald Mosley with his blackshirts—all combining to make a King's party and urging him to cling on and urge his case.

But, as the hours wore on, the fundamental instinct of loyalty and reason was again lord of his choice. How could he engage in stratagems against his Government and his Prime Minister? If he did, then, as Baldwin had said, he would divide the Commonwealth. He believed indeed still, and was long to believe, that if he allowed his friends to organize their propaganda, he would carry with him a majority—but even so, only at the cost of a deadly quarrel with the rest. He could not finally bring himself to do battle as ally of Mr. Winston Churchill and Sir Oswald Mosley, of Lady Houston and Mr. Rowse against so warm a friend as the Prime Minister, against whom these factions were now organizing their melodramatic propaganda, now with the cry,

> One, two, three, four, five,
> We want Baldwin, dead or alive

now with sandwich-men and fascist women bearing the device

GOD SAVE THE KING
FROM BALDWIN

Of such things the rumour came to him: they suggested that civil war might not stop just with words if armed fascists were to clash with others. Was he then to come forward with the trained bands of blackshirts at his back to do battle with his Prime Minister? God forbid. Was he to shatter the Crown which, with its jewelled circlet, symbolized the Divine authority of law and government above the legitimate contest of Parliament? Was he to raise the woman he loved to share a throne which faced invidious and angry question—was that to bring them happiness?

"This," he said in touching words, "was the question I answered in my soul that night. The answer was NO."

That, as far as he was concerned, was the end of the temptation set before him by misguided friends. He put their contentions, with Satan, behind him. And at last he slept.

When he saw Monckton next morning—it was now Saturday, 5th December—he gave instructions that the Prime Minister should be informed that the business of the afternoon would be formally to prepare for the Abdication. When he saw his lawyer, it was to ask for a courier to prepare him rooms in Switzerland.

Monckton, from the beginning, had done all he could to help the King; but he had seen that the abdication was the only alternative to renouncing Mrs. Simpson. He therefore was ready, as soon as the King arrived at a similar conclusion, to point out what it meant. The first was that the King must make practical plans with due resources: the second that he should do nothing to complicate the affair of the divorce which was now being shaken by a number of witnesses who spoke of coming forward with charges of collusion. None wanted the King to give up the throne for Mrs. Simpson only to find that by doing so he would be no nearer to marrying her. This point, which had been forced hard on the attention of his entourage very soon after the divorce, was now being pressed so hard that Mrs. Simpson's solicitor, as we saw, was being compelled to act. Indeed this danger had become so pressing that Monckton was forced to devise an expedient that would safeguard a ticklish situation and at the same time provide that when the King left England he should have the companionship and support he so eagerly coveted. As some had cherished the phantasy of the Dominion parliaments passing a series of bills for morganatic marriage, so it was now proposed to Baldwin that he should place before the House of Commons a proposal that was hardly more likely to commend itself to public opinion: this was a special Simpson Bill to allow the lady to shorten her decree *nisi* from six months to six weeks, counting from the date, 27th October, when she had obtained it from Mr. Justice Hawke at Ipswich. Those six weeks were already almost complete.

This meant that Saturday, 5th December, was a day of extreme pressure for Baldwin and for his chief legal adviser, Sir John Simon. On the one hand they had to prepare the act of Abdication: on the other they had to examine the question of the special Simpson Bill. As far as the Bill was concerned, it did not in itself violate any legal principle. Indeed the time was not far off when a period of six weeks would be all that the general law would require to complete a decree *nisi*. Monckton now arranged to discuss it with the two men who were acting as immediate advisers and agents for Baldwin: his Parliamentary Private Secretary, Major Thomas Dugdale, and his financial adviser, Sir Horace Wilson. He arranged to meet them at lunch in a club in St. James's Square. With them also was Sir Godfrey

Thomas who had had very little news of what was happening.

Monckton explained that he had been finding his complex and delicate task so difficult that his own nerves were getting worn out. To have to cope with the moods and demands of the King for practically every hour he was not conferring with the Prime Minister or the Government and to find that Edward VIII was determined to marry Mrs. Simpson as soon as possible, this was the experience which must have worn any mind, no matter how strong and how urbane. The natural tendency of Mr. Monckton's mind was to suit itself to the demands of clients: it was his special gift to be agreeable. But like Baldwin, he could not allow amiability to throw dust in the eyes of those who had to face the edge of the precipice.

He found the help he needed in Sir Horace Wilson, seconded to the Treasury and in actual fact a Special Secretary to the Prime Minister. Sir Horace owed his high position to something he shared with Baldwin's other special private adviser, Dr. Thomas Jones. They were both so full of heart, so shrewd, so well-informed, so well able to see the other man's point of view, and so, like Ernest Bevin, skilful at resolving clangour into harmonies. They both knew of Baldwin's intense sympathy with the King, his allowance for the claims of a tormented heart, his generosity to the lady in the matter of her divorce. So, when Sir Horace Wilson heard of the new proposal, he at once applied to it his arts of conciliation, and set to work on yet another compromise. He did so with especial sympathy for the harassing ordeal of the King's representative, and with a desire to meet his needs as well as those of the situation in general. Like the Prime Minister, whose mind he reflected, he was anxious to meet the King's wishes and proposal in any way they found practicable. He and Dugdale were quick to realize how sad and lonely the exile would be if he were out of the country and cut off from the companionship he craved; as much from personal sympathy as from a desire to eliminate any possibility of further complications, they immediately took up with a will, and with real sympathy, Monckton's ingenious proposal for this Simpson Bill. Sir Horace Wilson was so alive to the convenience it offered that he would be ready to do all possible to have it put forward in an acceptable way. The more awkward side of the proposal was to negotiate public opinion. Dugdale, as a Member of Parliament, was sufficiently close to the feeling of constituents to sense that any special concession to Mrs. Simpson would be indignantly resisted. When Baldwin consulted Simon, he too was warned that though the legal difficulties were not insuperable, to offer so large a concession to a woman who was already the object of such hostile comment was hardly likely to appeal to the Cabinet as a whole. Simon was not the only strong Free Churchman in the Cabinet: there were also Ramsay MacDonald, Kingsley Wood, Neville Chamberlain, and Walter Runciman to represent what Lord Kemsley had called the Nonconformist conscience. In that Cabinet also was such a leading Churchman as Lord Halifax. Nor was he alone, for there was also Sir Samuel Hoare. There was also the devout Low Churchman, Sir Thomas Inskip. It was not, therefore, a Cabinet which was likely to be accommodating to irregular love.

This then was one complex affair which Baldwin that Saturday had to discuss with Simon and Donald Somervell, the Attorney-General. The other was the actual arrangements for the Abdication for which the King had now given his definite instructions. Altogether that day Baldwin was in consultation with Simon for seven hours, as well as presiding at a Cabinet meeting at ten-thirty to endorse arrangements for the Abdication.

When law officers of the State set to work on that, they found their task weighted by the fact that they must work without a precedent; they must be not less careful about the precedent they were to establish. It was soon decided that when a King abdicates he gives up all the royal rights he has possessed, all his emoluments, privileges and titles, with those also of the Duchy of Cornwall. The Abdication meant legally the 'Demise of the Crown'.

In other words, the Sovereign abdicating must surrender every right and claim as completely as he would in dying: Jonathan Swift had correctly noted that a Prince's abdication could make no other sort of vacancy than would be caused by his death. By abdication, therefore, King Edward would become simply a royal prince, entirely dependent on his successor for all except his private possessions. He would not even have the right to marry: because by the Act of 1772, as we have seen, no Prince of the Blood could make a valid marriage without the Sovereign's permission. Nor would it be too easy for a new King to give this permission for it would violate the laws of the Church which any King in his coronation oath must swear to maintain. The more closely the legal authorities examined the situation, the more clearly they saw that they could not link the Abdication with a bargain made on the King's behalf.

If he wanted to go because his personal sense of obligation conflicted with his royal duties then he must go *unconditionally*. No matter how accommodating and sympathetic Baldwin might feel, he came at this point up against legal principles on which no legal authority could offer any compromise. This was the point to which he had ever again to adjust his plans in the seven hours of discussion which he had with Sir John Simon in the course of that exhausting day, a day which involved as much strain for him as the preceding one had done for the King. As for Walter Monckton, he had to manage the King at the same time as he conferred with the members of the Government, who when they looked at the new proposal felt they did not like it.

When therefore in the late afternoon of that heavy winter day Baldwin drove out once more to Fort Belvedere, he had no dainty dish to set before the King. Hardly had he entered than Monckton, who but an hour or two earlier had met Baldwin's secretaries at lunch and found them sympathetic, came in to speak direct of the project he had fathered—he wanted to secure Baldwin's personal support. Baldwin was so tired and so worn by the complexities which the day had already brought that he took the same line as Sir Horace Wilson had already done. At the end of the talk the Prime Minister and the King's lawyer went in through the darkness to London to press the proposal that the two Bills—one for Abdication, one for shortening the period required to make the decree absolute should be passed together. Baldwin accordingly called a meeting of important Ministers (it was not actually a Cabinet meeting) for the following morning, Sunday, at ten-thirty.

When Baldwin put before those Ministers the proposal he had so kindly taken up the evening before, he found that Simon had not exaggerated the weight of what people were apt to call the Nonconformist conscience, but which was the normal reaction of British morality. The time came when Baldwin actually found that the meeting was slipping from his control. One Minister after another insisted that he could not possibly support such a suggestion. These men knew already how fierce had been the reactions of the masses against Mrs. Simpson. Was the Government now to come before Parliament with the proposal that she should have a special bill to rush with a haste never yet permitted from one marriage to another? Up to then, they had kept from the papers any imputation of scandal in the King's irregular love for her: there had been no reflections on her own past and character. On that *The Times* had been particularly precise. But how could the public continue to gloss over the suspicion of misconduct if the immediate result of the Abdication was to place the departing King at once in the arms of a woman who at that moment was, and must for four months longer normally remain, the wife of another man? One member of the Cabinet after another spoke strongly in this sense. It was only when Baldwin came into agreement with them to remind them of his own standards of morals that he regained control over his team.

When the meeting had come to this decision, the Prime

Minister invited Monckton, who had been waiting in an ante-room, to come in and join it. It was then explained to him that his project must be dropped. It was put to him that it looked too much as though over the Abdication a bargain had been driven: also that it must offend the moralists, and throw a doubt on the stand the Government had been compelled to make.

Monckton was disappointed. He saw that yet more difficult tasks were to confront his exhausted energies. He was by no means certain that the King would stick to his decision to abdicate if that would not take him quickly to the woman he wanted. So he said that the King would probably go back to Churchill's particular plea and demand more time.

"How much ?" asked Ramsay MacDonald. "How many days ?"

Monckton's answer—"not days but weeks"—gave yet another indication of the way the King's mind was playing with the very debate which the Government felt it was their first obligation to avoid. It was not only the Government. By none was the Churchill proposal for a long discussion rejected with more skilful energy than by the Liberal agnostic, J. A. Spender. He was soon to publish his answer to the adjurations with which the ebullience of Mr. Winston Churchill had beguiled the King, to let the battalions march.

"Five months in which the King would be making up his mind in a blaze of publicity, and enterprising newspapers all over the world would be in eager competition to feed the appetite for sensation with rumours, true or false, about the state of his mind and the whereabouts and doings of the lady! Five months in which business would be held up, and the public mind distracted and politics being held in suspense by the possibility of a crisis between the government and the Crown. Five months of agitated canvassing for votes on one side or the other! This spectacle might be profoundly interesting to spectators like Mr. Shaw who like to see apple carts upset, but where, at the end of it all, would be the unity of Empire and Commonwealth, or even of the British people in allegiance to the throne ? . . .

"What is at issue is not this or that opinion about the desir-ability of the marriage in question, but the unity of the Country, Commonwealth and Empire."

Knowing this, the Cabinet had to turn to Monckton's new plea for time a deaf ear, and Monckton to preparing the King for some lonely months.

CHAPTER XXXII

THERE would be a lacuna in the story of the reign if nothing were told of how, apart from those who came into contact with the King, the papers and leisure of that Sunday played their part in the heart and mind of the whole people. For all were absorbed in the drama which only three days before had been disclosed to national discussion and which was now hastening from its hidden movement and heat to that series of seismic explosions which now struck and shocked the country.

Before the meeting of the Cabinet the Sunday papers had come out with an obvious intention to keep the public informed, and passionately occupied, over the weekend. With their pages recalling the week's happenings in detail, and many of them recounting what they knew of the King's past, as well, of course, as that which they had gradually been accumulating of that of Mrs. Simpson, the whole country buzzed with talk, and with views as families and groups huddle, by their firesides in the frosty weather. The day before that, Christmas shopping seemed out of place. Trade had been at a standstill, the shops losing millions of pounds. And this added its own weight in certain quarters to a crisis which in itself was all-absorbing.

Some recalled how the Archbishop of Canterbury had called them to prayer. At his request nothing was said of the crisis in Anglican pulpits—a good deal, however, was said in those of the Free Churches. Much of the discussion could again best be summed up in the words of J. A. Spender, which were the more telling that he was neither a supporter of the Government nor a believer in any form of Christianity. After referring to the fact that there would be no objection to the King marrying a commoner, even of comparatively humble status, he went on: "The marriage of the Sovereign to a woman who had two divorced husbands living raises an extremely different question. Beyond doubt it would cause a deep offence to immense numbers, including a great many who would raise no objection if it were a private individual. A public challenge would be thrown to religious susceptibilities, which, however obsolete they may be considered in this modern world, still have a strong hold on a great multitude. Many others would feel a sense of indignity offered to the great tradition of the Crown."

And then, referring to the dangerous controversy which has already been mentioned and which would involve the Government, the Church, the Monarchy and the Marriage Laws, and bring them all into relation with one person and one instance, he said that no Government could take the responsibility of exposing monarchy and empire to so dangerous a hazard.

Of course in the leisure of that Sunday many a voice was heard on the other side. It was not only the young who said "Let the King do as he likes!" Many a mother, many a maiden lady had thought of him as her heart's desire and given him a loyal love akin to worship. One of these wrote: "I for one will *never* acknowledge any other King while King Edward lives. I will recognize the woman he chooses for his wife as his Queen Consort. Let him who is without sin in any way cast a stone at the King." Those words were echoed in many a heart that day. Loyalty to him was so affectionate, in fact, that it was prepared to follow him whithersoever he went—to accept any choice without question provided it were his.

Others argued again less sentimentally, that, if the old standards of indissoluble marriage had been relaxed for the state, the King should certainly not be forced to conform to standards other than those of the law of the land. But others made the point that whereas those who did not care for the throne did not exact particular standards those who most honoured it with passionate loyalty demanded it should correspond with their highest ideals. Some questioned whether the choice were prudent. Was the King-Emperor of such vast dominions to be third husband to a woman who had twice failed to retain the fidelity of her spouse?

And then there were many who reflected on the principles of the Bible. Many recalled the Anglican Church and its law. Others remembered the vow the King had so lately taken in the House of Lords to be a faithful Protestant. Could a faithful Protestant flout his own Church? As one wrote to *The Times*, "If the King marries a *divorcée* without the sanction of the Church, of which he is defender, how can he retain his holy office of Kingship, having just infringed the regulations that he is supposed to enforce, or at least uphold?" That was the question uppermost in the minds not only of the Bishops, but of most sincere Christians. And, as we have seen, there was not much difference between it and the attitude of the agnostic Liberal, J. A. Spender.

Indeed this moral assessment was what proved strongest in the country, especially as Baldwin and Attlee had foreseen, in the provinces. The result was that when Members of the House of Commons came back to Westminster on the Monday morning from their country constituencies, there was a distinct hardening of opinion. It proved how right the Cabinet had been in its decision on the Sunday morning about the Simpson Bill which Monckton had suggested. The country would not have stood it. On this subject Lord Dalton* was particularly precise. "The Welsh miners," he wrote, "all deeply disapproved of the proposed marriage. Many strong words, even jeering words, were spoken against the King. The women were more emphatic and bitter than the men. The King they said was letting them all down by wanting to marry a woman like Mrs. Simpson." In Co. Durham also, he heard blunt words about her record. Besides, it would never have done either for the Government to lay themselves open to the charge that they had one law for the rich and another for the poor. Such had been indeed the reflection with which some had come out from the meeting of the Cabinet. General opinion was not less decisive on the question of the morganatic marriage. This view of Mrs. Simpson's hopes was stated cogently in *The Times* by Monckton's own college friend, Robin Barrington-Ward. "Is the constitution to be amended," he asked, "in order that she may carry in solitary prominence the brand of unfitness for the Queen's throne? Can anyone in the possession of his faculties imagine any Prime Minister moving, or any Parliament undertaking to support a provision so invidious and so distressing?" Barrington-Ward's question at this juncture did but echo in more forensic style the contention made in the *Daily Herald* by the Labour Member, Ellen Wilkinson.

The only prominent men who came forward as supporters of 'The Simpson Press' were the two men so opposed as Sir Oswald Mosley and Sir Stafford Cripps. This led to the statement that this support came from the 'worst sort of reaction'. In *The Times* it was termed "The foolish and deplorable project of misguided ingenuity". Let the King decide for himself.

And indeed, as we have seen, answering all these debates in his own soul, he had decided, and nobly decided.

Coming back to Westminster, with their opinions thus stiffened by the tonic of provincial opinion, Members of the House of Commons had made up their minds that the time had come to act with unity, swiftness and decision. The throne was now quivering beneath its occupant in the vast tremor and upheaval of subterranean fire and electric agitation which disturbed the Empire in its widths and depths. The time had passed when the promoters of 'A KING'S PARTY' could continue their endeavour to settle the restless occupant on its cold and uneasy stone. When therefore in the afternoon Mr. Churchill rose to press a motion which had already been twice rejected it was not surprising that he was howled down.

Members, having had their opportunities to read his printed statement on the Saturday, with its implication that he was acting as the King's advocate, had already been annoyed. He the

* Then the Rt. Hon. Hugh Dalton.

King's advocate! He the representative of the Court in the House of Commons! But a Member of the House was Vice-Chamberlain of the Royal Household as Lord Cromer was its Chamberlain in the House of Lords. It was the duty of the Vice-Chamberlain to inform the King night by night in a letter by hand of proceedings in Parliament. It was for the Vice-Chamberlain to bring to the Prime Minister any message from His Majesty. For Churchill to speak as the King's representative was therefore not in order. When he rose to speak his old friend, George Lambert, who was sitting beside him, tried to pull him down but he insisted on rising to press a point which had already been twice disposed of. The Speaker protested. But Mr. Churchill was in a fighting mood quelled only by the demeanour of the House which met him with cries of "Sit down!" and "Shut up!" His wild gesticulations were made in vain. His voice was drowned.

His reputation with all parties had fallen low when he was fighting the India Bills. It fell much lower now. His valiant battles for defence, his sounding eloquence were forgotten, and Members made their rash prophecy that never again would he have their respect! "Churchill," they said, "is finished." This also had its effect on international politics—for when Hitler heard later of his contentions he dismissed them with the words: "Churchill, a man whom England despises." This was one curious but important repercussion of this melodramatic reign.

In spite of this and the uncompromising attitude of the vast majority of the people to the idea of still according their loyalty not only to the throne but to the person of His Majesty, and from the Cabinet downwards still desired that he would make the choice which would re-establish the mutual attachment between him and his countless subjects.

Surely, they still said, he could give up this affair with Mrs. Simpson.

Or, if he could not, WOULD NOT SHE?

CHAPTER XXXIII

THE picture in Mrs. Simpson's mind after her arrival in Cannes has been painted by herself. We can see therefore pretty clearly from day to day how her thoughts were turning. One thing was uppermost in them—that she did not wish to push the King off his throne, and that she remained really disturbed by the amount of censure which she knew the King's most enthusiastic subjects were visiting on her own character and conduct. Before such expression of public opinion her courage failed.

But apart from what she herself discloses of her mind, the Government had at its disposal a close report, prepared by secret agents, of her long telephone talks with the King. Baldwin was averse to taking cognizance of these. And to tell the truth certain agents of the government acted independently of his instructions. Their reasons were two: first that the secret service had been for some time keeping close track of Mrs. Simpson, comparing her moves from day to day with what they knew of her previous record. The second was that for some time the domestic staff at Buckingham Palace had become so nervous of what was happening that they too kept the King's political advisers informed of what they thought was essential to the safety of their master and their country. Thus it was that through telephone operators, certain of Baldwin's advisers—though not at his orders —were aware of what advice Mrs. Simpson at this juncture was giving to the King.

Meanwhile in Cannes one of Mrs. Simpson's thoughts was that of a practical woman. The King had large sums banked which could be made available to him anywhere.

Not all of these investments were in his name. A number were in hers. Some inkling of this fact had got through to the staff at the time of the earliest retrenchments of the reign and given rise to the accusation that the King was cutting down on his Civil List in order to hand over the result to his favourite. It can be authoritatively stated that there is no ground for this suspicion. Simple business caution had been one reason for the early retrenchments. The sums that the King had placed at the disposal of Mrs. Simpson, though not inconsiderable, were never sequestrations from official funds; the sums he placed at her disposal were from his personal capital. In this the King maintained an impeccable standard of honour.

His minority, joined with the fact that the war had prevented him from quickly setting up a household, had combined with his natural acumen and the help of expert advisers to secure him in young manhood a fund of private capital from the economies of the funds of the Duchy of Cornwall which became his in 1911. To these he added the estates of Sandringham and Balmoral which at his father's death he inherited as personal possessions. Since these went to him as King, who must also have the large funds of the Civil List, George V had not bequeathed to him any sums by his own will. Those had gone in the main part to other children of the King, who were both on better terms with their father and who needed more as private supplement to what the State allowed them. But even so Edward VIII could contemplate abdication without qualms for his immediate comfort. All this Mrs. Simpson knew; but she was most anxious that the King should make all possible provision

180

for his future before he gave up the throne, if he gave it up at all. That she still thought could be avoided.

She was not the only person who thought in similar terms. Once it was clear to Beaverbrook that the country would not tolerate a King who was Mrs. Simpson's avowed husband whether she was Queen or not, he, desiring that his friend should not lose the throne, he wanted to bring pressure to bear on Mrs. Simpson. The loyalty of Lord Brownlow moved in the same direction. So in the course of that Monday, 7th December, it was gradually decided at Cannes that Mrs. Simpson should issue a statement that she was prepared to give the King up. On the Monday evening, at 'Lou Viei' Lord Brownlow read it to the reporters. It ran as follows:

"Mrs. Simpson throughout the last few weeks has invariably wished to avoid any action or proposal which would hurt or damage His Majesty on the throne.

"Today her attitude is unchanged, and she is willing, if such action would solve the problem, to withdraw from a situation which is unhappy and untenable." What is certain is that she was both in a state of panic and really intended to give up the King. She writes that she feared that if she expressed herself more strongly she would wound him she most wanted to help and to spare. Lord Brownlow adds that she gravely underestimated the King's pertinacity and overwhelming devotion.

As soon as her message reached Downing Street, it provoked the most earnest consideration. Did she really intend to save her lover at such cost to herself? If so, an acid proof could be immediately applied: would she give up the decree *nisi*? The only way to probe this question would be through her solicitor, Goddard. So he was immediately summoned to Downing Street for enquiry whether he would go and visit Mrs. Simpson at Cannes. As a matter of fact, he was already planning to do so, for the reason that the recurring threats of evidence of collusion had now taken the definite form of an 'Appearance' at Somerset House. That meant that a certain Francis Stephenson who lived at Ilford in Essex and who was a solicitor's clerk of seventy-four years of age had intervened with the assertion that he had reason to show why Mrs. Simpson's decree should not be confirmed. Of this the solicitor of the party affected had to be informed and he in turn was bound to report it to his client.

As soon as the King had wind of this he tried to prevent Goddard going. But by the evening of Tuesday, 8th December, Goddard was at 10 Downing Street. Baldwin saw that he had found a valuable ally.

Goddard at once agreed to go to Cannes and was flattered to hear that the Prime Minister would place a private aeroplane at his disposal. But with that came a difficulty, for his doctor had warned him that his heart was weak, and that he should not fly unless in the presence of a doctor who could give him any treatment that would prove necessary. Dugdale at this point had to look round for a doctor who was at that moment free to take the trip. Chance fell on a specialist in maternity cases who was, of course, perfectly able at the same time to take any necessary steps in dealing with the diagnosis and treatment of any strain on the heart that flying might cause. Those who made the arrangements for engaging him knew only that he was a qualified medical practitioner. It was not until his arrival at Cannes that the exact field of his special medical skill became known. But once it was known, it inevitably aroused the curiosity of the besieging journalists, and in a short time was reported in newspapers in widely different parts of the world.

Goddard's special task was first to warn his client of serious impediments which had come in the way of the decree *nisi* being made absolute. It was also to ascertain if her offer to withdraw from the situation which menaced the stability of the King on his throne meant that she would herself take steps not to proceed towards completing the decree, a step which was still open to her choice. By this time Baldwin attached the greatest importance to having this guarantee. Some information had reached his agents that there was a possibility of Mrs. Simpson withdrawing for the time in order that she might again appear on the scene when she and her admirer should deem the chances more propitious. If, however, she were still the legal wife of another, his government could face the future with comparative equanimity. Into this task Goddard threw himself with zeal.

His client to whom we are indebted for the fullest account of what next happened is perforce silent about this side of her interview with her solicitor. His report was that he found her not as in former times with zest for battle, but in a state of nerves, cowed and capitulating at every point to what he required. This she corroborates. Both sides agree that the difficulty came from the telephone at Fort Belvedere.

The first thing to deal with, however, was the story being prepared by the reporters whose avidity, so long kept in suspense, had now been fed with the most succulent viands. Mrs. Simpson's lawyer had arrived and with a gynaecologist! What implications! And to complete those how easy to transform Goddard's clerk into an anaesthetist! No, in all the wild gossip which the affair had caused and the sensation it had made none had for a moment hinted that the cause of her flight was what the present surmise entertained. It reduced the whole story to the lowest, crudest levels. And Lord Brownlow was at once sensitive to the effect this would have on the honour and dignity, already compromised enough, of his royal master. He must take every precaution that the journalists should make no more capital out of it. Loyalty itself, he was also profoundly concerned for the good name of the King's friend.

But to know Mrs. Simpson was to realize that one of her many attractions was a mischievous sense of humour which was never abashed at strong flavours. She dilates on this incident.

So anxious, however, was Lord Brownlow to give no further gobbets to the greed of the journalists who now, like vultures, swooped down on the purlieus of the villa for succulent meals, that he insisted that when Goddard arrived he should carry nothing that could look like a bag of surgical instruments, and that he should descend from his car well outside the gates so that every journalist could ascertain that this was so.

Therefore they must perforce realize that the operation Goddard had come to perform was not obstetric but legal. It was soon completed. Mrs. Simpson, as we saw, was in no fighting mood.

As soon as this proposal reached the ears of Fort Belvedere it was rejected incontinent. Allen spoke on the telephone to inform her that the Instruments of Abdication were already prepared. Later she spoke to the King himself saying that she had decided to give him up. He would not listen. He repeated that the arrangements for Abdication were complete. He was perfectly plain that the idea of a compromise and of playing for time were not such as he could any longer support. "The only conditions on which I can stay here," he said, "are if I renounce you for all time, and this of course I will not do." The King set this down in writing, and read it over the telephone. When he had laid down the receiver, his solicitor took it up and repeated it with emphasis. The lover had one aim and object immeasurably dearer than any other: it was to be with her and to be hers as soon as he could. No alternative plans, financial or other, weighed with him in the scales. He could no more think of giving her up than he could have carried on with the Government under the pretence that he had done so.

"I loved her so desperately," he says. It was, to tell the truth, a little more desperately than she thought prudence at the moment required. She had also been pressing that he should get an extra allowance of £25,000 a year from the Government; it was supported by his staff; but Baldwin, warned by his secret advisers that the request would be put forward in his next interview with the King, had to steel himself against it. He had learnt in his Cabinet meeting of the Sunday that he could wring no personal concessions of any kind from his Cabinet. But he knew only too well how desperate was the King's passion, and he was touched. He told his family that when the lover spoke of his love, his face had an expression of such beauty as if a young

Arthurian knight, a Galahad, were charging in white armour, with before him a vision of the Holy Grail and never again "would follow wandering fires". No reasoning, no pleading by his own family or by friendly counsellors could penetrate that "rapturous mist". With this dim brilliance on his inward vision, as mist and fog that evening hid the scenes of earth around Windsor and his home, the King read the precise phrasing of the Act of Abdication. He certainly meant to be straight with the Government and finish the thing once and for all.

Beaverbrook, it appears, had not kept closely enough in touch with the King to follow the dictates of this rapturous passion. When the news of Mrs. Simpson's withdrawal reached Fleet Street, the Beaverbrook papers brought out on their headlines the words

END OF THE CRISIS

The crisis was ending, but not in the sense that Beaverbrook had appeared to be supporting.

Nevertheless, the impressions left by his papers and that fact that the 'appearance' made by Francis Stephenson at Somerset House might persuade the King's solicitor to advise him to stay the Abdication lest he might fail to accomplish his legal union with Mrs. Simpson made Baldwin fear that the King's decision would waver at the last moment, a decision which had been all that week the prey of fractured nerves and panic alternations of agreement with impulses of desperation. Baldwin's feeling at that juncture was perhaps best summed up in three words that had escaped him the last time he had been driven away from Fort Belvedere. They were simply "Poor little devil!"

Full of sympathy for one whom he knew to be feeling a strain to which his resistance was unequal, Baldwin decided to go back on the Tuesday evening to Fort Belvedere, and thinking he might not bring calm to a troubled mind till the hours wore on, he gave instructions that his suitcases should accompany him so that he should be ready for an emergency. Baldwin had had a letter from Churchill saying that the King was in no fit state to voice a decision and that to extort one would be cruel and wrong. This had led to a rumour that the doctors were about to certify that the King was too ill for business. In any case it might mean that his will was again swithering. "I was frightened," said Baldwin. "I thought he might change his mind." He said that the King would probably have to wrestle with himself in a way he had never done before. "We may even have to see the night through together." It was still Baldwin's conviction that the final decision which the King claims in his narrative had been made in the hours after Churchill had left him was not yet decisive, if made at all. Such was the impression forced upon him by what he had heard from those of the communications which had passed with Mrs. Simpson, by Monckton's pressure for delay, and what he had himself observed of the restless and excited state of a worn man's nerves which were not too steady at the best of times. That was why he with his Parliamentary Private Secretary, Major Dugdale, drove down on the evening of Tuesday, 8th December to spend the evening—and if need were, the night—with the harassed King.

CHAPTER XXXIV

BALDWIN had hardly met His Majesty than he discovered that in spite of the extreme state of nerves in which "the little man", —as he so often called the object of his solicitude—had passed the day he was now perfectly clear that he intended to go through with the arrangements that had been already made. This was to Baldwin an immense relief. He would not need to wrestle through the night after all. The King reports that he had no intention of inviting him to do so, and this is not surprising. Although Baldwin had made the extremest efforts to meet every desire of the King, yet he had, as events proved, been obliged to veto each of the proposals made to him: the morganatic marriage, the broadcast, and the Simpson Bill.

These vetos might well have been regarded by Mrs. Simpson as acts of personal hostility which had been cleverly contrived to outwit the King at every turn. But the King's mind simply could not grasp the truth that he and Mrs. Simpson had so acted as to alienate public opinion and especially that of the Cabinet as a whole, strengthened as that was by the repercussion of feeling from the provinces over the weekend. No, she preferred to think it must all be Baldwin; so that is how he chose to set it down in his memoirs. "How lonely," he complained, "is a modern monarch in a struggle with a shrewd Prime Minister backed by all the apparatus of a modern state." But even those who were closest to him at the time of the Abdication were amazed by the tone in which his book spoke of Baldwin. Nothing he said at the actual time gave any hint of such feelings even to his closest friends.

He did not find him alone; his two brothers, the Duke of York, and the Duke of Kent, were there making the arrangements that must swiftly follow for signing the Act of Abdication and preparing for what would follow it. It was already the intention of the Duke of York to do all possible for the dignity of a brother with whom he had always been on good terms and whose versatility and liveliness he had envied and admired.

Major Dugdale, however, found the Duke of Kent astounded and dismayed at the point to which things had gone. He could not believe that his brother would give up such a heritage for such a cause.

He made violent complaints of how Mrs. Simpson had kept the King apart from his family. This, he said, was the first time the three brothers had been alone together for three years.

If the King had then any suspicions of Baldwin, he showed no sign of them. His dinner invitation sounded pleasant and cordial, and when after a bath he finally appeared at the table, he gave not the slightest sign of being either worried or embarrassed. He kept up a continual flow of sparkling conversation, which turned often to South America. The Duke of York was amazed. "Look at the way he carries it off," he said. "Isn't my brother wonderful, isn't he wonderful?" None of those at the table referred once to the reason of their meeting.

But although the King's demeanour was at that moment so gay that he left the Prime Minister with the impression that he really cared about nothing as long as he could leap all obstacles to his union with his adored, the King, on the other hand, could not help seeing how strained, how weary, how pale Baldwin was, and realized how much the whole affair had been costing to the heart as well as to the conscience of his Prime Minister.

Baldwin took his leave very soon after they rose from the table. And at that moment the King did find an opportunity to revert to the reason of the visit. He wanted to say some words of appreciation. So, "I know," he said, "that you and Mrs. Baldwin do not approve of what I am doing, but I belong to a different generation."

The old man's heart was wrung and in vibrant tones he answered: "Sir, it is quite true that there are no two people among your subjects who are more grieved at what has happened than we are, but you must always remember that there are no two people who hope more sincerely that you may find happiness where you believe it is to be found."

"Oh," answered the King in tones hardly less warm, "you are the only two people who have been around me in these last months to show that you really cared about my happiness." Of course those words, no matter how warm their tone at the time, were not literally true. Many around the King knew his struggle and cared for his happiness. But perhaps none had expressed their wish so warmly.

A day or two later Mrs. Baldwin wrote an affectionate letter, and when she had finished it added the words: "God grant him peace and happiness, but never understanding of what he has lost!"

In the House of Commons a day later Baldwin said of his

relations with his Sovereign: "It was not only between man and man a friendship of affection. I would like to tell the House that when we said goodbye to each other on Tuesday night at Fort Belvedere, we both knew, and felt and said to each other that that friendship, so far from being impaired by our discussions of the last week, bound us more closely together and would last for life." So much from Baldwin. It is the simple truth. As long as he lived no word of disagreement came from the other side. Before leaving England a few days later the King wrote a letter in his own hand in the warmest tones of appreciation. This letter remains in Baldwin's family. And, as has been said, it is in this tone he spoke to his closest friends at the time.

When Baldwin spoke, the King was well aware of what he said. But the King did not write till Baldwin was dead. How is it then that when *A King's Story* appeared a few years after Baldwin's death there is such a sharply etched account of the struggle of the worried monarch with a cunning strategist, as though in Baldwin he had always discerned not the heart of a friend, but the fang of a serpent?

The explanation is not too difficult. By that time the reputation of Baldwin had fallen, while that of Churchill had soared into an ether where it was invulnerable. So it had become easy to secure conviction for a story in which poor old Baldwin could be put on the stage to play the villain. Then by that time the writer had been married for fifteen years, and under the influence of the lady against whom Baldwin had undoubtedly been engaged; though in the end she had won a chief objective of her ambition, Baldwin had represented the pressure of the forces which made it impossible to attain its acme.

But no matter how affectionately King and Minister might speak to one another in taking farewell, there had been, even then, contending urges. In the one, royal obligations ingrained fought with the will to get all possible for a woman who wanted it; in the other, regard for the honour of the Crown wrestled with solicitude for a beloved figure. Courtesy did not belie sincerity when at the time they spoke of their warm feeling for each other. But in their aims for the future of Mrs. Simpson they were, none the less, at daggers drawn. One eagerly desired to have her Queen of England: the other was determined to prevent that.

A King's Story records the resentment of a thwarted pair after many years of married life had done their work in affecting his memory. It is therefore unfair to Baldwin, to Lang and to *The Times*. For the same reason it fails to record how Sir Winston Churchill had the support of Sir Stafford Cripps and Sir Oswald Mosley; and gives no hint of the way that Lord Monckton proved invaluable to the Prime Minister. The wholeness and balance of the truth would have marred the case he wanted to present. But in point of fact he was perfectly sincere in both the courteous and grateful words he addressed to the Prime Minister at the time and in the bitter ones he wrote after the Minister's death for his book: the former expresses the chivalry of his royal duties; the latter the pull of that personal passion to which, as he persuaded himself, every other claim should give way.

Most of those who were close to Baldwin understood and sympathized with the King: the further away they were the more they tended to be severe. Here and there in the Dominions they spoke of the prestige he had lost but what is most remarkable in the papers, especially in *The Times*, is the note of respectful sympathy. They passed no moral judgment, they realized like Baldwin that the King's dilemma was an affair of the heart on which it would be cruel to speak. "No word," said *The Times*, "has been penned without bitter distress of heart, and none without deep human sympathy for a man placed—as is every man at some time of his life—in the necessity of choosing between contradictory loyalties, both of which are entitled to command his conscience."

But when Baldwin was assessing the situation he could not disregard the warnings which from the beginning of the reign had reached him from the Royal Household, complaints of eccentricity, whimsicality, extravagance. All through his bachelor life, the King had woken little love in his domestic staff, and when three days later he left England not even his valet went with him. It is plain from *The Heart Has Its Reasons* that the lady was well aware of the extent to which this feeling had been extended to herself, and certainly she is under no delusion. As we have seen, they believed that it was she who was the reason why there had been cuts in staff and wages.

They also disliked her American innovations. But above all they resented the hurt she had brought on the household in which they had originally been so proud to serve.

Of this there has never been a hint in any English newspaper. There was, it is true, a claim which appeared in certain American ones that the information they had secured came from connections and postings in the domestic staff, but even then they did not imply what the lady implies: that the staff was hostile.

It was the Press of France and much more of the United States which was oblivious to the good name of the Crown. In Germany all references to the King were consistently favourable; and so they were in Italy. The reason for this was the leaders in those countries believed he was more on their side than most Englishmen. The impression went further, and it was soon to be mentioned in the House of Commons that Mrs. Simpson was in league with Ribbentrop, that Wallis in Wonderland had a soft corner for Adolf in Blunderland. A circumstantial report was current in certain official circles that this had played its part in the swift decision that Mrs. Simpson should leave England. But for this, of course, no proof whatever is forthcoming.

While the suspicion of her moves went thus to wild extremes, the explanation of them is really simple. She was completely misled by the circle who accepted her; she had no idea of public opinion in the large; she was still more ignorant of how the last sovereigns had developed the role of the Crown in the estimation of the country and therefore what the loyalty of the Commonwealth required of the Crown. Lord Brownlow has summed it well.

For, after all, the veneration of it was partly an exercise of and partly a substitute for religion. When her adorer said that he believed in God, he did not mean he understood how many expected to see in him a support for their conviction that conduct inspired by belief was the secret and aim of his noblest subjects.

So when on the evening of Tuesday, 8th December, Baldwin drove away for the last time from Fort Belvedere he was oblivious that the King could have any undercurrent of resentment. In spite of his distaste for the whole business of the Abdication, he could at least feel he had saved the dignity of the Crown. "This is making history," he said. "This is what I like." The two were never to meet again. But Baldwin must tell his story and he was determined that he should tell it in a way that reflected credit on the troubled man from whom he had just parted. He would suppress everything in that story which could affect its dignity.

When he returned to Downing Street, tired as he was, he had still to give an hour to the Home Secretary.

That same evening the King's Private Secretary went to the Archbishop of Canterbury in Lambeth Palace.

Very soon afterwards, the Prime Minister sent for Monckton, who was told that he was to receive a high honour, and one of the first acts of the new King was to make him a K.C.V.O. This disposes for ever of any idea that Monckton was not helpful to the Government, and indeed he had induced Mrs. Simpson to make certain sacrifices to the wishes of the new King.

CHAPTER XXXV

On the next day, Wednesday, 9th December, the King saw none of the Cabinet. But the Prime Minister was still extremely busy. At ten o'clock he received Simon once more, and an hour later met the Cabinet which sat for two hours to discuss the arrangements which the Abdication required, and to prepare for a successor. But before doing this, *they sent a formal communication begging the King to reconsider the message he had sent about deciding on abdication,* and this was delivered at Fort Belvedere while they sat. When the Cabinet had dispersed, Monckton returned once more to the King who immediately wrote in his own hand to the Prime Minister that he refused to reconsider his decision.

Meanwhile Sir John Simon, and Mr. Malcolm MacDonald, the Dominions Secretary of State, left the Prime Minister's house to walk over to the Dominions Office where the final messages to prepare for immediate Abdication were sent to the various capitals of the Commonwealth. The aim was that the Abdication should be simultaneously completed in each Dominion capital; though in the event this proved to be impracticable. The Imperial Parliament had passed its bill for Abdication before an equivalent Bill could be laid before the independent Parliaments of several Dominions who might have complained that their decision was forced. The machinery of co-ordination in obtaining a simultaneous decision so swiftly did not exist.

Parliament met as usual in the afternoon. Mr. Attlee voiced the increasing impatience and anxiety of the House; one of his supporters mentioned the grave financial inconvenience of the delay, its effect on the Stock Exchange, the markets, and above all the shops which found their Christmas trade brought almost to a standstill. This had already received the attention of the Cabinet which met once more as soon as the House of Commons gave them the opportunity. On the same afternoon also, the Royal Family gathered through the foggy air in the great Park of Windsor where the Duke of York was their host.

The Queen arrived shortly after lunch. She had had a racking week, but her poise never deserted her and Baldwin who also saw her several times was full of admiration at the way she combined dignity with the clearest estimate of the situation. The Duke of York returned to London in the evening to prepare to assume the Crown. A rumour spread that he was so loath to do this that there had been a proposal to appoint a Council of Regency to govern until such time as Princess Elizabeth should be of age to assume the Crown direct. But in reality such an idea was never entertained by the Duke of York: no such proposal was known to any of his household.

At midnight a weary Monckton arrived at Fort Belvedere with the Instrument of Abdication prepared by the Legal Officers of the Crown and ready for signature the following morning in the presence of the Royal Dukes. It was earlier in that day that the King and his solicitor had given over the telephone to Mrs. Simpson so uncompromising an answer to her proposal that he should remain on the throne.

On the following morning, Thursday, 10th December, the three Royal Dukes drove to Fort Belvedere. Before them were seven copies of the document the King was to sign and they were to witness. It ran as follows:

"I, Edward the Eighth, of Great Britain, Ireland, and the British Dominions beyond the Seas, King, Emperor of India, do hereby declare My irrevocable determination to renounce the Throne for Myself and My descendants, and My desire that effect should be given to this Instrument of Abdication immediately.

In token whereof I have hereunto set My hand this tenth day of December, nineteen hundred and thirty-six, in the presence of the witnesses whose signatures are subscribed." Then followed the names of the three brothers: Albert, Henry, George.

This was the document taken an hour after with its six duplicates to Buckingham Palace, and then on to Downing Street where the Prime Minister was waiting for it with the Home Secretary, the Lord Privy Seal, and the Secretary of State for the Dominions.

That day the heavy mist which had been for more than a week chilling and stifling England cleared away. By noon the December sun was shining with a frosty brilliance and in the pale light crowds began to surge towards the Houses of Parliament where the long awaited pronouncement of the Prime Minister was at last to be made. Every seat in the House of Commons and its galleries was taken by a quarter to three in the afternoon. When the Speaker took his seat, his mace before him, the chaplain began reading the stately cadence of official prayers—prayers most especially for the High Court of Parliament "Under our most religious and gracious King at this time assembled". He prayed that their deliberations might be guided for the advancement of God's glory, the good of His Church, the safety, honour and welfare of the Sovereign and his dominions, that "peace and happiness, truth and justice, religion and piety might be established among us for all generations". And then, prayers being ended, some fifty routine questions were asked, and answered to an impatient assemblage, before the Prime Minister, having entered with a scroll, to which were attached many red seals, rose from his seat, went to the Bar of the House, and made a deep bow to the Speaker: "A Message from His Majesty the King," he announced, "signed by His Majesty's own hand." Again he bowed low and delivered his papers to the Speaker who took them with trembling fingers. As he in turn began to read, all heads were bared.

The Royal Message, duly prepared by Sir John Simon, was phrased in these words:

"After long and anxious consideration I have determined to renounce the Throne to which I succeeded on the death of my Father, and I am now communicating this my final and irrevocable decision. Realizing as I do the gravity of this step, I can only hope that I shall have the understanding of my people in the decision I have taken and the reasons which have led me to it.

"I will not enter into my private feelings, but I would beg that it should be remembered that the burden which continually rests upon the shoulders of a Sovereign is so heavy that it can only be borne in circumstances different from those in which I find myself.

"I conceive that I am not overlooking the duty that rests on me to place in the forefront of the public interest when I declare that I am conscious that I can no longer discharge this heavy task with efficiency or with satisfaction to myself."

The Message then quoted the Act of Abdication expressing appreciation of the appeals made to the King to stay, but added that he saw that further delay would be dangerous to those whose happiness and prosperity were his constant wish. Confident that the course he had elected to follow was the best for the stability of the throne and the happiness of his Dominions, he finally offered thanks for the consideration which had always been shown to him and asked for it to be extended to his brother who was at once to succeed him.

No sooner had the Speaker finished reading than the Prime Minister again rose to move:

"That His Majesty's most gracious Message be now considered."

Then Stanley Baldwin began the most masterly speech of his life, delivered extempore from a few notes and coming very soon to a sentence that awakened a kindly amusement: "I have had but little time to prepare a speech so I must tell what I have to tell truthfully." But the speech that followed was one of the most subtle and adroit presentations of the story that a trained experience could have devised. It was the truth appropriately chiselled and decked in graceful garments so as to shield the King and save the imperilled honour of his throne. Its consummate art was as superbly concealed. It gave the impression of a simple man telling a plain tale without comment of praise or blame, and speaking straight from the heart. He had nothing with him but a few notes, and to tell the truth he had at lunch time been so tired and nervous that more than once he had dropped them and lost them. At lunch his trepidation had increased till Mrs. Baldwin said: "Just be yourself, Stan, and you'll be all right." She had not been mistaken. The task set before Baldwin was to explain what had happened in such a way as not to bring

—or leave room for—any accusation against the King. So, with that uppermost in his mind he launched into the story already told in these pages: "The whole of our discussions have been carried out with an increase, if possible, of that mutual respect and regard in which we stood."

He had had his two great anxieties: the effect in his own country of the criticism in the American press, and therefore for the integrity of the Monarchy. Though respect for the Monarchy had been growing for three generations, "it might not take so long in view of the criticisms to which it was being exposed to lose that power far more rapidly than it was built up, and once lost I doubt if anything could restore it."

The Prime Minister said then that if such criticism could do so much harm, no popularity would be strong enough to counter-act it—he spoke as one who was both His Majesty's first Minister and his friend, and the King had said to him not once but many times: "We must settle this matter together: I will not have anyone interfering."

But Baldwin had had to point out that once the divorce went through, gossip must come and surmise would lead to faction. Baldwin then went on in words already quoted in these pages to relate the next meeting on 16th November: the meeting where the King had said that he was determined to marry Mrs. Simpson at the cost of his crown. The next subject was the morganatic marriage with Baldwin's 'horseback opinion', as he phrased it to the King, that no Parliament in the Empire would accept it, but that he would question his own Cabinet, and the Parliaments and Governments of the Dominions—as indeed he had done.

Baldwin did not divulge to the House any hint of the other manoeuvres of the King. All he said was that "on hearing of the refusal the King said he was not surprised and never referred to the matter again: so the problem", said Baldwin, "was narrowed to the choice between two conflicting loyalties. We had many talks," said Baldwin. "And always on various aspects of this problem. The House must remember, it is difficult to realize, that His Majesty is not a boy, although he looks so young. We have all thought of him as our Prince, but he is a mature man with a wide and great experience of life and the world, and he always held before him three or four things which in these con-versations he repeated again and again—that if he went, he would go with dignity—he would not allow a situation to arise in which he could not do that. He wanted to go with as little disturbance of his Ministers and his people as possible. He wished to go in circumstances that would make the succession as little difficult as possible for his brother. And I may say that any idea to him of what might be called a King's party was abhorrent . . . I honour and respect him for the way in which he behaved."

That was the chivalrous way in which Baldwin chose to tele-scope the story. At that point he turned to his notes to read a few lines the King had sent up that morning for inclusion in the speech. "Duke of York. He and the King have always been on the best of terms as brothers, and the King is confident that the Duke deserves and will receive the support of the whole Empire." The King also sent a note to say a word of praise for Mrs. Simpson. But how would it help the King in the adroit presentation of his case that Baldwin was straining every nerve to make if he then added that although Mrs. Simpson had offered to give him up, he still insisted on putting her before every claim of the Crown and every expression of the personal loyalty of the people? Such a reference would have sprung a mine under the case which Baldwin was so generously and so skilfully presenting. It would have turned the whole effort into a farce if at that moment Baldwin had sought to enlist the tributes of the House to a woman whose part in the business had already outraged honest opinion in the House of Commons and in the constituencies its Members represented. What he did say was put in so tactful a way that he could while making a reference to her yet carry the House with him: "The King has told us that he cannot carry these almost intolerable burdens of Kingship without a woman at his side, and we know that this crisis, if I may use the word, has arisen now rather than later from that very frankness of His Majesty's character which is one of his many attractions."

The Prime Minister's loyalty then pushed him to another statement hardly accurate: that the King might have delayed mention of his marriage for months to come, but that he hastened the time to avoid the noise of discussion dangerous to the moral force of the Crown. Yet another inaccuracy did he loyally insert: that there had been no kind of conflict. He came back to firmer fact when he said he had done all he could to keep the King from abdicating, and that at the dinner party on the Tuesday evening, the little intimate circle around the King had assured him of it. Finally he said: "While there is not a soul among us who will not regret this from the bottom of his heart, there is not a soul here today who wants to judge. We are not judges. He has announced his decision. He has told us what he wants us to do, and I think we must close our ranks and do it . . .

"I am convinced that where I failed no one could have suc-ceeded. His mind was made up, and those who know His Majesty best know what that means."

He appealed to the House to act in the knowledge that its conduct that day was being watched by the whole world. They had to see that they so did their work as to maintain the integrity of this democracy and of the Monarchy which, as he had already said, was the sole link of their whole Empire and the guarantee of their freedom.

And now came the closing words: "Let us look forward and remember our country and the trust reposed by our country in the House of Commons, and let us rally behind the new King, stand beside him and help him—and let us hope that whatever the country may have suffered by what we are passing through, it may soon be repaired, and that we may take what steps we can in trying to make this a better country for all the people in it."

He had come to the end. He had told the story for which all were waiting and of which only the Cabinet knew more than the vaguest outlines: and in telling it with what seemed perfect frankness and simplicity—which seemed the more convincing from his speaking direct from his few notes, and rather as a friend confiding than as Minister making an oration, his manner, his tone and his words completely veiled his recurrence of courtly reticence. They conveyed rather to his listeners, who were the Lords and Commons of England, with the envoys of Foreign Courts and governments, that they had heard in words of classic simplicity not only the story of a drama both personal and royal—but at the same time the record of honour, taste, conscience, sympathy, allegiance. Absorption in the King's dilemma was merged in admiration for his Minister. Here then was a man whose tact and skill were one with a feeling heart— whose eloquence flowed from the depths of sympathy and honour within him. Here was a leader who had transformed a theme which could have scandalized many into an appeal for sympathy with a lover striving in the stress of the supreme passion of his life to do all his nature could compass to fulfil the demands of his office, while meeting whenever he needed it aid from the counsel of a discreet Minister who had perforce to represent the feelings of wide dominions; a Minister who balanced from hour to hour his affection for his Prince with the claims of an Empire's welfare.

For Stanley Baldwin, as he approached the verge of seventy, expressed in ideal words the best feelings of a far-flung people.

He had moved every heart before he resumed his seat in a tumult of respectful acclamation. There was nothing more to say than for the Leader of the Opposition to ask for the House to be suspended till its Members could consider the unique and moving story so tellingly told in the finest hour of a statesman's life.

As the tributes came in from the Empire he basked in a radiance of gratitude and praise. He deserved it.

CHAPTER XXXVI

WHEN at six in the evening the House of Commons reassembled, there was still much to hear of the country's opinion. First of all Mr. Attlee spoke, then the Liberal leader Sir Archibald Sinclair, then Mr. Churchill, Mr. Maxton, Colonel Wedgwood and the solitary Communist of the House, William Gallacher. George Buchanan followed and another from Scotland, the old soldier Sir Ian Fraser. Each had something to say on that which had to be taken into consideration in an account of the reign.

Mr. Attlee spoke of the sense of sorrow and personal loss among the King's peoples, the sympathy they felt for him not only because of an issue involving the strongest human emotions, but also because of the personal affection he had inspired. "We all know his personal charm, his courage, his sympathy with suffering—the wish of all his people is that he will have a busy and happy life"; and then he spoke of the severe shock the country had received, the time it would take to recover, the strain put on the Prime Minister, the loyalty of all the Royal Family.

Sinclair, the Scottish-American Liberal, spoke also of his sympathy with the Prime Minister: he paid tribute to the Duke of York and the pain that would be felt by all classes at the rupture of their relation with one to whom they were bound not only by formal and solemn ties but by the personal link of which Mr. Attlee had so eloquently spoken. So far the Opposition had spoken with a restraint that yet expressed respectful sympathy with the departing King and faithful attachment to the royal principle and the Royal Family. What remained to be heard from members of the House more independent? The Speaker now called on Mr. Churchill.

With intense curiosity members turned towards the man whom four days before they had silenced—silenced, as he himself admits, with a scorn almost unparalleled in the memory of the House. They were to be reassured.

"Nothing," began Churchill, "would be more certain than that recrimination at this time would be not only useless but harmful and wrong. What is done is done. What has been done, or undone, belongs to history and to history, as far as I am concerned, it shall be left." He would make only two observations: first that there had never been any constitutional issue. The King had been loyal to the letter and spirit of the Constitution, nay, he had voluntarily made a sacrifice for the peace and strength of the realm which went far beyond the bounds required by the law and the Constitution. That was the way

Churchill—the man who had most strongly urged the King to act independently of the Government—put the first point.

His second one was with regard to time. It had been proved that the King had had time to act freely and spontaneously in his own way. "As I have been looking at the matter, as is well-known, from an angle different from that of most honourable members I thought it my duty to place this fact also upon record." Who could have withdrawn more astutely from the pit into which he had fallen by his words about an Abdication being hastily extorted? Then he went on: "I should have been ashamed, in my independent and unofficial position, had I not cast about for every lawful means, even the most forlorn, to keep him on the throne of his fathers. In this Prince were discerned qualities of courage, of simplicity, of sympathy and above all of sincerity, qualities rare and precious which might have made his reign glorious in the annals of this ancient monarchy. It is the very acme of tragedy that these very virtues should in the private sphere have led only to this melancholy and bitter conclusion. But, though our hopes are withered, still I will assert that his personality will not go down uncherished to future generations." Finally Churchill spoke of offering to His Majesty's successor that strength which can come only from the love of a united nation and Empire.

He had spoken not only with his accustomed mastery of poetical and adjectival eloquence. Words, gleaming like diamonds and ringing like bells, had covered his retreat as effectively as salvoes of artillery.

The discussion was not over; now rose Jimmy Maxton, the Labour extremist. Brushing aside the thick lock of black hair which always gave a note of wildness to his strong and handsome features as it gushed over his white forehead and burning eyes, he began by referring to the strong emotions of the House as it reviewed its relation to a throne regarded as sacrosanct and everlasting. Sharing the human sympathies of the Prime Minister and acquiescing in what he had done with a big majority behind him, yet he could not forbear to mention the grave perils that confront a country if after its centralizing unifying figure was placed on high by the principle of heredity it were to break under the force of the circumstances which gather around him.

Then came Colonel Wedgwood not to take up the cudgels of his former challenge but to commend the choice which had been made. For nothing could have been worse than for the country to be ruled by a man with a grievance and hostile to the Ministers who had thwarted his aim and collecting around him friends ready to use his feelings against his own Ministers. That would be a dreadful alternative.

A ruddy Socialist from Glasgow rose to speak. His broad

197

Scotch voice and pleasant face combined to make an impression of youth in a love with truth; he looked, in fact, almost as young as the lean Prince whom they were all discussing, and breathed an echo from Burns: "An honest man's the noblest work of God." "I have listened to more cant and humbug than I have ever heard in my life. I have heard praise of the King which is not sincerely felt by any member in this House. I go further: who has not heard the tittle-tattle and gossip that is going about?" He not only accused the previous speakers of insincerity but he accused the authorities of desecrating the law; and in fact he brought up the accusation the Government were most anxious to avoid, that they were *accessories to collusive action* while having one law for royalty and another for the working man. "What are you talking nonsense about?" he asked. "You are setting aside your laws for a rich and pampered royalty."

The exact words of Geordie Buchanan are to be read in Hansard—they are too strong to be reproduced here; but they brought the Government back to what had been all through this melodrama a problem they could solve only by extremest reticence and which was at the heart of the constitutional dilemma with which they had to deal: to give in to the overpowering desires of the King and at the same time to keep intact the prestige and the unifying function of the Crown. The speech is also essential to the historic situation; for it expressed the qualms of many, and the indignation which for weeks to come was to bring Mrs. Simpson hundreds of letters expressing scorn.

A thought more or less similar to that which Geordie Buchanan had been expressing was set down two days before by one of the closest confidants of the Prime Minister: "We invest our royalties with qualities they do not possess, and we connive at the illusion—those of us who know better—because monarchy is an illusion which works. It has a pragmatic sanction. This King has done the popularity side of his job extremely well. He had a prodigious memory, a quick, if shallow, intelligence, and the sense of drama. But he dislikes work, and escapes from it and delays its performance."

Those were, of course, the difficulties which Baldwin confided to his closest friends about the Sovereign to whom he had through ten years given so much affection.

The difficulty was that in the regard felt for the Monarch by all sections of the people, they invest particular persons with a halo of sentiment. They idealize the Royal Family. But should any member of it take a step which suggests that he or she is not ready to pay the price demanded by the people's joy in the admiration it accords, then, of course, the Crown which plays so useful a part in imperial union would be transmuted from a symbol to a sham.

That is the warning which in their different voices and in their different spheres Geordie Buchanan, the Scots Labour member and Tom Jones, the retired professor who was *persona gratissima* at the centres of power—now set down. They had said the things which are not said, but which everyone knows. For a silent acquiescence in certain basic truths is the key to the British way of life.

Such truths are like those physical secretions essential to health and to mankind which after the uproar of youth a universal sense of decency permits only the scientist to mention. There are things so essential that while obvious they must remain shrouded in mystery. These are the springs of both life and its radiance.

The debate in the House of Commons could not end in disclosing the unspoken. An old soldier rounded off the affair with a word about the King's interest in the men who had fought in the war. So the debate which had been initiated in so masterly a style by Baldwin ended on no jarring note.

Thus, the Bill of Abdication was read for the first time in the House of Commons. In the House of Lords it fell to Lord Halifax as Leader of the House to speak first on the Abdication. He spoke of bewilderment, of sorrow, of the stern conflict of loyalties in the King's mind, of an untimely withdrawal of great gifts from the service of the state. Lord Snell following him said "it only remains for us to think of him in his happier days and to express sympathy with him in the difficult crisis he has to face"—he closed on one more tribute to the King's interest in the poor, the unemployed, the distressed. Lord Crewe spoke also of the personal appeal of the King's vigour, manliness and candour, but he also pleaded for reticence. Then followed the Archbishop of Canterbury: he did not ignore Lord Crewe's plea for reticence: on the contrary he repeated it. No renunciation comparable had been made in Britain's history. The motive that impelled it, he said, takes us into the region of the inner mysteries of human life and human nature. He spoke of infinite sorrow in accepting the King's decision, of the frankness and charm of his personality, of his embassies across the seas, his manifold services and their rich promise, saying that the thought of those inspired affection and admiration; he closed with a fervent prayer to the God of our fathers that He will take into His gracious mercy both the King that has been and the King that is to be.

So much the Archbishop saw fit to say in the House of Lords. After that he might well have remained silent: and if not silent he could have echoed those words over the air. But no: he chose to speak to the public over the air in a tone which, as we shall see, both tarnished his reputation and betrayed his Church.

CHAPTER XXXVII

ON the next morning, Friday, 11th December, the House met for the second reading of the Abdication Bill. At this session the Prime Minister pointed out that if a new King were to succeed then his children must be heirs to the throne, and King Edward must therefore renounce claims for any issue he might have. The legal authorities had been occupied with two possible eventualities: that of Mrs. Simpson at last having a child who could claim the Crown, and secondly of the abdicated Prince contracting a second marriage. They considered it essential both from the point of view of the elimination of such an issue and for the stability of the people's loyalty to the Royal Family as a whole that the regard of the whole people should turn to the household of the Duke of York.

At the same time it was held imperative that the new King at his accession should be freed from any responsibility for the marriage of his brother. The King was abdicating for the right to marry as he chose and he must have his freedom to do so guaranteed by Act of Parliament at the same time. The Prime Minister now explained how they had got over the difficulties raised by the Royal Marriage Act of 1772. The object of that Act, it was explained, was to provide a measure of control over the marriage of those who might themselves succeed to the throne, or whose descendants might succeed. It would be clearly wrong that the provisions of the Act should apply to Edward VIII if his descendants were to have no right to the throne. An interesting point that Baldwin did not mention was that only those in the line of succession had enjoyed the title of 'Royal Highness'.

The Labour Party made no demur to Baldwin's proposals, but Mr. Attlee explained why he supported the Bill. First of all he wanted the country to be free from the distraction of the last few weeks that it might cope with three urgent problems: the condition of the people, the state of the world and the great issue of peace. This was a most important point. The King's personal affairs had proved to be an immense obstacle to the state at a time which was critical, especially in Foreign Affairs. Had that year been free to take an immediate grasp of the issues which arose during the reign, it is possible that some of the sinister issues which so swiftly followed might have been obviated. This in later years was pushed so far as to assert that Mrs. Simpson was largely responsible for the war of 1939. It need hardly be said that such an idea was never current in the Labour Party. It came rather from theorists in America.

The Opposition Leader said he did not want to revert to the past; but he wanted to say a word for the future. "A real disservice has been done," he said, "to constitutional monarchy by over-emphasis and by adulation, especially in the Press." The Monarchy had been invested with a halo of magic: a false reverence had tended to obscure the real position. It is true that a rather unhealthy sentiment had been spreading among the people and they had so concentrated their interest on the Royal Family as to regard them as something other than human beings. Then he went on: "Some pomp and ceremony may be useful on occasions, but we believe that the note of the monarchy should be simplicity." Anticipating what the next reigns were to see, he spoke against class barriers and for more equality. For the country, for the Commonwealth and for the throne he believed it would bind more closely the people and their Sovereign.

This point was elaborated by four Labour members in speeches lasting an hour and a half.

After Sir Archibald Sinclair had talked of rallying round the throne for concern with the problem of the people's condition, James Maxton rose once more and this time to argue for an elected President as head of the state! His contention was that Socialists were for economic and social equality without further use for kings or courts or nobles. A King, he said, was the very head and front of class society. Had not the questions of the last few weeks made republicanism into a practical issue? For three reigns monarchy had proved an effective constitutional device, but what did they now see? Not merely the failure of a man with his passions and affections but the end of the myth that the royal family was free from the taints and weaknesses of ordinary men. At last Great Britain itself was seeing that revulsion from monarchy which had marked so many countries of Europe. Economic and social forces were at work to produce enormous changes, and the Government should not keep in the monarchy something which impeded them from running their course.

This speech was followed by one from another M.P. who made the sarcastic point that although the King was a man of mature age he was not considered competent in the choice of a wife. The monarchy, he thought, was losing its glamour: the Empire was now being held together not so much by the Crown as by economic interests. So far was he from appreciation of the monarchy that he even attacked the intervention of King George in 1931. He wanted a real democracy from top to bottom. He did not want the armed forces attached to the name of the King. He would like to see "an end to all this flummery".

Here was the case for republicanism! Sir John Simon rose at once with an answer: it was true, he admitted, that the British public had been shocked by what led to the Abdication. But the very reason they were shocked was because they loved and respected the monarchy. Yet the throne mattered much more than any individual. "If institutions were not greater than the inscrutable promptings of individual hearts, orderly development would be impossible." Constitutional monarchy was described as a device, but so was a Presidency. History did not show republicanism to be a guarantee of stability, nor necessarily was it combined with civil liberty. But the conception created by the genius of the people, and valued as a symbol of unity for the Commonwealth, would be vindicated by the new reign. A grievous incident in the history of an institution did not mean the breakdown of the institution itself. With the monarchy the will of the people still prevailed.

So did Sir John Simon express the idea which had ruled the mind of a Liberal in the crisis. But it was only part of the case for monarchy as the country had loved and valued it. Sir Austen Chamberlain now rose to develop this idea. He had been a Minister already in the distant days of Queen Victoria, and had watched many changes. He sat furthermore for a constituency of mean streets—but his constituents looked on the monarchy as a safeguard, the King as a friend.

The reason for this was that the monarchy was *not* a castle of class and privilege. It transcended class. It served the nation as a whole. When there was occasion for mean streets to rejoice, it was when the people shared through their honour and affection in the glory of the crown. The King is the people's King.

It was now once again the turn of the Communist. Gallacher, rising, made the piquant reminder that Joseph Chamberlain had once had republican leanings, and regarded monarchy as an idea less cherished than cultivated. He made another point of interest: aristocracy had sometimes overthrown the monarchy, the workers had never done so. This point certainly told rather in favour of the monarchy than otherwise. But, as Gallacher had said, the crisis of the monarchy was obscuring the far greater crisis of unemployment and the derelict areas.

Another Member, Cluse, who was also a Socialist, then elaborated this point: there were far more important affairs pressing for attention than to abolish the monarchy, and he did not want to impede them by mixing them up with the question of the monarchy.

Then a Glasgow Labour Member, G. D. Hardie, complained of the principle of heredity. Why bother about that? "If the nation was sane in its outlook, we would not now be wasting the time of the House of Commons in discussing this kind of stuff while so many people are poor and suffering." The debate closed with the significant words: "Since 1914 there has been a continual building up around the throne, but what has happened recently has done more for republicanism than fifty years of propaganda could do."

After hearing these words, with which few would have been inclined to disagree, on whichever side of the House they sat, the Abdication Bill and its corollary about the marriage was passed by a vote of 403 to 5.

The only thing that remained was to await equivalent legislation from the constituent parts of the Empire.

So we see that it was with an undercurrent of criticism of the monarchy itself that the debate in Parliament closed. There must always be minds which tend to identify the office with the person who holds it, and it is in fact impossible to press the distinction too far. Indeed none can combine respect for the throne with cavalier behaviour towards its actual occupant, and at the same time it is impossible for a sovereign to take questionable action without weakening the prestige of his position. The action which Edward VIII had taken tempted unsophisticated minds to ask what was the meaning and value of the wealth and panoply of the Court.

That was the question with which the Prime Minister, the Archbishop of Canterbury, the leaders of opinion and not least the officials of the Court, with the Private Secretary at their head, had had to deal from the beginning of the reign, and which had forced them to take action as the knowledge crystallized that the King was not only cultivating the society of—but actually proposing to marry—a lady who was still the wife of one of his most faithful subjects.

Through the ages the world has been indulgent to the vagrant hearts of princes; most had realized, as Queen Alexandra had done, that a Prince may be easily overcome by the alacrity with which attractive members of the other sex seek his favours. But for human nature to make allowances for the susceptibilities with which royalty sought compensation for its restraints is one thing. It was quite another for a sovereign to ask acceptance for a marriage in circumstances such as these. That was the point with which Government and Court had had to cope in their loyalty to the Crown. That was the point which made Labour members voice a very general question about the hereditary principle and the value of royal state.

As that point became more and more obvious, and the King, refused any compromise with what to him was romance, it was held that his departure should be in circumstances that would suggest neither dishonour nor conflict—and yet reduce discussion to a minimum.

So far all had been arranged with admirable skill. But it still remained to fix the details of the departure. It was decided that on the very day when the form of Abdication had been completed he who was chiefly concerned should leave Britain that evening in a destroyer, after the necessary formalities had been completed; and, though the Queen was against it, he insisted that he should go so far towards carrying out Mrs. Simpson's plan of appeal to the people as to make a final address over the air. To this the Government was perfectly agreeable.

For the Bill to become law, it must receive the Royal Assent. This was to be given by a Council specially appointed. The King therefore did not sign the Bill with his own hand. As soon as it was passed by the House of Lords, it was sent to the Council which was waiting for it and received it at eight minutes to two in the afternoon. Returned immediately to the House of Lord's, it was then given to the Clerk of the House, Sir Henry Baddeley, who announced it in the mediaeval formula:

LE ROY LE VEULT.

At the moment the Bill was being signed by the Commission appointed, he to whom it referred was again entertaining Mr. Winston Churchill on whom he relied to perfect the phrases of the pronouncement on which he himself had been working till late hours of the previous night. That next evening, his last in England for the time, he dined with the Royal Family at Royal Lodge as the guest of his brother whom his action had now made King in his stead. Before they left the table, a servant brought in the message that it was time to enter the car to take him to Windsor Castle where for some days Sir John Reith, the dour Scot who was head of the B.B.C., was waiting to introduce him to his listening country and an astonished world.

He began by explaining that he had long wanted to speak but had been constitutionally prevented as long as his reign lasted. But now he was King no longer, and he declared his allegiance to his brother. "This I do with all my heart."

Then he said:

"You all know the reasons which have impelled me to renounce the throne, but I want you to understand that in making up my mind, I did not forget the country or the Empire, which as Prince of Wales and lately as King, I have tried for twenty-five years to serve.

"But you must believe me when I tell you that I have found it impossible to carry the heavy burden of responsibility and discharge my duties as King as I would wish to do without the help and support of the woman I love."

And now he could insert the point he unjustly blamed Baldwin for not inserting in the Abdication speech in the House of Commons:

"I want you to know that the decision I have made is mine

and mine alone. This was a thing I had to judge entirely for myself. The other person most nearly concerned has tried up to the last to persuade me to take a different course."

Yes, it was chivalrous of him to say it; but strange that, even in the lapse of years, he should not have been able to see anything so obvious as how impossible it would have been for Baldwin to say this when he was arguing the whole time how scrupulous the King had been for the moral dignity of the Crown.

And now the royal speaker went on to say that for him everything had turned on the question of what in the end would be best for all. And the answer, he could say, "was much less difficult for me because of my sheer knowledge that my brother with his long training in the public affairs of this country and with his fine qualities will be able to take my place forthwith." Then he added two phrases he owed to Churchill. "He has the matchless blessing enjoyed by so many of you, and not bestowed on me, a happy home with his wife and his children" and: "Bred in the constitutional traditions of my father, I should never have allowed any such issue to arise." This followed on tributes to the Royal Family and to the Government: "During these hard days I have been comforted by Her Majesty, my Mother, and by my family. The Ministers of the Crown, and in particular the Prime Minister have always treated me with full consideration."

They had indeed: and it was only so that all constitutional complications had been avoided—they might not have been if *some* of his advisers had had their way. But the phrase he owed to Churchill that "he would never have allowed such an issue to arise" meant that his heart had at the crucial hour proved wiser than their counsels. Mr. Churchill's dignified phrase, therefore, served not one purpose only.

"Ever since I was Prince of Wales and later when I occupied the Throne," he went on, "I have been treated with the greatest kindness by all classes of the people, wherever I have lived, or journeyed through the Empire. For that I am very grateful.

"I now quit altogether public affairs and I lay down my burden. It may be some time before I return to my native land but I shall always follow the fortunes of the British race and Empire with profound interest [had not Churchill helped again here ?] and if at any time in the future I can be of service to His Majesty in a private station, I shall not fail.

"And now you all have a new King. I wish him and you, his people, happiness and prosperity, with all my heart. God bless you all. God save the King."

On the last words, the voice rose to a note shrill and tense. But for the rest, the announcement fitly closed his reign. He had done well to speak to his own people for a last time with his own voice, and tell them in his own words of the psychological malaise which overruled the demands of his august office. If it were rash of him to call another man's wife "the woman I love" few of his people would set themselves as judges of the dilemma which stormed upon his deferred awakening to the full life of the heart.

But now the general feeling was that it was better he should go. When Lord Brownlow told the Prime Minister how he had tried to persuade Mrs. Simpson to fly from Europe, the jocular answer was, "If you had succeeded I would have put you in the Tower of London for the rest of your natural life". By that time two things had been made clear to Baldwin: that the King would never have settled without her and secondly that he had shaken confidence in the Crown.

This thought was echoed in a saying often heard in different quarters: that for the British Empire never had a siren done such signal service.

CHAPTER XXXVIII

For there was one thing which Edward VIII had failed to gauge: the response of the young men in the Services. This was summed in the headlines of one newspaper: "The Fallen Idol".

After the Abdication, writes Sir Philip Gibbs, who fully appreciated the qualities of the departing Prince: "Something else happened in the English mind." It was anger . . . anger because he had "chucked his job". Sir Philip relates that on the afternoon of the Abdication there was a group of pilots of the R.A.F. who in their mess raised their voices, shouting and cursing, after they had heard the announcement on the wireless. "He has let us down," they shouted, "he has thrown up the sponge. He ought to have held on to his job." Wherever Sir Philip went, he heard words like those. "We gave him our loyalty and he has let us down."

But how did he let them down ? The Services' judgment on this point was expressed in a terse antithesis: "It is better to have a leader with guts and no morals than a fellow with morals and no guts." That was a judgment typical of the Air Force.

Later Sir Philip heard the voice of a general to whom the war of twenty years before had given fame. This general also knew and admired the qualities of the Prince. What he said was: "The truth is he has a wrong picture in his mind. He thought that if he fulfilled his public duty and made friends with the people—to whom he was really devoted—they would let him do as he liked in his private life. A King has no private life." There is some truth in this; but what should be added to it is that the King wanted to make his private life into his public life.

That was the point where the two lovers were so little competent to judge opinion. They trusted entirely to the sentimentalists who, of course, kept to their point; when Winston Churchill some three years later succeeded Neville Chamberlain as Premier a washerwoman in Oxford spoke for millions. "Thank heaven we have him at last for our Prime Minister. He never let that dear boy down."

As for the anger caused by the Abdication, the man departing produced his defence. Speaking of his decision to go rather than stay which meant to allow and encourage faction, he wrote: "I reject the notion put forward by some that faced with a choice between love and duty, I chose love. I certainly married because I chose love. But I abdicated because I chose the path of duty. I did not value the Crown so lightly that I gave it away hastily. I valued it so deeply that rather than risk an impairment of its prestige I surrendered it."

Such is the abdicating King's defence. We must not call it a sophistry. That it is subtle does not mean that it is insincere. But it implied a state of mind which had been at earlier stages obscure, and which, of course, plain minds, especially those of servicemen, completely failed at the time to comprehend. And of this, three years later, when the war began, and he met army men again, the dethroned sovereign became painfully aware.

On that last evening his mind was on other things. After finishing his discourse, he descended to the entrance of the great castle of his fathers, the castle by whose name he was henceforth to be known, and winding past the high chapel in which his father's body lay, he drove in the company of his friend Monckton across the Great Park and so among the birches and heather which surrounded Camberley and its college. He writes of crossing the wide stretch of heath where he had prepared twenty-two years before to serve as a Grenadier. But in this case he left the Portsmouth Road, for it goes through Aldershot, and not over the Hartford Flats.

From that region of woods which had been part of Windsor Forest it was but an hour to Portsmouth where the Navy, under Sir Roger Backhouse, expected his arrival. The Admiralty Yacht *Enchantress* was not available. The destroyer detailed to carry him from his country was not *Enchantress* but *Fury*.

On his arrival at the docks, though he was now but the shadow of an emperor, he was met with the courtesies due to his rank, and indeed with attentions with which he could not but be touched. Since none of his personal servants had chosen to accompany him he was provided with two stewards from the

Royal Yacht and after two devoted members of his household had taken their sad leave he remained with two others, Ulick Alexander and Piers Legh who accompanied him to Boulogne and who were indeed to remain with him all the way to Vienna.

A rumour was long current that he had paced the deck in misery. This however was the invention of some on the escort destroyer, *Wolfhound*, who envied the crew and the commander, Cecil Howe, of *Fury* to whom indeed the Prince talked alone for hours revolving many moods and memories; indeed he himself tells us how thoughts and emotions stormed through his mind as he went out to sea. He felt acutely the loss of home, country, kingship, all forgone. And surely we should do him wrong were we to think that he asked himself none of the questions which we all are apt to put in times of loss and affliction and which would invite our sympathy. In later years his face and expression witnessed that he was not always free from strain and suffering; but for the most part he appeared to remain sub-servient and absorbed in the love which had stripped from him his glory and taken the crown from his head.

CHAPTER XXXIX

IT is not the purpose of this book to trace the future of the pair who have been holding our attention. For that we should turn to *The Heart Has Its Reasons* as the Duchess of Windsor calls her witty memoirs of those many adventures in her life which both preceded and followed the Abdication which gave her a royal husband. Her book tells the story of her quiet wedding in the Château de Candé near Tours lent by M. Charles Bedaux, a French American, who, after being accused of collaborating with the Germans in the war, escaped execution by taking poison. It was the misfortune of the Duchess of Windsor to be taken up and perhaps exploited by Germans and German agents—more than once. Even the support of the British blackshirts which was so generously accorded to her was considered by some suspicious people to support their penchant for spy-hunting.

How was she married? The Church of England must perforce withhold its blessing on a new union for a woman where two men who had each been her legal husband are still living. But a buccaneering parson from Darlington in Yorkshire defied all the Bishops and arrived at Candé to say for her the marriage service of the Church of England which already at Baltimore in 1918 had bound her with its lifelong vows. This marriage ceremony took place on 3rd June, 1937; the day chosen was the birth-day of him who would have liked it least, King George V.

Later in the year the bride and bridegroom visited Germany, being entertained by Goering, Goebbels, Hess and finally Hitler himself. Hitler spoke volubly. The Duchess saw in this portent of the age the dominance of earnest eyes. Then her new husband made a great speech at Verdun eloquently appealing to all nations to avoid friction and ensure peace. But in all the Duke did towards warding off war, he was disappointed. In 1939 came the outbreak on which Hitler insisted against every attempt at reasonable accommodation. At that time the Duke and Duchess of Windsor were staying on the French Riviera when the British Ambassador in Paris, Sir Eric Phipps, telephoned from Paris the news that war had begun. The Duke walked to the shore where at noon he took his swim. We recall that he said: "Great Britain has declared war on Germany, and I am afraid that in the end this may open the way to world Communism."

In those words which fulfilled a warning given in 1935 by no other than Stalin and which subsequent events did much to endorse, he summed up the main political preoccupation of his short reign to her who had been the preoccupation which overrode all others. But this passion, consuming as it was, must not be allowed to obscure his desire to fill his place in a year when English politics had two immense aims: peace in Europe and the welfare of the people. No sooner had Parliament disposed of the Abdication and Succession than it turned to deal with the four motions the Abdication had interrupted: the weather, the state of the distressed areas, the grind of poverty and want in the Highlands and Islands of Scotland, and the need of baths at the head of the coalpits.

For such matters as these competed with the peril from Germany for the attention of the Government: the time had at last come when men had to recognize that they *were* their brothers' keepers. That new view remained and became more insistent in the succeeding years when the new Duke of Windsor seemed only to revisit England and its history like a ghost.

To such a point as the comfort and well-being of miners the eye of the King was ever open. The stability of the Crown depended not a little on how far a Prince had them so much at heart that he could take effective steps to see that they were before the eyes of the people who were in the position to press for the necessary changes. That he had many times showed a practical initiative in this direction was true, especially in relation to the estates of the Duchy of Cornwall. But on this particular instance of a harsh injustice to a body of men so essential to the work and well-being of the state as the miners, the private preoccupations of the King not only precluded him from stretching practical help so far but actually shelved the subject till he had departed.

When at Glasgow in the preceding March, he had spoken of the contrast between the comfort of the huge liner *Queen Mary* and the slums of the town. For he had knocked at the humblest doors. He was a Prince whose heart, like his father's, had been responsive to suffering: who once, in fact, finding a man so disfigured by war wounds that what should have been a face was a hideous misfeature had stooped and kissed him. But the impulsive moment had seldom been upheld by that type of sustained effort which made his mother formidable as an inspector of hospitals. Efficiency demands sacrifices.

Baldwin, as we saw, was aware of the untoward prospect. What of Queen Mary? She had no doubt hoped against hope. But at the end she had seen the truth very clear. It had been her lifelong habit never to make a speech, but now she decided to follow her son on the wireless; it was her message which covered the transition between the two reigns, and she spoke as one who was not more Queen than Mother, as she now addressed nation and Empire.

She thanked them for the sympathy and affection which had greeted her once again in the distress which filled a nation's heart when she thought that her dear son had deemed it his duty to lay down his charge, and suddenly to end a reign begun with hope and promise. "I know that you will realize what it has cost him to come to this decision; and that remembering the years in which he tried so eagerly to serve and help his country, you will keep a grateful remembrance of him in your hearts.

"I commend to you his brother summoned so unexpectedly and in circumstances so painful to take his place." She asked for them the unfailing trust and affection which had been accorded to herself; and she concluded: "It is my earnest prayer that in spite of, nay, through this present trouble, the loyalty and unity of our land and Empire may, by God's blessing, be maintained and strengthened."

That was the attitude of the nation as a whole. It responded to the appeal of the Queen, and learnt that it was founding its loyalty to the throne not on sentimental attachment to a romantic lover or to a paragon for democracy but on acceptance of a new King and Queen, who, if not heroic figures, understood the royal part and would put first those nobler cares to which it obliged them while he who preceded them saw the vintage of his honour pressed by other hands.

The contesting claims of sympathy, anger, curiosity and surprise prevented the people as a whole from passing a moral judgment on an affair so flavoured with the condiments of melo-drama. It was, however, inevitable that the clergy—and not alone the clergy—should preach sermons. One resists every-thing—so Oscar Wilde once said—except temptation: and the

Archbishop of Canterbury, who had spoken with wisdom and faultless taste in the House of Lords, now descended to giving the masses what he thought they ought to have. The Queen had given him an example of touching and acceptable words: he did not follow it. He spoke of pathos and tragedy. Catching up the coincidence that James II and Edward VIII had each abandoned their royal charge on the same day of the year, he compared them—each, leaving castle and throne, had gone out an exile. Then came seven words in which the Archbishop's aptitude for effect betrayed him: "In the darkness he left these shores."

That alas was not his worst: after speaking of years of eager service at home and across the seas he said: "It is the remembrance of these things which wrings from our hearts the cry: the pity of it, O! the pity of it."

The British Empire was not in that mood. The people in their hearts realized the strain they put on royalty in giving its common virtues the praise of the not merely good but godlike, and therefore deciding that what they condone in themselves is incompatible with the apotheosis they have conferred on mortals with personal endowments not necessarily above the average. What was the matter with the departed monarch was that, from an insufficient regard for appearances, his virtues had lost much of their lustre, and defects which many tolerate in secret drove him into exile. But the people, even when not sympathetic, were more puzzled than censorious.

When, therefore, the Archbishop called on their pity he jarred on their reserve. Still less did they want to hear condemnation. Dr. Lang said he was compelled to it for the sake of sincerity and truth. So he spoke of the King's circle standing rebuked and of the King he said things which, at least at that juncture, would have been better left unsaid. "He has surrendered his trust. With characteristic frankness he has told us his motive. It was a craving for private happiness. Strange and sad it must be that for such a motive, however strongly it pressed upon his heart, he should have disappointed hopes so high and abandoned a trust so great. Even more strange and sad it is that he should have sought his happiness in a manner inconsistent with Christian principles of marriage, and within a social circle whose standards and ways of life are alien to all the best instincts and traditions of his people."

That there had been a decline of standards was, of course, true. But those of freer morals did not want to 'stand rebuked' before the nation. And those who were loyal to the ways of the last court were not ready either to visit censure on a man who must have suffered, and who probably was still to suffer. Nor did they want to associate his venerated office with scandal.

So, in inveigling a discreet and able Archbishop into an error, whether of tact or tactics, the reign embittered certain followers of their own desires into echoing the last three syllables of his signature which was 'Cosmo Cantuar'.

The most widespread lampoon was this:

> My Lord Archbishop, what a scold you are,
> And when a man is down, how bold you are,
> Of Christian charity how scant you are
> You auld Lang Swine, how full of cant you are!

For this lampoon, not only cruel but insolent, it cannot be said that his sudden lapse of taste or judgment could account wholly. There were many who wanted an opportunity to attack the Church—and this they would have seized, with a sneer at the Archbishop, whether he had spoken or not. Those who did not want the Church to come out victor in so hazardous a duel were naturally very much annoyed; and it can hardly be denied that it was due from the Primate of an Established Church to tell the people something of what the Church and the Monarchy owed first to one another, and then together to the nation. The truth was that the people did still so much regard the Sovereign as a symbol of ideals as to invest him with qualities moral and religious. If not the head of the Church, he must offer an example worthy of the Church. That more than ever they demanded. He had not given it.

The Archbishop of York also made a pronouncement—in his diocesan paper. He said it was easy for a man, in any station, to fall in love with another man's wife—but whatever his walk in life, the only decent thing for such a man to do was to give her up. Here was straight speaking; but from that day to this, no fuss was made about it. The trouble with Lang was not only that he represented the Ten Commandments, but suggested one of them on a falsetto note.

Exactly two hundred years before, had men chosen to recall it, Henry St. John, remembered as Bolingbroke, had written the warning that against the lesser faults of character none must be so much on their guard as Princes. "As they are men," he wrote, "susceptible to impressions, liable to the same errors and exposed to the same passions, so they are likewise exposed to more and stronger temptations than others." The disadvantages of their elevation often outweigh its great advantages. "Thus for instance a little *merit* in a prince is seen and felt by numbers: it is multiplied as it were, and in proportion to the effect his reputation is raised by it. But then a little *failing* is seen and felt by numbers, too: it is multiplied in the same manner, and his reputation sinks in the same proportion."

But, to tell the truth, for years and years, almost the only warning words that ever came near the Prince were those of

A. G. Gardiner in 1926. Ten years had passed, and in that time the Prince had become further and further from advice. Ten years, to prove, each of them, how right Gardiner had been when he said: "The danger with princes is that they do not enjoy the chastening criticism to which the rest of us are mercifully subject. It is assumed that princes are beyond any comment except that of flattery, eulogy and adulation. This attitude of servility, curiously enough, has strengthened as the Throne has become more democratic in spirit and more restricted in function, and as the Press has become more free." In other words, the press used its freedom to sentimentalize and flatter: sometimes it should have hinted a warning, as Lord Altrincham did in later years.

That was the situation which the new King had to face. At first nothing but praise was given to the differences in his tastes and habits from those of his father. A veil was thrown over all else and it was assumed, in Mrs. Baldwin's way, that once he became King, he would take heart of grace from Henry V and put on with his royal supremacy a staidness to accord with it; and therefore that Mrs. Simpson would fade into the background of his life. But the contrast between his father and himself was such that question could not be silenced, even for one who set so high an estimate on his popularity as Lord Simon: Gently he had written his words of warning: "The life of King George is a striking proof of the influence which a constitutional sovereign can exert by the force of high character and by ceaseless devotion to duties which must often be wearisome and which never end. The new Monarch has a high sense of duty, too, as well as infinite energy, but he will find the continual succession of official duties irksome."

There came the doubt whether the master of Fort Belvedere would so discipline his retirement as to do what kingly state required; there was nothing wrong in him going out to relax there. "The world outside the Palace railings," wrote one who had been his friend more or less since his Oxford days, "had always interested the Prince. It was more entertaining and there was not nearly so much fuss." Then with another acute word about his tastes this friend, Philip Guedalla, wrote: "Busy people are apt to take refuge in the dubious distractions of detective fiction or the cherished privacy of weekend retreats. He chose the latter."

Yes, and why not? There he could release his physical restlessness and calm his nerves whether in gardening, in steam baths, or in the company his modern taste preferred. None objected to that. But, whether he were there or elsewhere, there were certain tasks he had to perform; his boxes, his interviews with Ministers, his reception of envoys and functionaries, the ceremonies of the Court. And, as there were certain duties with an inexorable demand, no less imperative were certain discretions for which he was unprepared. For him no angel of consideration came to 'whip the offending Adam out of him'. What had Gardiner written in 1926? "We do not ask for a brilliant King, but we need a king whose character we can respect, whose loyalty to his office is above suspicion and whose capacity is adequate." Yes, here were the three essentials which the Prince must add to all his popularity. Perhaps Baldwin had not been wrong when he confided so apologetically to Geoffrey Dawson that "the little man" had not "the faintest idea of how the country was governed".

Watching the complex drama of the reign, we have seen it as the year in which Hitler's Rhineland coup trumpeted the warning that Germany had crossed the Rubicon from post-war mind to that of pre-war. It was the return of Roosevelt for a second term which proclaimed that American democracy still beguiled by Russia was on the march towards world power. It was the year which showed for all to see that no matter how much nations might talk of their society and league at Geneva they were quite unwilling to join in taking the action needed to enforce justice and order. It was the year in which the prerogative traditionally vested in the Spanish Army gathered in successful strength against a combination of Moscow influence with a 'Popular Front'.

What did all that mean in the current of a single year's events but that America under Roosevelt with Russia under Stalin were being harnessed to take a tremendous part in world affairs? None could yet see that these two would combine to resist the furious genius of Hitler in his endeavour to compromise with the methods of both in order to make himself tyrant first over Germany, then over Europe. So it came about that what was to be called the United Nations meant in effect a balance of power between the two huge agglomerations which a hundred years before Alexis de Tocqueville had seen would be the world's two masters.

Such was the year in which the King of England, the foremost monarch of Europe, designed to marry an American; and he received the strongest support in his design from a Beaverbrook and a Churchill, each strongly linked with North America—well, that too was but a hint of how in the succeeding decade Churchill, willynilly, was to make Britain subservient to an America which joined with Russia, while Europe in five short years lost the supremacy she had, on Roman foundations, enjoyed for two thousand years. Such was the astoundingly swift reaction of the reign of Edward VIII to the successes attained by Hitler and by Mussolini. Yes, it was his passion for an American which drove him from the throne, not actually because she was American, but because her position and point of view came from American changes of law and morality—or at least of standards —which the British Empire found incompatible with its ideals. As American newspapers showed no mercy on his privacy, so his choice of American standards made him unacceptable to the British Empire.

At this point we can—if we look hard—discern how this personal melodrama of the reign which threw into sharp outline what is, and what is not, required from Britain's Royalty, fits into the pattern of those events and affairs which in that year most occupied the King's—or if not his, the Government's— political attention. Both indicate a sweeping change in the forces which controlled the civilized world, and these in turn affect the people's way of living. It was not the fault of Edward VIII if his nature was affected by the speed, the mechanization, the roar, racket and disruption which burst upon the world through that war which met and moulded his maturity. From the beginning he was a Royalty who set out to compromise with revolution, and in the essential particular himself became too much of a revolutionary for his people to stand.

"A country without the means of change," wrote Burke, "is without the means of conservation." The British people while they conserve much are always in the way of changing much. But here was one who in his nature was part and type of the disruption and insurrection through which he was projected like a ball hemmed in by the sides of an ever-moving plane, and pushed from side to side by its see-saw.

For while King George V and Queen Mary performed in a way so exemplary their royal duties, the land over which they reigned was being revolutionized. Its governments were more often called Conservative than otherwise, but the world's mood was changing without England really admitting it. "In the later years of George V," wrote Philip Guedalla, "nothing was quite what it pretended to be. Sparse remnants of the old nobility pretended to be rich: the rich pretended to be noble: sporting stockbrokers masqueraded as fox-hunting squires and practically everyone above a certain income-level indulged in some form of social impersonation. Professional success, commercial daring, American accretions, journalistic flair, financial shrewdness, ingenuity in politics, all these ingredients were represented in the House of Lords."

In other words, a revolution had even then been accomplished. The abdication of the aristocracy had been for fifteen years preceding that of the new King who represented the mood of the levelled modernized upper class of his time. He used his privileges in much the same way: and he, like them, faced a rebellion of the masses against the standards, not only of tradition but of the new *élite* which itself cared little for keeping the good of the past. And then he made his plans for representing what the majority of his people—or at least the most solid and reliable of them—found incompatible with what they needed from Royalty.

And somehow the feeling of that need was deep in the masses who were working for change. While the exile was driving from Windsor Castle to Portsmouth after the broadcast, a huge mob of Londoners gathered in the chill air of the December night. They marched towards the western end of Piccadilly where they knew they could greet their new King with roar and roar of acclamation. So tumultuous was it that he was almost taken aback, not knowing what it could mean. His wife who was suffering from a chill felt she must rise from her bed too to see this demonstration. What was behind it? Welcome? Relief? They wondered. But there was no mistaking that it meant gladness in the fact that they had a King and one whom they could keep till the end of his life. Once again, after ten days of tormented doubt, they had found someone who could centre their loyalty and give them the glow they felt of shared greatness in greeting a King.

At first he felt acutely the lack of that power of evoking the enthusiasm of masses which had been his brother's speciality. Physically he was not strong, and it was feared that his health might give way even before it did so fourteen or fifteen years later. He was shy and had an impediment in his speech which took a long training to overcome. Words in any case did not come readily to him. "What am I to say to them?" he would ask as he had to meet one set of functionaries after another. Like his father and his brother he had never been an intellectual, and those who had most to do with him found that in general knowledge, especially of history, he was, like his predecessor, so deficient that it reflected on the capacity of the tutor they had shared. "Hansell must have taught them damn all!" was the impatient comment of those who had now to fill in the gaps.

The new King was not well-known, as his brother had been. He had to be put in the forefront of his people's regard, and the whole prestige of the monarchy built up to what it was at the beginning of that fateful year. So month by month the Court officials, with Sir Alexander Hardinge at their head, set to work to link the Crown and the King personally with every dominant interest in the country. First there were the preparations for the Coronation which the whole world was prepared to welcome as the most glorious pageant that the world could offer: now the Bishops could make of it an occasion of that spiritual renewal of which Dr. Blunt had so spoken in the discourse which had opened Britain's doors to the pressing shouting talkers when the newspapermen could no longer hold them back. But with this came plan on plan to draw Crown and people together.

Men of note in all directions must be given honours. The Forces, the learned societies, the privileged bodies, the municipalities, the industries both in workers and leaders must all be got in touch with the King; and he be prepared to give them all he could of what his father had given. He had much to learn. In younger days he had played a game of tennis which a champion could call 'very useful'. He had done well at Southwold in bringing together boys of different strata in a camp on the Suffolk shore. But his two main assets were his conscience and his wife. She in her love for him and her own wish to do good gave him support and comfort, and he met it with a knightliness which put first his wish to be of service where he could for all varieties of his people. And he was soon found to be shrewd and able in the conduct of affairs. "Few people," writes Lord Halifax, "were endowed with judgment more wise and penetrating than his, rooted in simple and assured standards and frequently salted with humour uninhibited and robust." At his death "the recollection of the bleak inauguration of the reign fifteen years earlier; the grief now universal; the loyal devotion to be so fervently expressed at the Coronation of the young Queen and ready to do anything in its power to lighten the load now laid upon her: those concurrent emotions joined to the volume of sympathy that went out to Queen Elizabeth told how great a work with her help the King had accomplished in the re-establishment of the monarchy after the strain placed upon it by the events which brought him to the throne."

It was long before the affair of Edward VIII faded from the minds of men and women. They continued to talk of it in London, in the British Isles, in America, in the whole world. The protagonists were the subject of ever-renewed debate which followed for the most part along the lines which at one place or another in this study have already been suggested. But gradually as the talk rose and fell in the British Empire, the whole argument soon merged into grateful acceptance of the new King and Queen, with admiring love of their two daughters whom, as Queen Mary had said, the people had taken to their hearts even before the new reign began. And then came the preparations for the magnificent pageantry of the Coronation which was now pushed on, according to the earlier plan, with no queries nor complications whatsoever.

Soon it was discovered that any peculiar aptitudes for modern kingship in Edward VIII were of much less value to the Court, the Throne, the country, the Commonwealth, and international affairs than the simple rectitude of his brother, whose happy household gave all what they wanted as a focus for loyal affection.

For the first few months of the new reign the Coronation became an engrossing subject which for a time thrust into the background the stalking menace of Hitler. By 1939, however, all minds turned to the question of what was to be done with that. Baldwin had received at the Coronation the acclamation he deserved. Yet even amid the shouts which greeted him he had known that popular acclaim is fickle. The time was at hand when his lack of energy in Foreign Policy and the deficiencies of his new Foreign Secretary were to bring about a change of feeling.

When at last Hitler forced the war, men remembered that Churchill had clamoured for it when our forces were wholly unprepared, and this was now accounted rightness. The new King had to suit himself to what this new political leadership meant, and it was not long before the warning of his brother was proved to be not without foundation. The Monarchy had a new task: to adapt itself to a sweeping revolution in the life and economy of Britain as she sank from being a first-class nation into one on the verge of bankruptcy. And then they found that through this very bankruptcy certain necessary changes had been effected; while the upper classes were ruined and lost their splendour, and the educated classes were grievously restricted, the great masses of the people enjoyed a solid spread of welfare such as they had hardly dreamed. Into all this the Monarchy fitted by making certain sacrifices of its state.

In one sense the reign which followed was the most disastrous in English history. The sense of the greatness and wealth of the country as a paramount force in international affairs, exerted through a certain privileged class, not always wealthy but capable of going round the world to lead and govern it—all that suddenly collapsed. Great Britain lost her prestige, especially in Asia and Africa, and in that Arab world which joins them. That led to the hegemony of Red Russia on the one side, on the other of America. But so ably was the Monarchy conducted at this time that it could confront sweeping revolution without diminishing its popularity. It followed the lead of Attlee who saw it through those years of crisis to which the ruin of war inevitably led. For the Monarchy Lord Attlee did such yeoman service that he well deserved from it that Knighthood of the Garter which was given him in 1956 by the new Queen.

It was not until her accession that the country found an ideal sovereign—a figure who fascinated the gaze of all as they fixed it upon her pleasing youth, who had taken to herself a bridegroom who in his ability, his strength of character, his physical excellence, his concord with the trend of the time and his personal energy would have perfectly fulfilled the role of Prince even had he not already become father of a son and a daughter in whom the country delighted as twenty years before it had delighted in the two daughters of the Duke and Duchess of York. These, after 1936, as they were brought up, were never again to hear the mention of their uncle's name. Even so, the issue raised by King Edward VIII, whether the sovereign was to sanction the principle of divorce in relationship to a family honoured as an ideal was again pressed on the attention of the young Queen. This time, however, it was resolved in a sense exactly contrary to that taken by King Edward VIII; the decision brought honour to both his nieces, and this time received the hearty concurrence of Sir Winston Churchill as Prime Minister!

As far as the reign of King Edward VIII in itself is concerned, it proved, in spite of its shortness, to be one of the highest interest and moment to both the old and the new conceptions of the function of the Crown. If one cannot maintain the hypothesis that it was highly dangerous in the international tension of its time, it is none the less true that it preoccupied the Government with a constitutional problem to such an extent that it proved a serious impediment to efficient administration; the desires of the King made his Crown a subject of contention rather than a centre of unity.

He showed what price the Sovereign—with other members of the Royal Family—have to pay for the deference and the prestige the people so gladly accord them. They must always respect their own position, and hold in view the ideals which their people cherish. It is preferred they should not have capacities or aims far above the average nor will there be complaints if they fall a little below it.

The whole Empire loved King George V not because he had a majestic personality, looks, or winning ways, but because he did his duty with all his heart. His successor wanted to force on his peoples a choice of his own which many of them must question.

But although this reign showed certain things very clear, it does not provide evidence for moral judgment on either the Duke or the Duchess of Windsor. Not only was his an unusual temperament but it was subjected to the most severe strains. Similarly with regard to the Duchess, she was placed in a position so flattering that no woman who had her experiences of disappointment, doubt, and difficulty could have reserves to withstand the glittering enchantments, the ease or the power which were at last and suddenly showered on her by a prince more privileged than any other.

Set in the very forefront of the whole world's attention were two people who fitted each other. One was enabled to find solace where he had felt frustration, a solace which consoled him for the feelings of loneliness and void which for twenty years had made an irony of his popularity with the masses: the other was to exert her unusual capacities in the enchantment of Europe's royalest milieu. The union was not merely the full overpowering tide with which romantic attraction can flood afresh on men's maturer years: it had the resources of rank and fortune and was to stand the test of time.

We can see clearly how owing to the sphere in which they lived they were beguiled into discounting moral commands and in doing so they made huge errors in judging public opinion—and perhaps it is not surprising that once they had made them they persisted in them when, after spaces of first fifteen and then twenty years, they published their books. They brought out these statements of their case with extreme skill—and also sold them to immense advantage. Each, undoubtedly has told an absorbing story. But each ignores that other side which is essential to truth about the reign—essential, too, if there is to be justice to those who had to take cognizance of public opinion and to represent it. Neither the Duke nor the Duchess seem to realize the immense problem they set the Government and the Prime Minister and his personal staff whose case their books ignore; yet who can deny that the public conscience is an essential part of the history of anything it concerns? Besides, the whole truth of the story is more interesting than just one side of it; and this story gains in interest when one sees how great a part in it was played by that momentum of opinion which is not only 'Queen of the world' but which represents in this case the sound instinct of countless hearts and the staying power of families and of homes.

Until we know it, we have lost not only the significance of a reign which though so short can never be disregarded, much less forgotten. It not only had a political significance: it not only defined the function and freedom of the Crown: it not only suggests many significant thoughts about the relation of the United States to Europe and to the British Commonwealth of Nations: but it is, and it must ever remain, the sort of melodrama in which the human record is for ever outdoing the most complex and fertile inventions of genius.

EPILOGUE

THERE is no better way to assess the significance of the three hundred and twenty-five days of the reign of King Edward VIII than to turn to the first ten years of his niece, Queen Elizabeth.

She represents a people who combine individual enterprise with solidarity, and continuity with experiment. Not only because she is a very attractive young lady, not only because of the distinguished competence with which she royally acts, not only for the regard felt towards her as mother and wife as well as Queen, not only for the exemplary prudence and discretion of her Court, not only for her constitutional position according to the Statute of Westminster, does she inspire admiration and love. The affectionate attention, amounting indeed to insatiable curiosity, which watch over her and her family spring also from a fount of mystery: she is made unique by her hallowing and her crown, a hallowing which goes back to the time when Saxon England was moulded under Christian Kings; and to this a Pope added a title still jealously retained: Defender of the Faith. Not only is she supreme governor of her established Church, but in working for the unity of peace and concord of her dominions with themselves and the world she has the special charge and receives the heavenly grace of Him who from His throne beholds all the dwellers upon earth.

High indeed must be the ideals, high the standard of the Sovereign of Great Britain with her Commonwealth and Dominions.

References

As this book is an analysis of the events and of the constitutional problem of the reign of King Edward VIII, it must rely mainly on the many memoirs published by those who were closely concerned or on the journals and periodicals which played such an enormous part in the development of the final situation. The classic authorities on King George V are Sir Harold Nicolson and Mr. John Gore, on Queen Mary, Mr. Pope Hennessy and Sir George Arthur. But to these we are able to add the direct impressions of the Duke of Windsor himself in *A King's Story*. Obviously this book must be a main source for the history of the Reign and at certain points that of the Duchess provides a most valuable addition. One of the main tasks of this book is to collate these autobiographical accounts with other memoirs. The main sources are noted chapter by chapter below. But, as the preface has already stated, the book is the work of one who was at Oxford with the Duke and has been in personal relation with the immense majority of the persons mentioned in the narrative. He has thus received a constant stream of impressions and information completed by special enquiries made in the preparation of this book. Names are mentioned in the preface but of course they cannot be cited in printed footnotes. If the actual names of the best sources of contemporary information were to be compromised in this way journalism, history and even political conversation would become impossible. Knowledge can be obtained only by those whose judgment and reticence can be trusted. Where the historian has the right to know who was the authority for my private information he may consult Sir Charles Petrie to whom I have given a list of them, and who has done me the generous service of reading my proofs.

Chapter References to Printed Authorities

CHAP.
1. For the Duke of Windsor's youth, the best authorities are his own book, *A Windsor Tapestry* by Sir Compton Mackenzie, and *Edward VIII* by Hector Bolitho with constant references to leading journalists (such as Sir Philip Gibbs, who supplements my personal knowledge).

CHAP.

2. Madame St. Laurent: the best account is in *Queen Victoria* by Hector Bolitho. See also *Wicked Uncles* by R. Fulford. The references to King George and Queen Mary are especially in the authorities already mentioned, in particular John Gore's *George V*.

3. Personal knowledge contributes to this chapter. In addition to the *King George V* of Sir H. Nicolson and the *King George VI* of Sir J. Wheeler-Bennett the text mentions A. G. Gardiner's *Certain People of Importance*.

4. The chapter cites Nicolson op. cit., p. 414, *A King's Book*, A. W. Baldwin's *My Father*, pp. 138-40, John Gore, op. cit., pp. 360, 436, 419-21.

5. Nicolson, op. cit., pp. 365, 441-3, 461. For criticism of League of Nations see Comte de St.-Aulaire, *Genève contre la Paix*. For continuation of narrative mentioned in text, Hector Bolitho, op. cit., p. 150. *Why Edward Went* by W. B. Wells, *Lord Derby* by Randolph Churchill.

6. Personal judgment and observation in drawing on the memoirs of the Duke and Duchess.

7. The printed sources here are the memoirs of the Duchess, *My Father* by A. W. Baldwin and *Double Exposure*.

8. "There is a time when the finest intelligence in the world is less serviceable than the broad commonsense of the Grand Seigneur," F. S. Oliver *The Endless Adventure*, John Buchan *The King's Grace*, pp. 319-20.

9. The King on unwillingness for war: Lord Templewood's *Nine Troubled Years*, p. 159.

10. Templewood, op. cit., p. 190. Duff Cooper *Old Men Forget*; Duchess of Windsor, op. cit.

11. The conversation of the Baldwins with the King from Thomas Jones's *A Diary with Letters*, p. 164. Speeches in the House of Commons from Hansard.

12. Lord Simon's *Retrospect*. Sir Philip Gibbs's *Ordeal in England*, pp. 99-100.

13. As before.

14. Quotations from Stanley Baldwin, Sir Arthur Bryant *Stanley Baldwin*, pp. 158-9, T. Driberg's *Lord Beaverbrook*.

15. Quotations from Winston Churchill's *Step by Step*, p. 19, Hesse *Der Kampf um Deutschland*, translated into English as *Hitler and the English*. Flandin's answer: *Contemporary Review*, May, 1936, p. 616. Quotations from *A King's Book*, p. 286, Duchess of Windsor, op. cit., p. 309. The distinguished British authority is Sisley Huddleston in *Contemporary Review*, May, 1936. Parliament speeches from Hansard. *Contemporary Review*, April, 1936, p. 624.

16. Badoglio to Mussolini, Martelli, *Italy Against the World*, p. 231. "To Disturb the Peace of Europe", Martelli, op. cit., p. 299. "International Morality at Stake", op. cit., p. 284.
17. "200,000 sq. miles would provide for 200,000 inhabitants." *Morning Post*, 15th September, 1935.
    con Badoglio, *The War In Abyssinia*. E. W. Polson Newman, *Italy's Conquest of Abyssinia*.
18. Duke and Duchess of Windsor, op. cit. Lady Hardinge of Penshurst *The Path of Kings*.
19. As before.
20. As before.
21. "A perfect avalanche of mud and slime", Sir Evelyn Wrench, *Geoffrey Dawson*.
22. *A King's Book*, Hansard, *The New York Times*.
23. Note on the Dinner in Philip Guedalla's *The Fatefu Year*.
24. Sir Evelyn Wrench, op. cit.
25. Lord Templewood's *Nine Troubled Years*; the Hardinge Letter has been published both by the Duchess of Windsor and in *The Times*, though its copyright really belonged to the Crown.
26. This chapter is an analysis of the situation in the light of the books already cited with special reference to *Old Men Forget*.
27– The authorities are cited in the text.
28.
29. The graphologist's report with the accompanying comments is in the Dugdale Diary.
30. The principal source is the Duchess of Windsor, *op. cit.*
31. At this point the life of Archbishop Lang by Lockhart and the article on him in the D.N.B. by Dean Don, formerly his private secretary, become important sources.
32. At this point the Spender Articles become an additional source.
33. Hugh Dalton.
34. In addition to the works of the Duke and Duchess of Windsor the chief sources here are *My Father* by A. W. Baldwin and the information placed at my disposal by one or more of Baldwin's secretaries.
35. Is an analysis of the situation.

For the remaining pages the authorities are again made clear by the text.